Pathways to Knowledge

PATHWAYS
TO KNOWLEDGE

Private and Public

ALVIN I. GOLDMAN

OXFORD
UNIVERSITY PRESS

2002

OXFORD

UNIVERSITY PRESS

Oxford   New York

Athens   Auckland   Bangkok   Bogotá   Buenos Aires   Cape Town
Chennai   Dar es Salaam   Delhi   Florence   Hong Kong   Istanbul   Karachi
Kolkata   Kuala Lumpur   Madrid   Melbourne   Mexico City   Mumbai   Nairobi
Paris   São Paulo   Shanghai   Singapore   Taipei   Tokyo   Toronto   Warsaw

and associated companies in
Berlin   Ibadan

Copyright © 2002 by Alvin I. Goldman

Published by Oxford University Press, Inc.
198 Madison Avenue, New York, New York 10016

Oxford is a registered trademark of Oxford University Press, Inc.

Library of Congress Cataloging-in-Publication Data
Goldman, Alvin I., 1938–
Pathways to knowledge : private and public / Alvin I. Goldman.
p. cm.
ISBN 0-19-513879-1
1. Justification (Theory of knowledge)   2. Knowledge, Sociology of.   3. Consciousness.
I. Title.
BD212 .G65 2002
121—dc21   2001046411

1 3 5 7 9 8 6 4 2

Printed in the United States of America
on acid-free paper

For Bill Alston

*Valued friend and fellow traveler
down the pathways of epistemology*

Preface

From its beginnings epistemology has been concerned with two questions about knowledge: "What is it?" and "How do you get it?" Plato's answer to the first was that knowledge is true belief that is securely "tied down." His answer to the second was that knowledge is attainable by intellectual apprehension of the Forms. Subsequent epistemology centered more on the second question than the first, often quarreling over the feasibility, legitimacy, or reliability of proposed methods for gaining knowledge. Plato's theory of intellectual apprehension is a good example of a controversial method. The organizing theme of this collection of essays similarly centers around candidate methods, or "pathways," to knowledge. What are the available pathways, and which are the best ones, or acceptable ones, to follow? The question is not restricted, however, to knowledge. A close cousin of knowledge is warranted or justified belief, and many epistemologists are as interested in identifying proper pathways to justified belief as good pathways to knowledge. That question gets at least equal attention in this volume.

On the current epistemological scene the hottest debate about justification is the internalism/externalism debate. Chapter 1 enters that fray with a sustained critique of internalism. Externalism characteristically holds that beliefs acquire justificational status if they are produced by methods with certain "external" properties, properties that need not be known—and perhaps need not be knowable, or at any rate "directly" knowable—by the agent him- or herself. Internalism takes issue with this claim about proper methods or pathways. It holds that all justification-conferring properties ("justifiers," for short) must be accessible to the agent. Chapter 1 examines the most popular defense of internalism and finds it wanting.

Chapter 2 joins the recent renewal of interest in a priori warrant or knowledge. Epistemologists of a "naturalistic" stripe have commonly championed radical empiricism and heaped scorn on anything smacking of traditional rationalism. So can a naturalizing epistemologist like me countenance the a priori? Is there a pathway to knowledge that yields certain, infallible, and unrevisable results, as traditional accounts of the a priori suggest? Chapter 2 defends the a priori from the standpoint of moderate naturalism. It rejects the traditional characteristics of the a priori just listed, but finds it plausible that there are psychological routes to mathematical belief and logical inference that are sound and distinctive enough to license a separate subcategory of warrant. Tentative support for this contention comes from empirical research in cognitive science, the sort of work needed to identify the exact nature of these "pathways." Reliable processes for arithmetic and logical cognition may be part of our natural endowment.

Chapter 3 adopts the standpoint of virtue epistemology by construing epistemic virtues as processes, methods, or activities ("pathways") that promote or realize epistemic value. A question therefore arises whether epistemic value is fundamentally single or multiple. If it were single, then all epistemic virtues would be united by their relationship to one and the same value. At first blush, however, epistemic value seems to be multiple. Don't we value both true belief and justified belief? Aren't these distinct values? Even restricting attention to truth and falsehood, isn't there a pair of values at stake: getting true belief and avoiding false belief? So how could epistemic "unitarianism" get off the ground? Despite these challenges, chapter 3 argues that a pretty good case can be made for epistemic unitarianism.

Parts II and III (chapters 4–9) explore the legitimacy and significance of private and public pathways to knowledge. An almost ubiquitous feature of analytic philosophy is its appeal to intuitions, typically the philosopher's own intuitions. In almost every branch of philosophy, choices between competing theories rest substantially on whether the deliverances of these theories comport or conflict with intuitions. But how can an ostensibly subjective and private event like an intuition provide a pathway to philosophical knowledge? Outside of philosophy, educated people are often skeptical about the deliverances of intuition. Why should things be different here? Given such worries, one might expect to find a copious literature on the epistemic credentials of intuition, or the epistemic propriety of using intuition in the practice of philosophy. In fact, however, the literature on this topic is relatively sparse. Chapter 4, written with Joel Pust, tries to tackle the problem. Instead of urging the abandonment of intuition as a dubious source of evidence, it tries to show how to interpret philosophical theories as theories about which intuition, properly construed, can provide legitimate evidence.

Chapters 5 and 6 explore the legitimacy of another controversial pathway to knowledge: introspection. In the heyday of behaviorism and positivism, introspection was often regarded as the prototype of a *private* process or method that should be forsworn, at least for scientific purposes. It fails to satisfy the requirement that scientific knowledge—and perhaps all knowledge—should be based on *public* (intersubjective) data and public methods. Psychologists and philosophers of science are still queasy at the very mention of the word "introspection"; and many philosophers of mind, working in the long shadows of Wittgenstein and Ryle, favor functionalist accounts of mental states that try to avoid or minimize the role of "privileged access." There are two problems with the foregoing stricture against introspection. First, something like it (perhaps "internal monitoring") seems to be the way people normally determine their own conscious states. Second, the scientific study of consciousness currently enjoys not only renewed respectability but dramatically increased importance. The question then arises of how the scientific study of consciousness can proceed, or how its epistemology can be reconstructed. Does it rely—perhaps implicitly and indirectly—on introspective methods, or can it do entirely without them? If it does rely on introspection, is the use of such a private method legitimate? Chapters 5 and 6 explore this fundamental epistemological problem for the science of consciousness. I argue, first, that introspection is indeed required in the science of consciousness, because researchers must rely on the introspective reports of their subjects, and this reliance is in turn (tacitly) based on introspection of their own. Furthermore, introspection is indeed a private method, in a relevant sense of "private." Nonetheless, a private method can be a legitimate pathway to knowledge. The constraint of publicity, as a universal constraint on (scientific) method, should be rejected.

To say that publicity should be rejected as a universal methodological constraint is not to say that public or social methods of knowledge-acquisition are undesirable or unimportant. That would be a strange thing to say, given the massively social dimensions of knowledge. I made much of this theme in my previous book *Knowledge in a Social World* (Goldman 1999), and I return to it here in part III (chapters 7–9), which is devoted to types of social pathways to knowledge and justification.

The need for social routes to knowledge is dramatized in modern life by the rampant specialization of knowledge. Practical questions about daily life and public affairs cannot be confidently or responsibly answered without appeal to experts in one or another technical area of inquiry. How safe is the food we eat, the medicines we take? What will be the consequences of this or that use of the environment, of this or that energy policy, of this or that method of teaching children to read? These are familiar examples of the exploding number of questions that cannot be reliably answered without appeal to special expertise. No single person can possibly attain all the relevant forms of expertise; each of us must rely on others. But on whom, exactly, should we rely? Which experts, or alleged experts, should be trusted? Unfortunately, so-called experts often disagree, and when they do, they cannot all be right. Which one should the novice or layperson trust? Upon hearing two rival experts offer conflicting viewpoints, can the novice justifiably trust either one? How can such justified belief be attained? After all, novices often struggle to get even a bare comprehension of what experts are saying. When they do understand them, how can they appraise the relative merits of their esoteric arguments? This is, I believe, a fundamental problem in social epistemology. Perhaps it is a special case of the general epistemological problem of testimony, but it is particularly acute when a novice confronts conflicting expert testimony. This problem is addressed in chapter 7.

Interest in social epistemology is not confined to philosophers. Numerous disciplines investigate problems in the near neighborhood of what philosophers call social epistemology. Few of these extraphilosophical disciplines address the core epistemic concepts of "justification" or "knowledge" (in the truth-entailing sense) that preoccupy philosophers. Indeed, many members of these disciplines assume the vacuity of these concepts when construed in an "objectivist" fashion. Nonetheless, these disciplines actively explore the processes and mechanisms by which ideas and beliefs are socially constructed and transmitted. In this sense, they take a lively interest in one part of social epistemology's territory. Any systematic social epistemology would like an instructive model of how ideas and beliefs spread through society or culture. One such model or approach is called "memetics." The general idea is to import the Darwinian model of biological evolution into the domain of culture. "Memes" are units of culture that supposedly propagate along the same fundamental principles as "genes." A related approach is the disease or epidemiological model: ideas propagate like viruses through a population. In the case of memes the mechanism of replication is said to be imitation. In the disease model, transmission occurs by contagion. These approaches have at least surface plausibility, though they encounter many problems. To the extent that hearers trust the speech of others, they emulate or inherit those speakers' beliefs. Perhaps this is indeed like contagion. If this approach has promise, it would seem relevant to social epistemology. But could it really be relevant to the social pathways for *knowledge,* where "knowledge" is understood as *true* belief? This is not obvious. The possible usefulness of these models for social epistemology is critically explored in chapter 8.

The final essay of the volume is a synoptic and (largely) ecumenical treatment of alternative possible approaches to social epistemology. Both *Knowledge in a Social World* and chapter 8 treat social epistemology from a "veritistic" perspective, inquiring into the social practices that are good pathways to "knowledge" in the sense of *true belief.* Chapter 7 treats social epistemology from the perspective of justification theory, inquiring into the ways that a novice might be justified in accepting an expert's opinion. Both approaches extend classical epistemology into the social domain without abandoning the traditional epistemological concern for truth and justification. Not all writers on social epistemology, however, share this point of view. As noted above, many explicitly reject the presuppositions of traditional epistemology and construct social accounts of (what they call) knowledge along very different lines. It is worth tracing out these alternative conceptions, if only to bring the similarities and contrasts with "traditional" (objectivist) social epistemology into sharper relief. Furthermore, there are many research techniques to use in plying social epistemology, whether in traditional or nontraditional forms. All of these permutations are worth identifying, and that is the task undertaken in chapter 9.

As these prefatory comments indicate, I do not conceive of knowledge as being attainable by just a single pathway, or even a handful of pathways, but by a wide variety of sometimes independent and sometimes interconnected pathways. The upshot is that epistemology, by my lights, is not a narrow subject but a highly rich and diversified subject, perhaps more diversified than most treatments of it typically allow.

Tucson, Arizona   A.I.G.
February 8, 2001

Acknowledgments

1. "Internalism Exposed" first appeared in *The Journal of Philosophy* 96 (1999), pp. 271–293. Reprinted by permission of *The Journal of Philosophy*.

2. "A Priori Warrant and Naturalistic Epistemology" first appeared in *Philosophical Perspectives, 13, Epistemology* (1999), edited by James E. Tomberlin (copyright by Blackwell Publishers). Reprinted by permission of Blackwell Publishers.

3. "The Unity of the Epistemic Virtues" first appeared in *Virtue Epistemology*, edited by Abrol Fairweather and Linda Zagzebski, copyright 2001 by Oxford University Press, Inc. Used by permission of Oxford University Press, Inc.

4. "Philosophical Theory and Intuitional Evidence" first appeared in *Rethinking Intuition: The Psychology of Intuition and Its Role in Philosophical Inquiry* (1998), edited by Michael DePaul and William Ramsey. Reprinted by permission of Rowman and Littlefield Publishers.

5. "Science, Publicity, and Consciousness" first appeared in *Philosophy of Science* 64 (1997), pp. 525–545. © 1997 by the Philosophy of Science Association. All rights reserved.

6. "Can Science Know When You're Conscious? Epistemological Foundations of Consciousness Research." First published in the *Journal of Consciousness Studies* 7. 5 (May 2000), pp. 3–22. © Imprint Academic.

7. "Experts: Which Ones Should You Trust?", reprinted from *Philosophy and Phenomenological Research* 63 (July 2001). Copyright © International Phenomenological Society, 2001.

8. "Social Routes to Belief and Knowledge" first appeared in *The Monist* 84 (2001), pp. 346–368. Copyright © 2001, THE MONIST, Peru, Illinois, U.S.A., 61354. Reprinted by permission.

9. "What Is Social Epistemology? A Smorgasbord of Projects" appears here for the first time.

Contents

PART I

Internalism, the A Priori, and Epistemic Virtue

1

Internalism Exposed

1. Deontology, Access, and Internalism

In recent decades, epistemology has witnessed the development and growth of externalist theories of knowledge and justification.[1] Critics of externalism have focused a bright spotlight on this approach and judged it unsuitable for realizing the true and original goals of epistemology. Their own favored approach, internalism, is defended as a preferable approach to the traditional concept of epistemic justification.[2] In this chapter I turn the spotlight toward internalism and its most prominent rationale. Fundamental problems that lie at the core of internalism will be revealed and the viability of its most popular rationale will be challenged. Although particular internalist theories such as (internalist) foundationalism and coherentism will occasionally be discussed, those specific theories are not my primary concern. The principal concern is the general architecture of internalism, and the attempt to justify this architecture by appeal to a certain conception of what justification consists in.

I begin with a certain rationale for internalism that has widespread support. It can be reconstructed in three steps:

(1) The *guidance-deontological* conception of justification is posited.
(2) A certain constraint on the determiners of justification is derived from the guidance-deontological conception, i.e., the constraint that all justification-determiners must be *accessible to*, or *knowable by*, the epistemic agent.
(3) The accessibility or knowability constraint is taken to imply that only internal conditions qualify as legitimate determiners of justification. So justification must be a purely internal affair.[3]

What motivates or underlies this rationale for internalism? Historically, one central aim of epistemology is to guide or direct our intellectual conduct, an aim expressed in René Descartes's (1955) title, "Rules for the Direction of the Mind." Among contemporary writers, John Pollock expresses the idea this way:

> I have taken the fundamental problem of epistemology to be that of deciding what to believe. Epistemic justification, as I use the term, is concerned with this problem. Considerations of epistemic justification guide us in determining what to believe. We might call this the "belief-guiding" or "reason-guiding" sense of 'justification.' (1986, 10)

The guidance conception of justification is commonly paired with the deontological conception of justification. John Locke wrote of a person's "duty as a rational creature" (1959, 2: 413), and the theme of epistemic duty or responsibility has been echoed by many contemporary epistemologists, including Laurence BonJour (1985), Roderick Chisholm (1966, 1977, 1989), Richard Feldman (1988a), Carl Ginet (1975), Hilary Kornblith (1983), Paul Moser (1985), and Matthias Steup (1988). Chisholm defines cousins of the concept of justification in terms of the relation "more reasonable than," and he re-expresses the relation "p is more reasonable than q for S at t" by saying: "S is so situated at t that his intellectual *requirement*, his *responsibility* as an intellectual being, is better fulfilled by p than by q" (1977, 14). Similarly, Feldman says that one's epistemic duty is to "believe what is supported or justified by one's evidence and to avoid believing what is not supported by one's evidence" (1988, 254).

The guidance and deontological conceptions of justification are intimately related, because the deontological conception, at least when paired with the guidance conception, considers it a person's epistemic duty to guide his doxastic attitudes by his evidence, or by whatever factors determine the justificational status of a proposition at a given time. Epistemic deontologists commonly maintain that being justified in believing a proposition p consists in being (intellectually) required or permitted to believe p; and being unjustified in believing p consists in not being permitted, or being forbidden, to believe p. When a person is unjustified in believing a proposition, it is his duty not to believe it.

It is possible to separate the deontological conception from the guidance idea. In ethical theory a distinction has been drawn between accounts of moral duty that aim to specify what makes actions right and accounts of moral duty that aim to provide practical decision procedures for what to do.[4] If an account simply aims at the first desideratum, it need not aspire to be usable as a decision guide. Similarly, accounts of epistemic duty need not necessarily be intended as decision guides. However, when the deontological conception is used as a rationale for epistemic internalism of the sort I am sketching, it does incorporate the guidance conception. Only if the guidance conception is incorporated can the argument proceed along the intended lines to the accessibility constraint, and from there to internalism. This is why I shall henceforth speak of the "guidance-deontological" (GD) conception of justification.

I turn now to the second step of the argument for internalism. Following William Alston (1989, 189), I shall use the term "justifiers" for facts or states of affairs that determine the justificational status of a belief, or the epistemic status a proposition has for an epistemic agent. In other words, justifiers determine whether or not a proposition is justified for an epistemic agent at a given time. It seems to follow naturally from the GD conception of justification that a certain constraint must be placed on the sorts of facts or states of affairs that qualify as justifiers. If a person is going to avoid violating his epistemic duty, he must know, or be able to find out, what his duty requires. By "know," in this context, I only mean: have an *accurate*, or *true*, belief. I do not mean: have a *justified* true belief (or whatever else is entailed by the richer concept of knowledge). Admittedly, it might be possible to avoid vi-olating one's duties by chance, without knowing (having true beliefs about) what one's duties are. As a practical matter, however, it is not feasible to conform to duty on a regular and consistent basis without knowing what items of conduct constitute those duties. Thus, if you are going to choose your beliefs and abstentions from belief in accordance with your justificational requirements, the facts that make you justified or unjustified in believing a certain proposition at a given time must be facts that you are capable of knowing, at that time, to hold or not to hold. There is an intimate connection, then, between the GD conception of justification and the requirement that justifiers must be accessible to, or knowable by, the agent at the time of belief. If you cannot accurately ascertain your epistemic duty at a given time, how can you be expected to execute that duty, and how can you reasonably be held responsible for executing that duty?[5]

The knowability constraint on justifiers that flows from the GD conception may be formulated as follows:

(KJ)   The only facts that qualify as justifiers of an agent's believing p at time t are facts that the agent can readily know, at t, to obtain or not to obtain.

How can an agent readily know whether candidate justifiers obtain or do not obtain? Presumably, the agent must have a way of determining, for any can-didate class of justifiers, whether or not they obtain. Such a way of knowing must be reliable; that is, it must generate beliefs about the presence or absence of justifiers that are usually (invariably?) correct. Otherwise, the agent will often be mistaken about what his epistemic duty requires. The way of knowing must also be "powerful," in the sense that when justifiers obtain it is likely (certain?) that the agent will believe that they obtain; at least he will believe this if he reflects on the matter or otherwise inquires into it.[6] As we shall soon see, internalists typically impose additional restrictions on how justifiers may be known. But the minimal, generic version of KJ simply requires justifiers to be the sorts of facts that agents have *some* way of knowing. In other words, justification-conferring facts must be the sorts of facts whose presence or absence is "accessible" to agents.[7]

Given the KJ constraint on justifiers, it becomes fairly obvious why internalism about justification is so attractive. Whereas external facts are facts that a cognitive agent might not be in a position to know about, internal facts are presumably the sorts of conditions that a cognitive agent can readily determine. So internal facts seem to be the right sorts of candidates for justifiers. This consideration leads to the third step of our rationale for internalism. Only internal facts qualify as justifiers because they are the only ones that satisfy the KJ constraint; at least so internalists suppose.

One possible way to criticize this rationale for internalism is to challenge the GD conception directly. This could be done, for example, by arguing that the GD conception of justification presupposes the dubious thesis of doxastic voluntarism, the thesis that doxastic attitudes can be "guided" by deliberate choices or acts of will. This criticism is developed by William Alston (1989, chap. 5), and I have sympathy with many of his points. However, the voluntarism argument against the GD conception is disputed by Feldman (1988a) and John Heil (1983), among others. Feldman, for example, argues that epistemic deontologism is not wedded to the assumption of doxastic voluntarism. Many obligations remain in force, he points out, even when an agent lacks the ability to discharge them. A person is still legally obligated to repay a debt even when his financial situation makes him unable to repay it. Perhaps epistemic obligations have analogous properties.[8] Since the complex topic of doxastic voluntarism would require chapter-length treatment in its own right, I set this issue aside and confine my attention to other issues. Although I do not accept the GD conception of justification, I take it as given for purposes of the present discussion and explore where it leads. In any case, what is ultimately crucial for internalism is the accessibility requirement that the GD conception hopes to rationalize. Even if the GD conception fails to provide a good rationale, internalism would be viable if some other rationale could be provided for a suitable accessibility requirement.

2. Direct Knowability and Strong Internalism

The initial KJ constraint was formulated in terms of knowability plain and simple, but proponents of internalism often add the further qualification that determinants of justification must be *directly* knowable by the cognitive agent. Ginet, for example, writes as follows:

> Every one of every set of facts about S's position that minimally suffices to make S, at a given time, justified in being confident that p must be *directly recognizable* to S at that time. (1975, 34)

Similarly, Chisholm writes:

> [T]he concept of epistemic justification is . . . internal and immediate in that one can *find out directly*, by reflection, what one is justified in believing at any time. (1989, 7, emphasis added and original emphasis deleted)

Thus, Ginet and Chisholm do not endorse just the minimal KJ constraint as earlier formulated, but a more restrictive version, which might be written as follows:

(KJ_{dir})   The only facts that qualify as justifiers of an agent's believing p at time t are facts that the agent can readily know *directly*, at t, to obtain or not to obtain.

An initial problem arising from KJ_{dir} is this: What warrants the imposition of KJ_{dir} as opposed to the looser constraint, KJ? KJ was derived from the GD conception on the grounds that one cannot reasonably be expected to comply with epistemic duties unless one knows what those duties are. How does such an argument warrant the further conclusion that *direct* knowledge of justification must be available? Even indirect knowledge (whatever that is) would enable an agent to comply with his epistemic duties. So the second step of the argument for internalism cannot properly be revised to feature KJ_{dir} in place of KJ. Proponents of KJ_{dir} might reply that direct forms of knowledge are more powerful than indirect knowledge, but this reply is unconvincing. The power requirement was already built into the original version of KJ, and it is unclear how directness adds anything of significance on that score. Whether KJ_{dir} can be derived from GD is a serious problem, because the argument for internalism rests on something like the directness qualification; I shall say more about this later. For now I set this point aside in order to explore where KJ_{dir} leads.

What modes of knowledge count as direct? At least one form of direct knowledge is introspection. A reason for thinking that introspection is what Chisholm means by direct knowledge is that he restricts all determiners of justification to conscious states:

> A consequence of our "internalistic" theory of knowledge is that, if one is subject to an epistemic requirement at any time, then this requirement is imposed by the *conscious state* in which one happens to find oneself at that time. (1989, 59–60)

Since he restricts justifiers to conscious states, it is plausible to assume that direct knowledge, for Chisholm, means introspective knowledge, and knowledge by "reflection" coincides with knowledge by introspection.[9] At least in the case of Chisholm, then, KJ_{dir} might be replaced by KJ_{int}:

> (KJ_{int})   The only facts that qualify as justifiers of an agent's believing p at time t are facts that the agent can readily know *by introspection*, at t, to obtain or not to obtain.

Now the only facts that an agent can know by introspection are facts concerning what conscious states he is (or is not) currently in, so these are the only sorts of facts that qualify as justifiers under KJ_{int}. This form of internalism may be called *strong internalism*:

> (SI)   Only facts concerning what conscious states an agent is in at time t are justifiers of the agent's beliefs at t.

Strong internalism, however, is an unacceptable approach to justification, for it has serious, skepticism-breeding, consequences. This is demonstrated by *the problem of stored beliefs*. At any given time, the vast majority of one's beliefs are stored in memory rather than occurrent or active. Beliefs about personal data (e.g., one's social security number), about world history, about geography, or about the institutional affiliations of one's professional colleagues, are almost all stored rather than occurrent at a given moment. Furthermore, for almost any of these beliefs, one's conscious state at the time includes nothing that justifies it. No perceptual experience, no conscious memory event, and no premises consciously entertained at the selected moment will be justificationally sufficient for such a belief. According to strong internalism, then, none of these beliefs is justified at that moment. Strong internalism threatens a drastic diminution in the stock of beliefs ordinarily deemed justified, and hence in the stock of knowledge, assuming that justification is necessary for knowledge. This is a major count against this type of theory.

Feldman (1988b, 98–99) anticipates this problem because his own account of having evidence also implies that only consciously entertained factors have evidential force. Feldman tries to meet the threat by distinguishing between occurrent and dispositional senses of epistemic terms. (Feldman actually discusses knowledge rather than justification, but I shall address the issue in terms of justification because that is the target of our investigation.) Feldman is not simply restating the familiar point that "belief" has occurrent and dispositional senses. He is proposing that the term "justified" is ambiguous between an occurrent and a dispositional sense. Feldman apparently claims that in the case of stored beliefs, people at most have dispositional justification, not occurrent justification.

There are two problems with this proposal. First, if having a disposition to generate conscious evidential states qualifies as a justifier of a belief, why wouldn't this extend from memorial to perceptual dispositions? Suppose a train passenger awakes from a nap but has not yet opened his eyes. Is he justified in believing propositions about the details of the neighboring landscape? Surely not. Yet he is *disposed*, merely by opening his eyes, to generate conscious evidential states that would occurrently justify such beliefs. So the dispositional approach is far too permissive to yield an acceptable sense of "justified."[10] Second, can an internalist, especially a strong internalist, live with the idea that certain dispositions count as justifiers? Having or not having a disposition (of the requisite type) is not the sort of fact or condition that can be known by introspection. Thus, the proposal to supplement the occurrent sense of "justified" with a dispositional sense of "justified" is simply the abandonment of strong internalism.

3. Indirect Knowability and Weak Internalism

The obvious solution to the problem of stored beliefs is to relax the KJ constraint: allow justifiers to be merely indirectly knowable. This yields KJ_{ind}:

> (KJ_{ind}) The only facts that qualify as justifiers of an agent's believing p at time t are facts that the agent can readily know at t, either directly or indirectly, to obtain or not to obtain.

The danger here is that indirect knowledge might let in too much from an internalist perspective. How are externalist forms of knowledge to be excluded, e.g., perceptual knowledge? Clearly, internalism must propose specific forms of knowledge that conform with its spirit. It is fairly clear how internalism should deal with the problem of stored beliefs. Simply allow knowledge of justifiers to include memory retrieval. Stored evidence beliefs can qualify as justifiers because the agent can know that they obtain by the compound route of first retrieving them from memory and then introspecting their conscious contents. This yields the following variant of the KJ constraint:

> ($KJ_{int+ret}$) The only facts that qualify as justifiers of an agent's believing p at time t are facts that the agent can readily know, at t, to obtain or not to obtain, *by introspection and/or memory retrieval.*

This KJ constraint allows for a more viable form of internalism than strong internalism. We may call it *weak internalism*, and initially articulate it through the following principle:

> (WI)   Only facts concerning what conscious and/or stored mental states an agent is in at time t are justifiers of the agent's beliefs at t.

WI will certify the justification of many stored beliefs, because agents often have other stored beliefs that evidentially support them. A person who believes that Washington, D.C. is the capital of the United States may have a stored belief to the effect that a map of the United States he recently consulted showed Washington as the capital. The latter stored belief is what justifies the former one. So weak internalism is not plagued with the problem of stored justified beliefs. Weak internalism seems to be a legitimate form of internalism because even stored beliefs qualify, intuitively, as internal states.

Although weak internalism is better than strong internalism, it too faces severe problems. First is *the problem of forgotten evidence*.[11] Many justified beliefs are ones for which an agent once had adequate evidence that she subsequently forgot. At the time of epistemic appraisal, she no longer possesses adequate evidence that is retrievable from memory. Last year Sally read about the health benefits of broccoli in a *New York Times* science-section story. She then justifiably formed a belief in broccoli's beneficial effects. She still retains this belief but no longer recalls her original evidential source (and has never encountered either corroborating or undermining sources). Nonetheless, her broccoli belief is still justified, and, if true, qualifies as a case of knowledge. Presumably, this is because her past acquisition of the belief was epistemically proper. But past acquisition is irrelevant by the lights of internalism (including weak internalism), because only her current mental states are justifiers relevant to her current belief. All past events are "external" and therefore irrelevant according to internalism.

It might be replied that Sally does currently possess evidence in support of her broccoli belief. One of her background beliefs, we may suppose, is that most of what she remembers was learned in an epistemically proper manner. So doesn't she, after all, now have grounds for the target belief? Admittedly, she has *some* evidence, but is this evidence sufficient for justification? Surely not. In a variant case, suppose that Sally still has the same background belief—viz., that most of what she remembers was learned in an epistemically proper manner—but she in fact acquired her broccoli belief from the *National Enquirer* rather than the *New York Times*. So her broccoli belief was never acquired, or corroborated, in an epistemically sound manner. Then, even with the indicated current background belief, Sally cannot be credited with justifiably believing that broccoli is healthful. Her past acquisition is still relevant, and decisive. At least it is relevant so long as we are considering the "epistemizing" sense of justification, in which justification carries a true belief a good distance toward knowledge. Sally's belief in the healthfulness of broccoli is not justified in that sense, for surely she does not know that broccoli is healthful given that the *National Enquirer* was her sole source of information.

The category of forgotten evidence is a problem for weak internalism because, like the problem of stored beliefs facing strong internalism, it threatens skeptical outcomes. A large sector of what is ordinarily counted as knowledge are beliefs for which people have forgotten their original evidence.

In reply to the problem of forgotten evidence, Matthias Steup offers the following solution.[12] An additional requirement for memorial states to justify a belief that p, says Steup, is that the agent have adequate evidence for believing the following counterfactual: "If she had encountered p in a questionable source, she would not have formed the belief that p." Steup's suggestion is that in the *National Enquirer* variant, Sally fails to have adequate evidence for this counterfactual, and that is why her broccoli belief is not justified. My response to this proposal is twofold. First, the proposed requirement is too strong to impose on memorially justified belief. It is quite difficult to get adequate evidence for the indicated counterfactual. Second, the proposed requirement seems too weak as well. Sally might have adequate evidence for the counterfactual but still be unjustified in holding her broccoli belief. She might have adequate evidence for the counterfactual without it being true; but if it is not true and the rest of the story is as I told it, her broccoli belief is not justified. So Steup's internalist-style solution does not work.

A second problem confronting weak internalism is what I call *the problem of concurrent retrieval*. Principle WI says that *only* conscious and stored mental states are justifiers, but it does not say that *all* sets or conjunctions of such states qualify as justifiers.[13] Presumably, which sets of such states qualify is a matter to be decided by reference to $KJ_{int+ret}$. If a certain set of stored beliefs can all be concurrently retrieved at time t and concurrently introspected, then they would pass the test of $KJ_{int+ret}$, and could qualify as justifiers under the principle of indirect knowability. But if they cannot all be concurrently retrieved and introspected at t, they would fail the test. Now it is clear that the totality of an agent's stored credal corpus at a time cannot be concurrently retrieved from memory. So that set of stored beliefs does not qualify as a justifier for purposes of weak internalism. Unfortunately, this sort of belief-set is precisely what certain types of internalist theories require by way of a justifier. Consider holistic coherentism, which says that a proposition p is justified for person S at time t if and only if p coheres with S's entire corpus of beliefs at t (including, of course, the stored beliefs). A cognitive agent could ascertain, at t, whether p coheres with her entire corpus only by concurrently retrieving all of her stored beliefs. But such concurrent retrieval is psychologically impossible.[14] Thus, the critically relevant justificational fact under holistic coherentism does not meet even the indirect knowability constraint, much less the direct knowability constraint. Here is a clash, then, between a standard internalist theory of justification and the knowability rationale under scrutiny. Either that rationale is indefensible, or a familiar type of internalism must be abandoned at the outset. Nor is the problem confined to coherentism. Internalist foundationalism might also require concurrent retrieval of more basic (or low-level) beliefs than it is psychologically feasible to retrieve.

4. Logical and Probabilistic Relations

As these last examples remind us, every traditional form of internalism involves some appeal to logical relations, probabilistic relations, or their ilk. Foundationalism requires that nonbasically justified beliefs stand in suitable logical or probabilistic relations to basic beliefs; coherentism requires that one's system of beliefs be logically consistent, probabilistically coherent, or the like. None of these logical or probabilistic relations is itself a mental state, either a conscious state or a stored state. So these relations do not qualify as justifiers according to either SI or WI. The point may be illustrated more concretely within a foundationalist perspective. Suppose that Jones possesses a set of basic beliefs at t whose contents logically or probabilistically support proposition p. This property of Jones's basic beliefs—the property of supporting proposition p—is not a justifier under WI, for the property itself is neither a conscious nor a stored mental state. Nor is the possession of this property by these mental states another mental state. So WI has no way of authorizing or permitting Jones to believe p. Unless WI is liberalized, no non-basic belief will be justified, which would again threaten a serious form of skepticism.

Can this problem be remedied by simply adding the proviso that all properties of conscious or stored mental states also qualify as justifiers?[15] This proviso is unacceptably permissive for internalism. One property of many conscious and stored mental states is the property of *being caused by a reliable process*, yet surely internalism cannot admit this archetypically externalist type of property into the class of justifiers. How should the class of properties be restricted? An obvious suggestion is to include only formal properties of mental states, i.e., logical and mathematical properties of their contents. But should *all* formal properties be admitted? This approach would fly in the face of the knowability or accessibility constraint, which is the guiding theme of internalism. Only formal properties that are knowable by the agent at the time of doxastic decision should be countenanced as legitimate justifiers under internalism. Such properties, however, cannot be detected by introspection and/or memory retrieval. So some knowing operations suitable for formal properties must be added, yielding a liberalized version of the KJ constraint.

How should a liberalized KJ constraint be designed? The natural move is to add some selected computational operations or algorithms, procedures that would enable an agent to ascertain whether a targeted proposition p has appropriate logical or probabilistic relations to the contents of other belief states he is in. Precisely which computational operations are admissible? Again problems arise. The first is *the problem of the doxastic decision interval.*

The traditional idea behind internalism is that an agent is justified in believing p *at time t* if the evidential beliefs (and perhaps other, non-doxastic states) possessed *at t* have an appropriate logical or probabilistic relation to p. In short, justification is conferred simultaneously with evidence possession. Feldman makes this explicit: "For any person S and proposition p and time t, S epistemically ought to believe p at t if and only if p is supported by the evidence S has at t" (1988a, 254). Once the knowability constraint is introduced, however, simultaneous justification looks problematic. If justification is contingent on the agent's ability to know what justifiers obtain, the agent should not be permitted to believe a proposition p *at t* unless she can know *by t* whether the relevant justifiers obtain. Since it necessarily takes some time to compute logical or probabilistic relations, the simultaneity model of justification needs to be revised so that an agent's mental states at t only justify her in believing p at $t + \varepsilon$, for some suitable ε. The value of ε cannot be too large, of course, lest the agent's mental states change so as to affect the justificational status of p. But ε must be large enough to allow the agent time to determine the relevant formal relations.

These two conditions—(1) avoid mental change, but (2) allow enough time to compute formal relations—may well be jointly unsatisfiable, which would pose a severe problem for internalism. Mental states, including perceptual states that generate new evidence, change very rapidly, and they could easily change before required computations could be executed. On the other hand, although mental states do change rapidly, the agent's belief system might not be epistemically required to reflect or respond to each change until interval ε has elapsed. Some doxastic decision interval, then, might be feasible.

Is there a short enough decision interval during which justificationally pertinent formal properties can be computed? Coherentism says that S is justified in believing proposition p only if p coheres with the rest of S's belief system held at the time. Assume that coherence implies logical consistency. Then coherentism requires that the logical consistency or inconsistency of any proposition p with S's belief system must qualify as a justifier. But how quickly can consistency or inconsistency be ascertained by mental computation? As Christopher Cherniak (1984) points out, determination of even tautological consistency is a computationally complex task in the general case. Using the truth-table method to check for the consistency of a belief system with 138 independent atomic propositions, even an ideal computer working at "top speed" (checking each row of a truth table in the time it takes a light ray to traverse the diameter of a proton) would take 20 billion years, the estimated time from the "big-bang" dawn of the universe to the present. Presumably, 20 billion years is not an acceptable doxastic decision interval!

Any reasonable interval, then, is too constraining for garden-variety coherentism (see Kornblith 1989). The knowability constraint again clashes with one of the stock brands of internalism. Dyed-in-the-wool internalists might be prepared to live with this result. "So much the worse for traditional coherentism," they might say. "We can live with its demise." But this does not get internalism entirely off the hook. There threaten to be many logical and probabilistic facts that do not qualify as justifiers because they require too long a doxastic interval to compute. Furthermore, it is unclear what is a principled basis for deciding what is too long. This quandary confronting internalism has apparently escaped its proponents' attention.

A second problem for logical and probabilistic justifiers is *the availability problem*. Suppose that a particular set of computational operations—call it "COMP"—is provisionally selected for inclusion alongside introspection and memory retrieval. COMP might include, for example, a restricted (and hence noneffective) use of the truth-table method, restricted so as to keep its use within the chosen doxastic decision interval.[16] This yields a new version of the KJ constraint:

$(\text{KJ}_{\text{int}+\text{ret}+\text{COMP}})$ The only facts that qualify as justifiers of an agent's believing p at time t are facts that the agent can readily know within a suitable doxastic decision interval *via introspection, memory retrieval, and/or COMP*.

Now, the KJ constraint is presumably intended to apply not only to the cleverest or best trained epistemic agents but to all epistemic agents, including the most naive and uneducated persons on the street. After all, the point of the knowability constraint is that justifiers should be facts within the purview of every epistemic agent. Under the GD conception, compliance with epistemic duty or responsibility is not intended to be the private preserve of the logical or mathematical elite. It is something that ought to be attained—and should therefore be attainable—by any human agent. The truth-table method, however, does not seem to be in the intellectual repertoire of naive agents, so it is illegitimate to include COMP operations within a KJ constraint. Unlike introspection and memory retrieval, it is not available to all cognitive agents.

It may be replied that computational operations of the contemplated sort would be within the *capacity* of normal human agents. No super-human computational powers are required. Computing power, however, is not the issue. A relevant sequence of operations must also be *available* in the agent's intellectual repertoire; that is, she must know which operations are appropriate to obtain an answer to the relevant (formal) question.[17] Since truth-table methods and other such algorithms are probably not in the repertoire of ordinary cognitive agents, they cannot properly be included in a KJ constraint.

A third problem concerns the proper methodology that should be used in selecting a KJ constraint that incorporates computational operations. As we see from the first two problems, a KJ constraint that conforms to the spirit of the GD rationale must reflect the basic cognitive skills or repertoires of actual human beings. What these basic repertoires consist in, however, cannot be determined a priori. It can only be determined with the help of empirical science. This fact fundamentally undermines the methodological posture of internalism, a subject to which I shall return in section 7.

Until now, I have assumed a *universal* accessibility constraint, one that holds for all cognitive agents. But perhaps potential justifiers for one agent need not be potential justifiers for another. Justifiers might be allowed to vary from agent to agent, depending on what is knowable by the particular agent. If two agents have different logical or probabilistic skills, then some properties that do not qualify as justifiers for one might yet qualify as justifiers for the other. Indeed, the constraint $KJ_{int+ret+COMP}$ might be read in precisely this agent-relativized way. The subscripts may be interpreted as indicating knowledge routes that are available *to the agent in question*, not necessarily to all agents.

If KJ constraints are agent-relativized as a function of differences in knowledge skills, this means that two people in precisely the same evidential state (in terms of perceptual situation, background beliefs, etc.) might have different epistemic entitlements. But if the two agents are to comply with their respective epistemic duties, each must *know* which knowledge skills she has. This simply parallels the second step of the internalist's original three-step argument. If one's epistemic duties or entitlements depend on one's knowledge skills (e.g., on one's computational skills), then compliance with one's duties requires knowledge of which skills one possesses. There are two problems with this approach. First, it is unlikely that many people—especially ordinary people on the street—have this sort of knowledge, and this again threatens large-scale skepticism. Second, what is now required to be known by the agent is something about the *truth-getting* power of her cognitive skills—that is, the power of her skills in detecting justifiers. This seems to be precisely the sort of *external* property that internalists regard as anathema. How can they accept this solution while remaining faithful to the spirit of internalism?[18]

5. Epistemic Principles

When the KJ constraint speaks of justifiers, it is not clear exactly what these comprehend. Specifically, do justifiers include epistemic principles themselves? I believe that principles should be included, because epistemic principles are among the items that determine whether or not an agent is justified in believing a proposition, which is just how "justifiers" was defined. Furthermore, true epistemic principles are items an agent must know if she is going to determine her epistemic duties correctly. Knowledge of her current states of mind and their properties will not instruct her about her epistemic duties and entitlements unless she also knows true epistemic principles.

How are epistemic principles to be known, according to internalism? Chisholm (1990) says that central epistemic principles are normative supervenience principles, which (when true) are necessarily true. Since they are necessary truths, they can be known a priori; in particular, they can be known "by reflection":

> The internalist assumes that, merely by reflecting upon his own conscious state, he can formulate a set of epistemic principles that will enable him to find out, with respect to any possible belief he has, whether he is justified in having that belief. (Chisholm 1989, 76, emphasis omitted)

This passage is ambiguous as to whether (correct) epistemic principles are accessible on reflection just to epistemologists, or accessible to naive epistemic agents as well. The latter, however, must be required by internalism, because justifiers are supposed to be determinable by all epistemic agents.

Are ordinary or naive agents really capable of formulating and recognizing correct epistemic principles? This seems highly dubious. Even many career-long epistemologists have failed to articulate and appreciate correct epistemic principles. Since different epistemologists offer disparate and mutually conflicting candidates for epistemic principles, at most a fraction of these epistemologists can be right. Perhaps none of the principles thus far tendered by epistemologists is correct! In light of this shaky and possibly dismal record by professional epistemologists, how can we expect ordinary people, who are entirely ignorant of epistemology and its multiple pitfalls, to succeed at this task?[19] Nor is it plausible that they should succeed at this task purely "by reflection" on their conscious states, since among the matters epistemic principles must resolve is what computational skills are within the competence of ordinary cognizers. I do not see how this can be answered a priori, "by reflection."

A crippling problem emerges for internalism. If epistemic principles are not knowable by all naive agents, no such principles can qualify as justifiers under the KJ constraint. If no epistemic principles so qualify, no proposition can be justifiably believed by any agent. Wholesale skepticism follows.

6. The Core Dilemma
for the Three-Step Argument

In this section I raise doubts about whether there is any cogent inferential route from the GD conception to internalism via an acceptable KJ constraint. Here is the core dilemma. The minimal, unvarnished version of the KJ constraint does not rationalize internalism. That simple constraint merely says that justifiers must be readily knowable, and some readily knowable facts might be external rather than internal. If *all* routes to knowledge of justifiers are allowed, then knowledge by perception must be allowed. If knowledge by perception is allowed, then facts of an external sort could qualify for the status of justifiers. Of course, no epistemologist claims that purely external facts should serve as justifiers. But partly external facts are nominated by externalists for the rank of justifiers. Consider properties of the form: being a reliable perceptual indicator of a certain environmental fact. This sort of property is at least partly external because reliability involves truth, and truth (on the usual assumption) is external. Now suppose that a certain auditory perceptual state has the property of being a reliable indicator of the presence of a mourning dove in one's environment. Might the possession of this reliable indicatorship property qualify as a justifer on the grounds that it is indeed readily knowable? If every route to knowledge is legitimate, I do not see how this possibility can be excluded. After all, one could use past perceptions of mourning doves and their songs to determine that the designated auditory state is a reliable indicator of a mourning dove's presence. So if unrestricted knowledge is allowed, the (partly) external fact in question might be perfectly knowable. Thus, the unvarnished version of the KJ constraint does not exclude external facts from the ranks of the justifiers.

The simple version of the KJ constraint, then, does not support internalism. Tacit recognition of this is what undoubtedly leads internalists to favor a "direct" knowability constraint. Unfortunately, this extra rider is not rationalized by the GD conception. The GD conception at best implies that cognitive agents must know what justifiers are present or absent. No particular *types* of knowledge, or *paths* to knowledge, are intimated. So the GD conception cannot rationalize a restrictive version of the KJ constraint that unambiguously yields internalism.

Let me put the point another way. The GD conception implies that justifiers must be readily knowable, but are internal facts always *more readily* knowable than external facts? As discussed earlier, probabilistic relations presumably qualify as internal, but they do not seem to be readily knowable by human beings. An entire tradition of psychological research on "biases and heuristics" suggests that naive agents commonly commit probabilistic fallacies such as the "conjunction fallacy" and use formally incorrect judgmental heuristics, e.g., the representativeness heuristic and the anchoring-and-adjustment heuristic (Tversky and Kahneman 1982, 1983). If this is right, people's abilities to detect probabilistic relationships are actually rather weak. People's perceptual capacities to detect external facts seem, by contrast, far superior. The unqualified version of the KJ constraint, therefore, holds little promise for restricting all justifiers to internal conditions in preference to external conditions, as internalism requires.[20]

7. The Methodology of Epistemology: Empirical or A Priori?

Internalism standardly incorporates the doctrine that epistemology is a purely a priori or armchair enterprise rather than one that needs help from empirical science. Chisholm puts the point this way:

> The epistemic principles that [the epistemologist] formulates are principles that one may come upon and apply merely by sitting in one's armchair, so to speak, and without calling for any outside assistance. In a word, one need only consider one's own state of mind. (1989, 76)

Previous sections already raised doubts about the merits of apriorism in epistemology, even in the context of the theoretical architecture presented here. I now want to challenge the viability of apriorism in greater depth.

Assume that, despite my earlier reservations, an internalist restriction on justifiers has somehow been derived, one that allows only conscious states and certain of their non-external properties to serve as justifiers. How should the epistemologist identify particular conscious states and properties as justifiers for specific propositions (or types of propositions)? In other words, how should specific epistemic principles be crafted? Should the task be executed purely a priori, or can scientific psychology help?

For concreteness, consider justifiers for memory beliefs. Suppose an adult consciously remembers seeing, as a teenager, a certain matinee idol. This ostensible memory could have arisen from imagination, since he frequently fantasized about this matinee idol and imagined seeing her in person. What clues are present in the current memory impression by which he can tell whether or not the recollection is veridical? This is precisely the kind of issue that internalist epistemic principles should address. If there are no differences in features of memory states that stem from perceptions of real occurrences versus features of states that stem from mere imagination, doesn't this raise a specter of skepticism over the domain of memory? If there are no indications by which to distinguish veridical from non-veridical memory impressions, can we be justified in trusting our memory impressions? Skepticism aside, epistemologists should surely be interested in identifying the features of conscious memory impressions by which people are made more or less justified (or prima facie justified) in believing things about the past.

Epistemologists have said very little on this subject. Their discussions tend to be exhausted by characterizations of memory impressions as "vivid" or "non-vivid." There is, I suspect, a straightforward reason for the paucity of detail. It is extremely difficult, using purely armchair methods, to dissect the micro-features of memory experiences so as to identify telltale differences between trustworthy and questionable memories. On the other hand, empirical methods have produced some interesting findings, which might properly be infused into epistemic principles in a way entirely congenial to internalism. Important research in this area has been done by Marcia Johnson and her colleagues (e.g., Johnson and Raye 1981; Johnson, Foley, Suengas, and Raye 1988). I shall illustrate my points by brief reference to their research.

Johnson calls the subject of some of her research "reality monitoring." She tries to characterize the detectable differences between (conscious) memory traces derived from veridical perception of events versus memory traces generated by mere imaginations of events.[21] Johnson and Raye (1981) propose four dimensions along which memory cues will typically differ depending on whether their origin was perceptual or imaginative. As compared with memories that originate from imagination, memories originating from perception tend to have (1) more perceptual information (e.g., color and sound), (2) more contextual information about time and place, and (3) more meaningful detail. When a memory trace is rich along these three dimensions, this is evidence of its having originated through perception. Memories originating from imagination or thought, by contrast, tend to be rich on another dimension: they contain more information about the cognitive operations involved in the original thinkings or imaginings (e.g., effortful attention, image creation, or search). Perception is more automatic than imagination, so a memory trace that originates from perception will tend to lack attributes concerning effortful operations. Johnson and Raye therefore suggest that differences in average value along these types of dimensions can form the basis for deciding whether the origin of a memory is perceptual or non-perceptual. A memory with a great deal of visual and spatial detail, and without records of intentional constructive and organizational processes, should be judged to have been perceptually derived.[22]

Epistemologists would be well-advised to borrow these sorts of ideas and incorporate them into their epistemic principles. A person is (prima facie) justified in believing in the real occurrence of an ostensibly recalled event if the memory trace is strong on the first three dimensions and weak on the fourth dimension. Conversely, an agent is unjustified in believing in the real occurrence of the recalled event if the memory trace is strong on the fourth dimension but weak on the first three dimensions. All of these dimensions, of course, concern features of conscious experience. For this reason, internalist epistemologists should be happy to incorporate these kinds of features into their epistemic principles.

Let me distinguish two categories of epistemologically significant facts about memory experience that empirical psychology might provide. First, as we have seen, it might identify types of representational materials that are generally available in people's memory experiences. Second, it might indicate which of these representational materials are either reliable or counter-reliable indicators of the veridicality of the ostensibly recalled events. Is the reliability of a memory cue a legitimate issue from an internalist perspective? It might be thought not, since reliability is usually classed as an external property. However, epistemologists might use reliability considerations to decide which memory characteristics should be featured in epistemic principles. They need not insert reliability per se into the principles. There is nothing in our present formulation of internalism, at any rate, that bars the latter approach. Any KJ constraint provides only a necessary condition for being a justifier; it leaves open the possibility that additional necessary conditions, such as reliable in-dication, must also be met. Indeed, many internalists do use reliability as a (partial) basis for their choice of justifiers. BonJour (1985, 7) says that the basic role of justification is that of a *means* to truth, and he defends coherence as a justifier on the ground that a coherent system of beliefs is likely to correspond to reality. This point need not be settled definitively, however. There are already adequate grounds for claiming that internalism cannot be optimally pursued without help from empirical psychology, whether or not reliability is a relevant consideration.

8. Conclusion

Let us review the parade of problems infecting internalism that we have witnessed, though not in their order of presentation. (1) The argument from the GD conception of justification to internalism does not work. Internalism can only be derived from a suitably qualified version of the KJ constraint because the unqualified version threatens to allow external facts to count as justifiers. No suitably qualified version of the KJ constraint is derivable from the GD conception. (2) A variety of qualified KJ constraints are possible, each leading to a different version of internalism. None of these versions is intuitively acceptable. Strong internalism, which restricts justifiers to con-scious states, is stuck with the problem of stored beliefs. Weak internalism, which allows stored as well as conscious beliefs to count as justifiers, faces the problem of forgotten evidence and the problem of concurrent retrieval. (3) The question of how logical and probabilistic facts are to be included in the class of justifiers is plagued by puzzles, especially the puzzle of the doxastic decision interval and the issue of availability. (4) Epistemic principles must be among the class of justifiers, but such principles fail internalism's knowability requirement. (5) The favored methodology of internalism—the armchair method—cannot be sustained even if we grant the assumption that justifiers must be conscious states.

Internalism is rife with problems. Are they all traceable to the GD rationale? Could internalism be salvaged by switching to a different rationale? A different rationale might help, but most of the problems raised here arise from the knowability constraint. It is unclear exactly which knowability constraint should be associated with internalism, and all of the available candidates generate problematic theories. So I see no hope for internalism; it does not survive the glare of the spotlight.

Notes

An earlier version of this chapter was presented at the Central Division meeting of the American Philosophical Association, in Pittsburgh, April 25, 1997. My commentator on that occasion was Matthias Steup, and I am much indebted to him for valuable correspondence on this topic. I am also grateful to Tim Bayne and Holly Smith for very useful suggestions.

1. Prominent statements of externalism include Armstrong 1973; Dretske 1981; Goldman 1986; Nozick 1981; and Plantinga 1993a, b.

2. Major statements of internalism include BonJour 1985; Chisholm 1966, 1977, 1989; Foley 1987; Lehrer 1990; and Pollock 1986. In addition to relatively pure versions of externalism and internalism, there are also mixtures of the two approaches, as found in Alston 1989; Audi 1993; and Sosa 1991.

3. Plantinga also traces internalism to the deontological conception: "If we go back to the source of the internalist tradition, . . . we can see that internalism arises out of deontology; a deontological conception of warrant . . . leads directly to internalism" (1993b, 24–25). Alston (1989, 236) proposes a slightly different rationale for internalism, although his rationale also proceeds via the knowability constraint. Alston suggests that the concept of justification derives from the interpersonal practice of criticizing one another's beliefs and asking for their credentials. A person can appropriately respond to other people's demands for credentials only if he knows what those credentials are. So it is quite understandable, says Alston, that justifiers must meet the requirement of being accessible to the agent. Clearly, this is one way to derive the accessibility constraint without appeal to the deontological conception. But Alston is the only one I know of who advances this ground for the accessibility constraint. In any case, most of the problems I shall identify pertain to the accessibility constraint itself, which Alston's rationale shares with the deontological rationale.

4. For example, Bales (1971) distinguishes between two possible aims of act-utilitarianism: as a specifier of a right-making characteristic or as a decision-making procedure. He defends utilitarianism against certain critics by saying that it does not *have* to perform the latter function.

5. Some internalists explicitly reject externalism on the grounds that it cannot be used as a decision guide. For example, Pollock says: "[I]t is in principle impossible for us to actually employ externalist norms. I take this to be a conclusive refutation

of belief externalism" (1986, 134). Pollock would not subscribe to the full argument for internalism I am discussing, however, because it is committed to the "intellectualist model" of epistemology, which he disparages.

6. For the distinction between reliability and power (phrased slightly differently), see Goldman 1986, chap. 6.

7. Jack Lyons points out that to comply with one's epistemic duty it suffices to know *that one has* (undefeated) justifiers for proposition p; one does not have to know *which* justifiers these are. So the argument is not entitled to conclude that knowledge of particular justifiers is required by epistemic duty. Practically speaking, however, it is difficult to see how a cognitive agent could know that relevant justifiers exist without knowing which particular ones exist. So I shall pass over this objection to the internalist line of argument.

8. Feldman's response, however, undercuts the step from the GD conception of justification to the knowability constraint. If epistemic duty does not require that the agent be *able* to discharge this duty, there is no longer a rationale for the knowability constraint. A different line of response to the voluntarism worry is taken by Lehrer (1981), who suggests that epistemological analysis should focus not on belief but on *acceptance*, where acceptance is some sort of action that is subject to the will.

9. Other epistemologists who restrict justifiers to conscious states or discuss access in terms of introspection include Moser (1985, 174); Feldman (1988b); and Audi (1989).

10. Feldman might reply that there is an important distinction between memorial and perceptual dispositions; but it isn't clear on what basis a principled distinction can be drawn.

11. This sort of problem is discussed by Harman (1986); Senor (1993); and Audi (1995).

12. Steup's proposal occurred in a commentary on an earlier version of this paper, presented at the Central Division meeting of the American Philosophical Association, April 25, 1997.

13. Obviously, one would need to reject the principle that the knowability of fact A and the knowability of fact B entail the knowability of the conjunctive fact A and B.

14. The "doxastic presumption" invoked by BonJour (1985, 101–6) seems to assume that this is possible, but this is simply an undefended assumption. Pollock (1986, 136) also raises the problem identified here, though in slightly different terms.

15. More precisely, the contemplated proviso should say that the possession of any property by a mental state (or set of mental states) qualifies as a justifier. This reading will be understood wherever the text talks loosely of "properties."

16. Because of the contemplated restriction, there will be many questions about formal facts to which COMP cannot deliver answers. Thus, formal facts that might otherwise qualify as justifiers will not so qualify under the version of the KJ constraint that incorporates COMP.

17. Propositional (or "declarative") knowledge of the appropriate sequence of operations is, perhaps, an unduly restrictive requirement. It would suffice for the agent to have "procedural" skills of the right sort. But even such skills will be lacking in naive cognitive agents.

18. It might be argued that internalism's spirit leads to a similar requirement even

for universal versions of a KJ constraint, not just for agent-relativized versions. Perhaps so; but so much the worse for the general form of internalism.

19. A similar worry is expressed by Alston (1989, 221–22).

20. It is not really clear, moreover, why logical or probabilistic facts intuitively count as "internal" facts. They certainly are not internal in the same sense in which mental states are internal. This is an additional problem about the contours of internalism.

21. Memory errors are not confined, of course, to confusions of actual with imagined events. There are also errors that arise from confusing, or blending, two actual events. But this research of Johnson's focuses on the actual/non-actual (or perceived versus imagined) problem.

22. They also recognize that people can compare a target memory with memories of contextually related events to assess the target's veridicality. This kind of "coherence" factor is a stock-in-trade of epistemology, however, and hence not a good example of the distinctive contributions psychology can make to this subject. I therefore pass over it.

2

A Priori Warrant and Naturalistic Epistemology

1. Introduction

Epistemology has recently witnessed a number of efforts to rehabilitate rationalism, to defend the existence and importance of a priori knowledge or warrant construed as the product of rational insight or apprehension (Bealer 1987; Bigelow 1992; BonJour 1992, 1998; Burge 1998; Butchvarov 1970; Katz 1998; Plantinga 1993). This effort has sometimes been coupled with an attack on naturalistic epistemology, especially in BonJour 1994 and Katz 1998. Such coupling is not surprising, because naturalistic epistemology is often associated with thoroughgoing empiricism and the rejection of the a priori. In this chapter, however, I shall present a conception of naturalistic epistemology that is entirely compatible with a priori justification or knowledge. The resulting conception, I claim, gives us a better appreciation of the respective merits of the rational and the empirical, as well as a better understanding of how moderate epistemological naturalism comports, at least in principle, with moderate rationalism. This chapter defends moderate rationalism; but it does not defend everything rationalists have often wanted, only what it is reasonable to grant them.

The a priori is traditionally regarded as a type of *knowledge*, and sometimes as a type of *truth*. I shall follow the practice of recent discussants who treat the a priori primarily as a species of *warrant* or *justification* (I use these terms interchangeably). This has several advantages. First, it properly allows for the possibility that a belief might have a priori warrant but fail to be true, and hence fail to be a piece of knowledge. Second, it sidesteps, or at least marginalizes, the question of what else is required for knowledge beyond justified true belief. Third, it highlights the fact that unlike the necessary/

contingent distinction, which is a distinction between types of truth, the a priori/a posteriori distinction is fundamentally concerned with sources of warrant or justification, not types of (true) propositions. It is not wrong to use the term "a priori" as a predicate of propositions, e.g., as a predicate that applies to any proposition for which a person *might* have a priori warrant. But such a use is derivative from the central, epistemic sense of "a priori."

2. What Is Naturalistic Epistemology?

Many things can be meant by "naturalism" and "naturalistic epistemology." Some forms of naturalism involve metaphysical theses—for example, the thesis that everything in the world either is physical or supervenes on the physical—and some forms of naturalism involve methodological doctrines— for example, the doctrine that proper methodology is purely empirical.[1] I am concerned here with specifically epistemological forms of naturalism and shall therefore try, as far as possible, to skirt issues of metaphysical naturalism. Although rationalism might invite certain forms of metaphysical anti-naturalism, I shall remain largely neutral on these metaphysical issues. Epistemological naturalism itself comes in many varieties and flavors however, none of which is uniquely correct or authoritative.[2] I begin by first characterizing some radical forms of naturalistic epistemology which I do not endorse and then turn to a more attractive form of epistemological naturalism that I cheerfully embrace.

The first form of radical epistemological naturalism will be called *scientistic naturalism*:

(SN)   Epistemology is a branch of science. The statements of epistemology are a subset of the statements of science, and the proper method of doing epistemology is the empirical method of science.

This formulation of naturalistic epistemology is obviously drawn from Quine's description of the subject in "Epistemology Naturalized" (Quine 1969). He there describes naturalistic epistemology as a "chapter of psychology and hence of natural science" (82). It studies a certain input-output relation involving a particular "natural phenomenon, viz., a physical human subject" (82).

My principal dissatisfaction with this description of naturalistic epistemology is that no branch of empirical science, including psychology, takes on the (normative) tasks of specifying the criteria, conditions, or standards for *justification* and/or *knowledge*. But surely at least part of epistemology's mission is to undertake these tasks. Thus, as many critics of Quine have pointed out (e.g., Kim 1988), his conception of naturalistic epistemology omits too much of what is distinctive of epistemology. Some might argue that the sciences of probability or statistics do address the question of standards of justification or warrant. However, these are not usually considered *empirical* sciences, and they are not the sciences Quine mentions in saying that epistemology should be a branch of science. Furthermore, it is controversial whether either of those sciences (or branches of mathematics) offers a theory of justified or warranted belief.

The second form of radical epistemological naturalism is what I shall call *empiricist naturalism*. I formulate it as follows:

> (EN)   All justification arises from empirical methods. The task of epistemology is to articulate and defend these methods in further detail.

Unlike (SN), (EN) has the virtue of addressing the nature of justification, which (SN) ostensibly dodges. (EN) also properly assigns to epistemology the task of clarifying appropriate epistemic methods. (EN) also differs from (SN) in not equating epistemology with some branch of empirical science. To that extent, it is a bit weaker than (SN). At the same time (EN) is stronger than (SN) insofar as it makes a more unequivocal commitment to empiricism. (SN) does not say that *all* justification arises empirically—in fact, it says nothing about justification at all. (SN) specifies that the study of *epistemology* must be empirical, but it is noncommittal on whether the warrant for *all* subjects is empirical.

The obvious problem with (EN) is that it is far from clear that an adequate epistemology must hold that all warranted belief is empirical. Rejection of thoroughgoing empiricism, however, should not automatically exclude one from a defense of epistemological naturalism. There is a moderate conception of epistemological naturalism, I submit, that is perfectly compatible with non-empirical warrant.[3]

The naturalism I recommend is a fusion of two theses, the first concerning the generic source of epistemic warrant and the second concerning the nature of the epistemological enterprise. Here is my formulation of *moderate naturalism*:

> (MN)   (A) All epistemic warrant or justification is a function of the psychological (perhaps computational) processes that produce or preserve belief.
> (B) The epistemological enterprise needs appropriate help from science, especially the science of the mind.

Thesis (A) fits with the rather minimal metaphysical point that epistemic agents are natural phenomena, namely, physical organisms. It goes beyond this claim, moreover, in locating the source of warrant in the psychological or computational processes by which beliefs are formed and preserved. This thesis about warrant (originating, I believe, in Harman 1973 and Goldman 1979) corresponds to what Kitcher (1992) calls the *psychologistic* conception of epistemological naturalism. BonJour (1994) argues that psychologism is not a very distinctive ingredient of epistemological naturalism because "it is hard to believe anyone has ever disputed [it]" (290). "Minimal psychologism," says BonJour, involves little or no departure from traditional epistemology. If "traditional epistemology" means the history of pre-20th-century epistemology, then I would agree. Indeed I have elsewhere emphasized that psychologism dominated the great sweep of historical epistemology (Goldman 1985, 1986, 6). But in our own era—that is, in the 20th century—epistemological psychologism has been frequently attacked. During the positivist era epistemic concern with the "genesis" of a belief was considered a fallacy: Reichenbach (1938) and his successors drew a sharp distinction between the the context of discovery—to which causal questions were admitted as relevant—and the context of justification—to which causal questions were deemed irrelevant. Nor was the rejection of psychologism confined to the positivist period. Among recent epistemologists, Chisholm criticizes the causal approach (1989, 82–84) and erects standards of justification that ignore a belief's causes. Similarly, Lehrer labels it a "causal fallacy" to confuse a person's reason for belief with the cause of his believing it (1990, 169).

Thesis (B) of moderate naturalism merely says that the epistemological enterprise "needs help" from science. (MN) thereby differs from (SN) in not identifying epistemology with any branch or sub-branch of science, and in not limiting epistemology to narrowly scientific questions. But it shares with (SN) the idea that empirical science has important contributions to make to epistemology (more on these contributions later).

The most salient feature of (MN) for present purposes is that it makes no commitment to any thoroughgoing form of empiricism. It leaves it entirely open that rational insight or rational apprehension might be among the sources of epistemic warrant. In particular, since rational insight or apprehension might be a variety of belief-generating causal process, the door is not closed to rationalistic warrant. Others who have defended a moderate conception of naturalism have not looked so kindly on the a priori. For example, Kitcher embeds the following thesis in his favored form of naturalism: "Virtually nothing is knowable a priori, and in particular, no epistemological principle is knowable a priori" (1992, 76). Similarly, Devitt identifies naturalism with the view that "there is only one way of knowing, the empirical way that is the basis of science (whatever way that may be). So I reject *a priori* knowledge" (1996, 2). In contrast to Kitcher and Devitt, the form of moderate naturalism I advocate—when combined with the conception of a priority I shall defend—does not take so dismissive an attitude toward the a priori. Certainly the formulation of epistemological naturalism contained in (MN) does not automatically exclude a priori sources of warrant as inevitably obscure, mysterious, occult, or epistemically disreputable.

3. Features of A Priori Warrant

Certain properties have been historically associated with the a priori that might indeed be in tension with epistemological naturalism. Let us review these historically salient properties and ask whether they really must be retained in any sensible account of a priority. Following the lead of other recent writers, I argue that many of these properties—especially those posing the most serious conflict with naturalism—are inessential to a priori warrant and should be abandoned.

Six properties are traditionally associated with a priori knowledge or warrant: (1) a non-experiential, i.e., non-perceptual, source or basis, (2) necessity, (3) a subject-matter of abstract, eternal objects, (4) infallibility, (5) certainty, and (6) rational unrevisability (incorrigibility). The first of these properties—having a non-perceptual source—is unquestionably essential to a priority. The second of the six properties, necessity, is another firmly entrenched feature of a priority according to historical treatments. I am uncertain whether some sort of involvement in necessity is essential to the a priori. An appropriate restriction involving necessity is difficult to formulate, but I do not preclude the possibility of identifying one. It is a delicate matter that will be explored below but not firmly settled.

The third property associated with the a priori is that its subject-matter should be abstract, eternal objects, such as numbers, universals, or meanings. Here I want to stick to my earlier resolve to stick to the *epistemological* questions concerning the a priori and avoid the *metaphysical* questions. Thus, I want to remain neutral on the issue of what the subject-matter of the a priori has to be. To be more precise, although I am willing to concede that only beliefs on certain topics or in certain domains will qualify as warranted a priori, I want to remain neutral on the question of what the *truth-makers* are in those domains. I want to be able to concede the possibility of a priori warrant about arithmetic without taking a position on what numbers are or must be. Given this desire for metaphysical neutrality, it is obviously unacceptable to make an abstract subject-matter a necessary condition for a priority.[4]

Concerning the three remaining properties, I join several contemporaries in rejecting the traditional notion that a priori warrant must possess them. I consider them in the order listed, beginning with infallibility. A mode of justification is infallible if its use always leads (perhaps necessarily) to truth. I interpret this to mean that whenever a person believes a proposition with sufficient a priori warrant, then that belief is true. By "sufficient" I mean enough warrant that it would qualify a belief for knowledge if it were true and satisfied other Gettier-averting conditions (see Casullo 1988). However, there are many historical and everyday cases that comprise counterexamples to infallibility—cases in which people had sufficient a priori warrant for beliefs that have subsequently been recognized as false. BonJour (1998, 111–12) presents three categories of such counterexamples. First, certain claims of mathematics and logic were at one time regarded as self-evident by all leading authorities but are now regarded as false, e.g., Euclidean geometry and naive set theory. Second, there are a priori claims of rationalist metaphysicians that cannot all be true because they conflict with one another. For example, reality cannot consist both of a system of timeless, windowless monads and also of one indivisible absolute mind. If these examples are not wholly convincing because it isn't transparent that the foregoing beliefs were warranted, we may turn to BonJour's third category. There are routine errors in calculation, proof, and reasoning. When adequate care is taken in such matters, a reasoner's belief is presumably sufficiently justified on a priori grounds, but this still does not preclude all mistakes.

The next traditional property of a priori justification is certainty: the highest possible level of warrant. According to the tradition, propositions known (or warranted) a priori are self-evident, and self-evidence is typically taken to imply certainty. To require a priority to yield certainty is presumably to say that a priori justification comes in only one degree: the highest. So every a priori justified belief must be at least as well justified as any belief whatever; and if, as is commonly maintained, all empirical beliefs are less than certain, then all a priori beliefs must have greater justification than all empirical beliefs. Is this consequence plausible? Routine beliefs about mathematics and logic are presumably justified a priori. But if they are fallible, as conceded earlier, can they really be certain? Must they all be better justified than any perceptual belief whatsoever, including the belief that there is a telephone on the table before me? That is counterintuitive.

The sixth traditional property of a priority is rational unrevisability. Quine famously wrote that "no statement is immune from revision" (1961, 43), and he associated revisability with empiricism. A priori statements, if there were any, would be statements that are rationally immune to revision. Putnam (1979) makes rational unrevisability a condition of a priority in saying that an a priori truth is one that "it would never subsequently be rational to reject no matter how the world turns out (epistemically) to be" (1979, 433). Similarly, Kitcher's account of a priori knowledge implies that if a person has a priori warrant for proposition p at time t, then nothing he can undergo after t would rationally undermine this warrant:

We can say that a proposition is unrevisable for a person at a time in case there is no possible continuation of that person's experience after that time which would make it reasonable for her to change her attitude to the proposition. The explication makes it apparent why one might think that propositions which a person knows a priori are unrevisable for that person. If you have a priori knowledge that p, then you have an a priori warrant for a belief that p. Assuming that the warrant is available independently of time, then, given any continuation of your experience, you would have available to you a warrant which would continue to support belief. Hence, it would never be reasonable for you to abandon p in favor of its negation. Whatever trickery your experience may devise for you, you will always be able to undergo a process which will sustain the belief. (1981, 222)

Examining the unrevisability thesis, Casullo (1988) distinguishes strong and weak versions of unrevisability. The strong version says that if S is justified in believing that p a priori, then the statement that p is rationally unrevisable in light of *any* future evidence. The weak version says that if S is justified in believing that p a priori, then the statement that p is rationally unrevisable in light of any future *experiential* evidence. Casullo proceeds to give convincing counterexamples to each of these unrevisability constraints on the concept of a priori warrant.[5] Charlie believes that p entails q after reflecting on a valid proof of this entailment, so presumably he has a priori warrant for this belief. But suppose there is a pseudoproof that p entails $\sim q$ such that if this pseudo-proof were brought to Charlie's attention, he would not detect any flaws in it or be able to discount it in any other fashion. Then his current a priori warrant for the original entailment is rationally revisable; this warrant *could* be defeated. Nonetheless, Charlie still possesses a priori warrant for the entailment now. This case refutes the strong unrevisability thesis. To refute the weak unrevisability thesis, Casullo presents an example involving defeating evidence of a neurophysiological sort. Like Charlie, Phil bases a logic belief on a certain proof he has carefully considered. But if Phil were to be apprised of a certain brain scan of his logical thinking, this information would undermine his warrant for trusting his own thought process—although we may suppose that the brain scan is flawed and his logical thinking is impeccable. Phil really does have a priori warrant for his belief, although that warrant is subject to *empirical* defeat. Notice that the mere fact that a source of warrant is subject to empirical defeat does not show that it itself is empirical. Introspective warrant for a belief about one's bodily sensations might be defeasible by neurophysiological observations; but this does not imply that the original warrant is not introspective.

For all of these reasons, properties (4), (5), and (6), which are often associated with a priority, should be peeled away from that concept. Once this surgery is accomplished, epistemological naturalism should be much less repelled by the prospect of the a priori. Infallibility, certainty, and unrevisability may indeed be unlikely bedfellows of naturalism, because the prospect is dim that any natural causal process is either infallible, certain, or closed to correction. But once these features are deleted from the defining characteristics of the a priori, naturalists can find it much more palatable.

Another feature of rational insight, however, might frighten off naturalists. This is the perceptual model of rational insight, in which the objects of rational insight are somehow cognized in a fashion analogous to the perception of physical objects. Perception is a causal process, in favorable cases, a process that causally connects a perceived object with the perceiver's mental experience. If rational insight is understood on this model, it must consist in a causal connection between the realm of rationally knowable objects and the knower's cognitive awareness. But it is highly doubtful, from a naturalistic perspective, that such causal connections could obtain. Benacerraf (1973) crystallized this problem in the domain of numbers. If numbers are Platonistic entities, can they really have a causal connection with people's mental lives? This problem seems particularly threatening to the form of naturalism adopted here, because (MN) endorses a causal theory of warrant. How can this form of naturalism be reconciled with a priori knowledge?

A crucial step in the reconciliation is to distinguish two types of causal processes, what I shall call *intra-mental processes* and *trans-mental processes*. Intra-mental processes occur wholly within the mind; trans-mental processes include links that are external to the mind as well as links that are internal. Warrant-conferring processes, as envisaged by (MN), are intramental processes; they don't encompass objects outside the mind (although the contents of their constituent states may *refer* to such objects). Thus, a priori warrant does not require the sort of trans-mental, perception-like process that Benacerraf was discussing.[6]

If a priori warrant does not require a perception-like causal connection between mental apprehensions and extra-mental realities that these apprehensions are about, how can they (non-accidentally) get the truth about the extramental realities (which is required for *knowledge*)? Bigelow (1992) suggests one possibility: necessities in the world might be "reflected" in the minds of the agents who are seeking to understand that world. "[A] necessary link between representations may . . . mirror a necessary link in the world, between the things which they represent. This harmony between representations and things represented is the source of the a priori character of mathematical knowledge" (1992, 155). Here again we see that a priori warrant and a priori knowledge are not committed to assumptions that will inevitably repel a conscientious naturalist. Of course, if the truth-makers of mathematical propositions are abstracta, that will presumably worry a metaphysical naturalist. But as long as we focus on epistemological naturalism, which sets metaphysical issues aside, there is no cause for concern.

Let us review where we stand. Properties (4), (5), and (6) have been carefully peeled away from the a priori, and property (3) has been scrupulously set aside. Does this leave us with a precise enough specification of a priori warrant, precise enough to distinguish it from other forms of warrant? We are left with two ingredients for distinguishing a priori from other forms of warrant, and it is unclear whether these two ingredients are adequate to the task.

The first ingredient for characterizing a priori warrant is a negative feature: the *absence* of an experiential or perceptual basis of belief. Even this feature, of course, needs to be clarified if it is to serve as a necessary condition for a priority. As is often pointed out, the ability to comprehend a proposition may require perceptual experience to learn its constituent concepts. We don't want such perceptual concept-learning to count against the possibility of a priori warrant for belief. This much understood, we must next ask whether a non-experiential, non-perceptual basis for belief is a *sufficient* condition of a priority. Burge contends that it is:

> A warrant . . . is *a priori* if neither sense experiences nor sense-perceptual beliefs are referred to or relied upon to contribute to the justificational force particular to that warrant. (1998, 3)

This is a negative characterization of the a priori: a warrant is a priori if it is *not* perceptual. Such a negative condition, however, will not do. To take just two examples, memory warrant and introspective warrant are both forms of non-perceptual warrant, but neither is a priori. A belief formed purely by memory, as when one recalls having had a certain (non-sensory) thought, does not have perceptual warrant; but neither is its warrant of the a priori variety. Similarly, introspection can give rise to warrant, but its type of warrant is neither perceptual nor a priori. Introspection should not be regarded as a species of perception, especially for present purposes, because it has no distinctive type of sensory experience associated with it. Of course, many objects of introspection—e.g., pains, itches, and tickles—have sensory qualities, but introspection per se does not. One can introspect thoughts without any accompanying sensory quality. So one cannot equate a priori warrant with non-perceptual warrant.[7]

Instead of marking a priori warrant by the absence of sensory phenomenology, perhaps it can be marked by a positive form of phenomenology, a phenomenological mode unique to the a priori. This move was popular among traditional rationalists, and still finds favor among a few contemporary theorists. According to Plantinga (1993), when one *sees* that a proposition is necessarily true, one forms a belief "with that peculiar sort of phenomenology with which we are all acquainted, but which I can't describe in any way other than as the phenomenology that goes with seeing that such a proposition is true" (106). Is this approach well-motivated? Is there a single distinctive phenomenology that accompanies all (purely) logical thought, mathematical thought, and other forms of cogitation that rationalists like to subsume under the a priori? This seems very doubtful. I do not reject the idea that rational thinking, when fully conscious, has phenomenological dimensions (see Goldman 1993). But I see no reason to suppose that a single distinctive form of phenomenology accompanies every a priori warranting process.

Reliance on phenomenology, then, does not seem to capture the a priori. Can the situation be improved by adding the necessity ingredient? The simplest appeal to the necessity ingredient would be the following condition:

A belief has a priori warrant only if the proposition believed is necessary.

One problem with this proposal is that Kripke (1980) has argued that a person can have a priori warrant even for contingent propositions, e.g., "the standard meter stick is one meter long." This example does not convince everyone, however, so I shall not press it. A second difficulty is more decisive. Since a priori warrant is not infallible, it is possible to have a priori warrant for propositions that are not in fact true and hence not necessary.

A different way of bringing necessity into the picture is through the following condition:

A belief in p has a priori warrant only if the doxastic agent also believes that p is necessary.

Is this condition acceptable? It seems to me implausible. Ordinary people often believe arithmetic propositions without believing them to be necessary. Unlike philosophers, they do not reflect on matters of modal status. The proposition $2 + 5 = 7$ just strikes them as true, not *necessarily* true. So there are many cases in which this condition is not met.

A third possible way to introduce necessity into the picture is more promising:

A belief in p has a priori warrant only if p belongs to a family or domain of propositions each of which is either necessarily true or necessarily false.

Propositions of arithmetic comprise a family of propositions that meet this condition, and so do propositions of logic. They are precisely the sorts of propositions for which people can have a priori warrant.

Even if we accept this necessary condition of a priority, however, it does not combine with the non-perceptual-basis condition to yield a sufficient condition of a priori warrant. That is to say, the following proposal is not correct:

A belief in p has a priori warrant if (1) the basis for this belief is non-perceptual and (2) p belongs to a family or domain of propositions each of which is either necessarily true or necessarily false.

Obviously, a belief can meet the first of these conditions without being warranted a priori, indeed, without being warranted at all. For example, the belief might be based on mere wishful thinking, or sheer guesswork. Even beliefs in truths of logic and arithmetic might have this kind of source. The combination of non-perceptual basis and appropriate modal status does not suffice to confer a priori warrant on such beliefs.

We have not succeeded, then, in explicating the concept of a priori warrant. Does that scuttle epistemic rationalism? No. The fundamental idea of a priori warrant is the idea of purely rational warrant, warrant based on "pure thought." This intuitive idea has not been shown to be devoid of merit. We should not jettison the assumption that it refers to a definite phenomenon (or set of phenomena) simply because we cannot yet provide a fully illuminating characterization of it. For one thing, it may be impossible to elucidate what a priori warrant is until we have an account of warrant in general. So let us turn next to that task.

4. Reliabilism, Warrant, and the A Priori

Thesis (A) of moderate naturalism identifies psychological processes as the generic source of all epistemic warrant. This is hardly a complete theory of warrant, however, so more must be said about warrant before we can fully assess the prospects for a priori warrant from the perspective of moderate naturalism. Here I shall defend a theory I have put forward earlier, a version of process reliabilism. Process reliabilism fits very comfortably, of course, into the category of naturalistic approaches specified by (MN)(A). I have not built it explicitly into (MN)(A) because many other psychological-process accounts of warrant are in principle available. Any such theory is plausibly regarded as naturalistic—at least as having one naturalistic component. Reliabilism does not exhaust naturalistic approaches to warrant, though it is the only such approach I view as correct.

The version of reliabilism I wish to endorse here is *two-stage reliabilism* (for details, see Goldman 1992). Two-stage reliabilism offers the following reconstruction of our standards for epistemic warrant. During various periods of a community's evolution, the criterion of reliability is applied to various belief-forming processes and methods, which are individuated in some rough-and-ready fashion.[8] Certain belief-forming processes pass the test of reliability—or are thought by the community to pass it—and other belief-forming processes do not pass it. Basing expectations about future battles on the features of animals' entrails, for example, was regarded as a sound method in some communities. When a process or method is judged to have a high proportion of true outputs, it is viewed as a warrant-conferring process or method. Thus, the root or "Ur" criterion of warrant is reliability of belief-formation. (Notice that the criterion appealed to is reliability, not judged-reliability or believed-reliability. Actual reliability is the criterion that the community tries to apply, though it may fail to apply that criterion correctly.) I shall call this first stage of the epistemological story the *standard-selection* stage, because it involves the selection of approved epistemic standards, viz., the approved belief-forming processes or methods that confer epistemic warrant. The second stage of the epistemological story is the *standard-deployment* stage. In this stage, members of the community apply the chosen standards by judging whether individual beliefs (either actual or hypothetical) are warranted as a function of whether they are arrived at (or sustained) by approved processes or methods. According to my hypothesis, although standards are chosen by the (judged) reliability of processes in the actual world, the chosen standards are then applied "rigidly." That is, each of the approved processes or methods is deemed warrant-conferring in any possible world in which it operates. (This will only be relevant when the judged belief is a hypothetical belief, e.g., one supplied in a philosophical example.) This reconstruction helps account for intuitive judgments about justifiedness that pose problems for other versions of reliabilism, e.g., the justifiedness of beliefs in Cartesian demon worlds (see Goldman 1992).[9] The following sorts of processes are examples of approved belief-generating processes, at least in our epistemological community: perceptual processes in the several sense modalities, remembering, introspecting, and (many forms of) reasoning or calculating. I have tried to reconstruct the way in which communities and individuals select and deploy their standards of warrant or justification. But, it will be asked, when are beliefs *really* justified, as opposed to being *held* justified by this or that community? A natural response is: a belief is "really" justified if and only if it results from processes (or methods) that really are reliable, and not merely judged reliable by our present epistemic community.[10] Thus, we should be prepared to change our standards of justification if we find reason to believe that processes or methods previously thought reliable are really unreliable, or if we find that previous ways of individuating or grouping modes of belief-formation do not cut the cognitive mind "at its joints," which could affect assessments of reliability.

Now one family of these justification-conferring processes is a good candidate for conferring a priori warrant, i.e., the family of reasoning or calculational processes. If this proposal is accepted, then beliefs formed exclusively by such processes—for example, beliefs formed by purely arithmetic or logical reasoning—would be warranted a priori. Furthermore, we might expand the ambit of the a priori by following the lead of BonJour. BonJour suggests that instead of restricting a priori warrant to *beliefs*, we might also allow *inferences* to have a priori warrant (BonJour 1998, 4–6). Adapting this idea to my process approach, we may say that certain sorts of processes, including inferential processes, are *a priori warranters*. (Non-inferential processes might also qualify as a priori warranters, e.g., processes for apprehending "basic" necessary truths, which are not derived inferentially from other such truths.) This proposal is not meant to imply that whenever an agent uses a process that is an a priori warranter, any belief-output of the process is *wholly* a priori. On the contrary, if one starts with a set of believed premises that originate in perception and then applies an inferential a priori warranter to that set of beliefs, the resulting conclusion belief does not have *pure* a priori warrant. Nonetheless it seems instructive to say that such a conclusion belief has an *element* or *component* of a priori warrant, simply because there is one strand of its warrant that is a priori.

It should be noted that when dealing with inferential processes, we need to qualify the reliabilist criterion slightly (see Goldman 1979). Here the criterion of warrant conferral should not be simple reliability but *conditional reliability*. An inferential process should not be expected to have a high truth-ratio of output beliefs when the input beliefs are false. It is only necessary that its output beliefs have a sufficiently high truth-ratio for those cases in which the input beliefs (premises) are all true. This conditional understanding of reliability for inferential cases will be presumed in the remainder of the discussion.

There are several objections I can anticipate to my entire approach. First, epistemological internalists will undoubtedly want to object to the fundamental reliabilist contours of the approach. Setting aside the distinctive features of two-stage reliabilism, internalists characteristically deny that *de facto* reliability of belief-forming processes suffices to give them warrant-conferring power. A belief does not attain justificational status merely by resulting from reliable processes; that makes the believer's justification too "external" to him. Instead, the believer must also possess a *metajustification*: he must be justified in believing that his processes are reliable. A leading proponent of this metajustification requirement has been BonJour (1985).

Interestingly, when it comes to a priori warrant, BonJour explicitly rejects the appropriateness of metajustification (1998, 142–47). In defense of this move, he says that a metajustification would have to be either a priori or empirical. If it were a priori, it would be circular; if it were empirical, the a priori would lose its presumed status as an "autonomous" mode of justification. I shall not explore in detail these reasons for rejecting the metajustification requirement, though I find them unconvincing. But I do wish to register surprise that BonJour does not recognize this position as a reversal of his long-standing dissatisfaction with externalism. It is curious that he continues to think of himself as a champion of internalism (see 1998, 1, 96–97) even with respect to the a priori, despite his abandonment of the metajustification requirement.

My own reason for rejecting the metajustification requirement was given in Goldman 1979.[11] It is too demanding a constraint on justification that an ordinary cognizer should possess such a metajustification. This is particularly so in the domain of the a priori. It is very unlikely that someone who has never studied philosophy could produce a satisfactory justification for the reliability of his inductive or deductive inference procedures. To conclude from this, however, that ordinary, philosophically untrained people have no inferential warrant would be a dramatic capitulation to skepticism.

A different kind of objection to the reliabilist approach to a priori warrant would be an objection to its *contingent* character. Is it sufficient for an inferential process to have a priori warrant that it be (conditionally) reliable in the actual world? Isn't a stronger requirement appropriate, namely, that it be *necessarily* reliable: reliable in every possible world?[12] Such a requirement would not constitute a retraction of our earlier insistence that a priori warrant be compatible with fallibility. The current proposal does not require *perfect* reliability in every possible world; it merely requires a "sufficiently" high truth-ratio in every possible world. This proposal feels quite appropriate for mathematical and deductive reasoning processes, but it looks excessive for inductive processes. Yet it is definitely plausible to hold that inductive reasoning processes (of certain types, at any rate) can be a priori warranters. Clearly, inductive connections between propositions are not epistemically accessible by perception, memory, or introspection; they seem to be accessible only by some species of "reason." The problem is that for any inductive process mapping premise beliefs into conclusion beliefs, there will be possible worlds in which the process is unreliable (that is, has very low reliability). However, it is possible to construe inductive inference as tracking *probabilistic* relations between premises and conclusions, and these probabilitistic relations might hold in all possible worlds.[13] So forms of inductive reasoning might be candidates for a priori warranters even if necessary reliability is required for a priori warrant. For this reason, I am not ready to dismiss the demand for necessary reliability as a condition on a priori warranters. An alternative approach, however, would say that since we have already admitted the fallibility of a priori warranting processes, error possibilities are already on the table in the sphere of the a priori. If a priori warrant is compatible with error in the actual world, why shouldn't it be compatible with further error—perhaps even *un*reliability—in other possible worlds? So I shall not try to resolve this matter fully.

Still another possible worry about our account is whether it can be suitably supplemented to handle a priori *knowledge*. Granting that the primary notion of a priority is that of warrant rather than knowledge, an account of a priori warrant must be "upgradable" into an account of a priori knowledge. Does the reliability theory have such a potential?[14] The simplest way to complete a reliabilist account of knowledge is to add both the standard truth requirement and a no-relevant alternatives requirement.[15] Admittedly, the no-relevant-alternatives condition will not do much work whenever the beliefs in question are beliefs in necessities, because counterfactuals involving the negations of necessities are either trivially true or at least difficult to evaluate. So it will be hard to show that anyone ever violates the no-relevant-alternatives condition if he already believes a necessary truth. For the very same reason, however, it does not seem that anyone with a true, a priori warranted belief in a necessity genuinely faces any further threat to knowledge. So there simply is no real "work" for the no-relevant-alternatives condition to do in that class of cases.

In the final segment of this section, I want to raise a further complication for the account of a priori warrant. I earlier introduced, with little comment, a distinction between belief-forming *processes* and *methods*. Now I want to say more about that distinction and its relevance to the theory of a priori warrant. By a "process" I mean something that is part of a person's fundamental cognitive architecture. By a "method" I mean something that is not part of one's fundamental cognitive architecture, but something learned, typically by cultural transmission. For example, a truth-table procedure for determining which sentences are tautologies is unlikely to be a process in the foregoing sense; it is unlikely to be of a person's fundamental cognitive architecture. Someone might acquire such a method by learning, however, and this method would presumably be a paradigm case of a necessarily reliable method. Is such a method an a priori warranter?

I think not. Consider the case of Carroll's tortoise (Carroll 1895). He apparently has no native, intuitive power to detect logical relationships. If he were persuaded to accept such relationships on Achilles's authority, his belief in such relationships might be warranted; but it would not qualify as a priori warrant. Let us return to human beings and to the truth-table method. By my lights, two cases must be distinguished. In one case Harry learns the truth-table method from Ellen, who simply explains how to use it without explaining why it is (necessarily) reliable. Harry simply accepts its reliability from Ellen on trust; he does not use his prior reasoning powers to "see" that it is reliable. In a second case Harry learns the truth-table method from Eileen, who explains why the method is (necessarily) reliable, an explanation that Harry fully comprehends and appreciates in virtue of his prior reasoning powers. In the first case it seems clear that the truth-table method of forming beliefs about tautologies is not an a priori warranter. For one thing, the method is acquired in part by perception (of Ellen's testimony), and that perception is not an incidental or eliminable feature of Harry's acceptance of the method.[16] In the second case Harry seems to have a priori warrant for his belief that the method is (necessarily) reliable, because he himself determines its reliability by pure reasoning powers. This might suffice to make the method itself an a priori warranter. But I am not fully convinced of this. Guided by historical treatments of the a priori, I am inclined to say that only basic mental faculties have the power to confer a priori warrant. In other words, only "processes" in the present sense, are a priori warranters. However, I might be prepared to concede that methods can also become a priori warranters if their (necessary) reliability is determined by a priori means.

In either case, it turns out that the underlying source of all a priori warrant must reside in appropriate processes, which are features of our fundamental cognitive architecture. Do people actually *have* such processes? If so, exactly *which* such processes do they have?

5. Naturalism, Cognitive Science, and the A Priori

The form of epistemological naturalism I have endorsed, moderate naturalism, claims that epistemology needs help from science, especially the science of the mind; but I have not yet fully explained why science should enter the picture. The remarks at the end of the previous section indicate the direction of the rationale, as applied specifically to the question of the a priori. But let me back up a little to give the rationale more fully. Two-stage reliabilism is a reconstruction of ordinary people's conception and standards of justification. As indicated, however, epistemology should not rest content with lay people's standards of warrant. There are several reasons why a scientifically-infused epistemology might plausibly part company with folk epistemology. First, the folk presuppose some categories of belief formation, some types of belief "sources." But it is doubtful that the folk have landed upon an optimal classification of belief-forming processes. There is ample reason to suspect that scientific psychology is needed to cut the operations of cognition "at their joints." This is one reason to seek help from psychology. Second, according to two-stage reliabilism, the folk have somehow identified certain belief-forming processes as having relatively high truth-ratios and identified other belief-forming processes as having relatively low truth-ratios. But it is debatable whether all of these assessments are accurate. A scientific understanding of exactly how the indicated processes work might lead us to a different assessment of their truth-producing capacities (just as the study of perceptual illusions can shed light on matters of reliability). Third, if philosophers want to distinguish a priori from other types of warranters and specify which are which, then, for reasons sketched at the end of the last section, psychology needs to tell us which processes are parts of our fundamental cognitive architecture and which are used in acquiring new reasoning methods. Finally, rationalist philosophers have identified a single kind of putative knowledge source that they call (roughly) "rational intellection." A more scientific approach to cognition might make fruitful headway into this terrain, not by rejecting such a source altogether, but by revealing that the supposedly single source of rational insight is really comprised of an assemblage of different mechanisms.

I begin with the subject of numerical or arithmetic cognition. Might there be psychological evidence that supports the existence of a psychological capacity for reliable (even necessarily reliable?) numerical cognition? Yes, there might; indeed, there actually is such evidence. I should preface my exposition of this evidence by pointing out that the possible capacity I shall discuss does not speak to the apprehension of numbers in the full-blown Platonistic sense. It may only be a capacity to discern relations of *numerosity* among sets of objects. From my point of view, nothing more is needed for a priori numerical cognition.

In the last 10–20 years it has been shown that both animals and human infants as young as five months are sensitive to number (see Wynn 1992a). Rats are able to determine the number of times they have pressed on a lever, up to at least 24 presses. Birds have similar abilities. Canaries were trained to select an object based on its ordinal position in an array. Out of 10 cubicles spaced along a runway, they had to walk along the runway and choose the cubicle that held, say, the fifth aspirin (Pastore 1961). In another study, Church and Meck (1984) showed that rats can compute small numerosities, such as two plus two. Similar findings have now been made among human infants. Using the standard technique of gauging surprise by length of looking time, Wynn (1992b) found that five-month-old infants can correctly detect elementary arithmetic relationships, such as $1 + 1 = 2$ and $2 - 1 = 1$. Infants saw arithmetic operations of placing or removing (adding or subtracting) items from a display area, though a screen initially prevented them from seeing the result of the operations. When an "impossible" result was revealed to them (e.g., $2 - 1 = 2$), the infants manifested surprise (as measured by comparative looking time). All this evidence points to innate arithmetic powers among animals and human infants.

How might they execute their arithmetic computations? One hypothesis, directed primarily at animals but possibly involving children as well, is that a single mechanism underlies the ability to determine numerosity and also the ability to measure duration. This is the so-called "accumulator theory" advanced by Meck and Church (1983), based on a model by Gibbon (1981). The proposed mechanism works as follows:

> [A] pacemaker puts out pulses at a constant rate, which can be passed into an accumulator by the closing of a mode switch. In its counting mode, every time an entity is experienced that is to be counted, the mode switch closes for a fixed interval, passing energy into the accumulator. Thus, the accumulator fills up in equal increments, one for each entity counted. In its timing mode, the switch remains closed for the duration of the temporal interval, passing energy into the accumulator continuously at a constant rate. The mechanism contains several accumulators and switches, so that the animal can count different sets of events and measure several durations simultaneously.

The final value in the accumulator can be passed into working memory, and there compared with previously stored accumulator values. In this way the animal can evaluate whether a number of events or the duration of an interval is more, less, or the same as a previously stored number or duration that is associated with some outcome, such as a reward. (Wynn 1992a, 323–24)

Evidence that the same mechanism underlies timing as well as counting processes includes the fact that methamphetamine increases rats' measure of duration and of numerosity by the same factor.

Another nativist theory of numerical competence has been advanced by Gelman and colleagues (e.g., Gelman and Gallistel 1978; Gelman and Greeno 1989). She has proposed that young children possess an innate concept of numbers governed by three counting principles that define correct counting. One principle states that items to be counted must be put into one-to-one correspondence with a set of (innate) mental counting tags; a second principle says that these tags must be used in a fixed order; and the third principle states that the last number tag used in a count represents the cardinality of the counted items.

Wynn points out that in the accumulator model, numerosity is inherently embodied in the structure of the hypothesized representations. The relationships between the representations exactly reproduce the relationships between the quantities they represent. For example, four is one more than three, and the representation for four (the magnitude of fullness of the accumulator) is one more increment than the representation for three. Thus, a mechanism of this sort would mirror the structure of the facts that are represented. This makes it a kind of mechanism well suited for reliable numerical calculation. As Wynn also points out, addition could be achieved in an accumulator mechanism by transferring the energy from two accumulators into an empty third accumulator.

These are only two theories, of course, of numerical cognition in infants and animals. I am not claiming that either theory has been proved to be correct. But if either theory were correct, there would be an innate mechanism of a priori numerical cognition that at least approaches the desiderata of some rationalist philosophers. There is nothing to suggest that such mechanisms would have any sort of trans-cognitive causal relation with numbers construed as abstract entities. And there might not be any distinctive phenomenology accompanying the operation of either mechanism (although, on the other hand, there *might* be such a phenomenology). But both of these traditional desiderata were already dismissed here as inessential to a priori cognition.

I turn next to deductive logic, a subject to which psychologists have devoted considerable attention, yielding a proliferation of theories. Certain of these theories comport fairly nicely, at least at first blush, with the claims of a priorist philosophers. One going psychological theory is that ordinary people have something like natural-deduction systems built into their heads (Rips 1994, 1995; Braine, Reiser, and Rumain 1984), quite possibly innately (Macnamara 1986). They possess at least *some* sound natural-deduction rules and have operating systems that enable them to apply such rules to proffered sets of sentences to assess their derivability. When a person "intuits" that P is derivable from P-AND-Q, she may be deploying a sound mental rule of inference or proof. Since the deployment of such a mental rule would constitute a reliable process—even a necessarily reliable process—it would pass the test of a reliabilist conception of the a priori. Another approach to mental logic claims that people execute logic tasks by constructing mental models and seeing whether a proffered conclusion is true in all models in which the premises are true (Johnson-Laird and Byrne 1991). This approach might also sit comfortably with a priorist conceptions, although the process of constructing appropriate models is in general quite difficult. Only for certain types of logic tasks would the process be successful (the same holds for the proof-theoretic approach).

Neither of these approaches, however, has clear-cut support from a majority of current researchers. Other psychological approaches to logic cognition offer frameworks quite alien to traditional epistemological thinking and alien to the prospects of a priori warrant in this domain. One approach suggests that skills at conditional logic, for example, are not at all innate, but instead are learned by an inductive process from particular contingencies between events (Holland et al. 1986, 281–82). Support for this viewpoint is adduced from the fact that in a famous type of test for conditional reasoning, the Wason selection task, there are well-known "content effects". Subjects presented with a form of the task involving arbitrary and unfamiliar subject-matter perform quite poorly, whereas subjects given the same task (same from a logical perspective) employing familiar subject matter perform quite a bit better. A possible explanation for these content effects is that people lack domain-general competence at conditional logic, but acquire a certain level of competence through an inductive learning process.[17] Adherents of this approach might concede that a few people—those adequately trained in pure logic—ultimately achieve wide-ranging competence. But this only shows that people can acquire reliable *methods* (in my terminology) for executing formal logic tasks. It does not show that anyone has *innate processes* of the sort that may be needed for a priori warrant in matters of deduction. I have, of course, left the door open to the idea that learned methods might be a priori warranters. But they can serve as a priori warranters, I suggested, only if the learning processes themselves can demonstrate that deductive methods are *necessarily* reliable. It is not clear how this could be achievable under the inductive learning approach currently under discussion.

A recently developed approach to logic cognition, and perhaps the most extreme approach, endorses the idea that there are innate or genetically endowed reasoning mechanisms. But this approach, championed by Cosmides and Tooby (Cosmides 1989; Cosmides and Tooby 1994), denies that our genetic endowment includes any sort of abstract or domain-general capacity for deductive reasoning (or for inductive reasoning either). On the contrary, it hypothesizes that our genetic cognitive endowment consists of highly specialized "modules," each of which is dedicated to a narrow cognitive task that proved adaptive in our evolutionary history. They specifically argue that the capacity to reason correctly with conditionals is restricted to tasks that involve the detection of "cheaters," that is, the detection of people who have violated the terms of a social contract or social exchange. According to Cosmides and Tooby, lay people only succeed at those permutations of the Wason selection task in which the logically correct response coincides with effective cheater-detecting choices. For example, subjects are given problems in which they have to decide which information-revealing cards need to be examined in order to determine whether a conditional sentence holds true in a certain situation. According to Cosmides, people succeed at this task only when the content of the conditional is a social-contract type of rule on which somebody might "cheat," i.e., when the rule's content is of the kind: "If you take the benefit, then you pay the cost."

This thesis may sound far-fetched to philosophical ears, but it has at least initial support from intriguing experimental evidence. For example, Cosmides (1989) found that when subjects were given *switched* social contract rules, i.e., rules of the form "If you pay the cost, then you take the benefit," they chose cards appropriate to cheater detection rather than to the principles of logic. Logic required the choice of a certain pair of cards (in a group of four) to determine whether or not the specified conditional holds. Instead, given the switched social-contract rules, subjects ignored the logically correct cards and chose those suited to cheater detection.[18]

If Cosmides and Tooby were right about logic cognition in general, the prospects for a priori warrant in the deductive reasoning domain would indeed be dim. True, people would have innate processes enabling them to form logically accurate beliefs for *some* tasks. But these processes would also lead to logical errors in other tasks; so it is questionable whether the processes would be sufficiently reliable to qualify as epistemic warranters. It is even more doubtful that they would meet the condition of *necessary* reliability, which I have (tentatively) endorsed for a priori warrant. All this would apply *if* the Cosmides-Tooby story were correct, but I am pretty dubious about it, at least as a full story of human logical competence. Cosmides and Tooby have not, to my knowledge, addressed human abilities to solve simpler logic tasks, e.g., tasks involving AND-elimination. AND-introduction, or IF-elimination (Modus Ponens). Rips (1995) provides evidence for substantial lay competence with these sorts of reasoning principles. So I am not arguing that empirical studies in fact imperil the prospects for a priori warrant in the domain of deductive logic. I am only arguing that empirical studies could *in principle* imperil such prospects.

A final domain that might be investigated here is that of inductive or probabilistic inference. A good deal of psychological research has raised questions about the capacity of naive judgment to conform with principles of probability. Doubt on this score has been the main message of the influential "biases and heuristics" approach of Tversky and Kahneman (1982, 1983). However, a careful treatment of this literature and some of the critical discussion of it (e.g., Gigerenzer 1991) poses difficult issues, both about the interpretation of probability and about the interpretation of a large body of psychological research. There is also a special problem of assessing the import of these findings in terms of the reliabilist framework advanced here. So although this terrain might prove fertile ground for illustrating my earlier points about the pertinence of empirical psychology, I shall rest content with the earlier illustrations.

There is one additional point, however, that is worth emphasizing. The traditional rationalist picture, I think, is that a priori insight or apprehension is one homogeneous type of cognition, ostensibly intended to explain knowledge of logic, mathematics, meaning relationships, and so forth. But if the accumulator device, say, is a good example of the sorts of mechanisms and processes that lie at the roots of rational intellection, there is unlikely to be a *single* faculty of rational intellection. Obviously, the accumulator device is only useful for counting and related numerical operations. It is wholly incapable of subserving any of the other functions traditionally ascribed to rational insight. So there would have to be other mechanisms and processes that subserve those functions. Thus, a sober cognitive science of rationality might have to postulate not only a numerical device, but separate devices for deductive logic, inductive or probabilistic relationships, and so forth. There would be processes of intellection$_1$, intellection$_2$, intellection$_3$, and so forth. In this fashion, naturalistic epistemology—that is, epistemology that exploits the resources of cognitive science—would in some measure support the ideas of traditional rationalism, but would also transform rationalism into a form entirely respectable by contemporary scientific lights.

6. Philosophical Analysis, Intuitions, and Empirical Science

In this section I consider some objections to my thesis of moderate naturalism. I have defended moderate naturalism from the vantage-point of process reliabilism, but is this an adequate defense? Some critics might complain that they don't accept process reliabilism as an adequate analysis (or reconstruction) of justified belief. So why should they be persuaded by my brief for the role of science in epistemology? Other critics might complain that although process reliabilism is a credible theory, the basic epistemological task of *establishing* process reliabilism is itself a task for conceptual analysis; and I have done nothing, they would add, to show that the enterprise of conceptual analysis needs help from empirical science. Furthermore, they would continue, conceptual analysis is really a purely a priori enterprise, because it rests fundamentally on a priori *intuition*. Conceptual analysis consists of offering accounts of certain concepts, in the case of epistemology, epistemological concepts. These candidate accounts are tested by seeing whether their implications accord or fail to accord with our intuitions. Thus, a priori intuition is the method for assessing philosophical analyses. No empirical science need be consulted.

Now I agree that intuitions about cases play precisely the evidential role in testing conceptual analyses that the foregoing argument maintains. But I am not convinced that this establishes that philosophical methodology is, or should be, wholly a priori. (The reply I proceed to offer is adapted from a more extended treatment of conceptual analysis presented in chapter 4.)

I regard intuitions—i.e., intuitional states of the type in question—as conscious, spontaneous judgments. They either are beliefs or they readily give rise to beliefs when not overridden by independent information. I will understand them in the latter fashion, as states that tend to generate beliefs. As used by philosophers, intuitions are typically about whether particular cases are or are not instances of a particular concept. For example, someone reflecting on one of Gettier's (1963) cases may have the intuition that Smith's true justified belief that p is not an instance of *knowledge*. One important question is how we should construe this talk of "concepts." The construal I advocate, for present purposes, is that a concept is some sort of non-conscious psychological structure or state that is distinctively associated with the cognizer's deployment of a certain natural-language predicate, in this case, the predicate "knows."[19] Such structures or states have contents, and hence particular examples—either actual or hypothetical examples—either instantiate those contents or fail to instantiate them. Now when someone has an intuition that case C is (or is not) an instance of concept K (as he represents or understands K), does that intuition qualify as *evidence* for the claim that C *is* an instance of K? In other words, does the occurrence of this intuitional state *justify* the belief to which it naturally gives rise, that C is an instance of K? Certainly this is what philosophers generally assume and I have no quarrel with it. Furthermore, it meshes perfectly with my process reliabilist approach to justification. The reason such a belief is justified is because the process by which it is generated is a generally reliable process. Usually, when beliefs are formed via intuitions in this sort of way, those beliefs are true: C *does* instantiate the content of the person's concept K. Admittedly, intuitions can sometimes go astray. When an intuition is produced by the person's semantical theory about concept K, rather than as an expression of K itself, then the intuition can easily be mistaken. But if the intuition arises from a spontaneous application of concept K itself, the intuition will usually be right, as will the belief it generates. The fact that this is a reliable process accords quite well with the standard philosophical assumption that such intuition-based beliefs (about particular cases) are warranted beliefs.

So far I take myself to be in substantial agreement with the imagined critic. But the critic proceeds to assert that the intuition-based beliefs in question are not only warranted but are warranted *a priori*. This is what he means in saying that the evidence for conceptual analyses resides in a priori intuition. This is where I part company with the critic. I do not see why this warrant should be considered an a priori form of warrant. On the view I would propose, intuitive "access" to certain features of a (non-conscious) concept—for example, access to the fact that it is instantiated by a certain case C—is akin to perception. Better yet, it is a form of *interoception*. Since a concept, on my construal, is a non-introspectible structure or state of one's cognitive system, it is part of oneself. An intuition that reflects or reports something about that structure or state is analogous to a sensation that reflects or reports upon some condition of the body, e.g., the position of a limb. When intuitions are understood in this fashion, as analogous to inner perceptual experience, there is no longer any reason to think of them as a priori warranters. They are indeed warranters, just not a priori warranters.[20]

Another reason to reject the suggestion that intuitionally generated beliefs are warranted a priori is that the propositional contents of intuitions are neither necessarily true nor necessarily false. If I am right, the contents of these beliefs are of the form, "C satisfies the content of my concept that I express with the predicate 'K'." That sort of proposition is neither necessarily true nor necessarily false, since it is quite contingent what content one does associate with 'K'. So if a priori warranters must be processes directed at domains involving necessity, we have an additional reason to reject the idea that philosophical intuitions—that is, intuitions about concept instantiations—have a priori warrant. Of course, this is not to say that they have *empirical* warrant either. I am not claiming that the intuitional warranting of propositions about concept satisfaction is a form of external perception.

Much of what I have said about concepts and their relationship to intuitions is similar to the views of Bealer (1987, 1996b, 1998). The main point of departure is that Bealer regards intuitions as sources of *a priori* evidence, whereas I do not. Some may regard this as a terminological matter which should not be blown out of proportion. But Bealer seems to pin his case for (pure) rationalism in philosophical method substantially on this point, so it is worthy of close attention.

I must here add the point that philosophical theorists are not interested simply in their own personal concepts associated with a given natural-language predicate. They are not merely interested in their own concepts associated with "justice," "personal identity," or "freedom." They are surely interested in the concepts possessed by others as well, including non-philosophers. To obtain this information, philosophers must rely on others' verbal reports of their intuitions, reports that must be empirically observed in order to be utilized. In this fashion, even the gathering of intuitional evidence assumes an empirical guise.[21]

This is not the principal point I wish to make, however, in support of the contention that empirical investigation, in particular cognitive science, has a role to play in epistemological analysis (and philosophical analysis generally). A further line of argument runs as follows.[22] Epistemological analysis involves the generation and testing of hypotheses about epistemic concepts, such hypotheses as "Knowledge is justified true belief." In principle, there are always indefinitely many hypotheses that might be advanced; and for any finite set of intuitions about cases, there are, in principle, indefinitely many hypotheses that would be compatible with those intuitions. Can cognitive science play a role in choosing among such hypotheses? Yes. Cognitive scientists investigate the form that concept representations tend to take, for example, whether they consist in sets of necessary and sufficient conditions, or weighted features, or sets of individual exemplars (see Smith and Medin 1981). Findings on this topic can bear on the relative plausibility of alternative hypotheses that epistemologists might float about epistemic concepts. For example, psychologists study how much context can affect a variety of intuitive responses to cognitive tasks. To take just one example, researchers have found that subjects' judgements about their own level of happiness is swayed by the temporary accessibility of stimuli that shape their choice of a comparison standard. Subjects were influenced, for example, when a handicapped confederate was visible to them while they filled out the happiness report (Schwarz and Strack 1991). Such information about context effects can be relevant in assessing the relative plausibility of "contextualist" versus "invariantist" hypotheses about the meaning of "know."[23] Once it is granted that conceptual analysis has the task of laying bare the semantical features of items that are "hidden" within a cognitive system—items that are neither directly observable nor directly introspectible—it should become credible that scientific investigation is in principle relevant to the task.

If anyone doubts the hiddenness of concepts (in my sense of that term), I recommend the instructive discussion by Peacocke (1998), whose term "implicit conception" corresponds to what I mean by "concept." Peacocke points to Leibniz's and Newton's grappling with the notion of the limit of a series, a notion that they certainly used and understood (as well as anybody of their time) and yet could not explicate adequately. Only in the mid-nineteenth century was a clear, unproblematic explication achieved. But even the humble word "chair" is not so trivial to explicate. Thinkers can be good at classifying cases but bad at articulating the principles guiding their classifications. Peacocke argues persuasively (to my mind) that implicit conceptions are psychologically real, subpersonal, contentful states that are useful in explaining (*inter alia*) classificational dispositions. He also sees the spirit of his enterprise as closely aligned with cognitive science, and cites a couple of cognitive scientists as proceeding in this spirit.[24]

7. Transcending the A Priori/A Posteriori Dichotomy

I conclude this chapter with some remarks on the need to transcend the traditional dichotomy between a priori and a posteriori knowledge. In speaking of a dichotomy I refer to the familiar fact that according to the tradition, all knowledge or warrant is *either* a priori or a posteriori. It cannot be both. As a matter of pure definitional stipulation, this is unproblematic. A belief either has *some* perceptual elements in its warranting history or it has *none*. If it has some, its warrant is a posteriori; if not, its warrant is a priori. This is a tenable classificational scheme, but is it very instructive? From the perspective of this chapter, it is not. A significant number of people's beliefs have a warranting history that includes *both* perceptual and ratiocinative processes. By calling such beliefs "empirical," the classificational system automatically gives pride of place to the first of these components. To my mind, this is misleading. Should it be replaced with a classification system according to which beliefs with *some* ratiocination in their warranting history are a priori and those with *no* ratiocination in their warranting history are a posteriori? This would be just as inegalitarian and objectionable as the standard taxonomy. We need an epistemology that puts the two sources of warrant on a more balanced footing. The traditional terminology of "empiricism" and "rationalism" is equally misleading. As traditionally used, "rationalism" is the proper label for an epistemology which holds that *some* (non-analytic) beliefs are warranted a priori. But if only *one* such belief exists, wouldn't the label "rationalism" inflate the significance of the a priori?

What should we call an epistemology that gives roughly equal credit to perceptual and ratiocinative sources of warrant: *empirico-rationalism*? Unfortunately, the label "empirico-rationalism" tends to suggest that *all* warranted beliefs are warranted by perception, ratiocination, or a combination of the two. That, as we have seen, is false. Pure memory beliefs have only memorial warrant; they have neither perceptual nor ratiocinative warrant. Similarly, purely introspective beliefs have only introspective warrant; they too are devoid of either perceptual or ratiocinative ingredients. So it is best to reject not only the traditional options of empiricism and rationalism but even the appealing but simplistic synthesis of empirico-rationalism. Warrant is just a complex and multi-dimensional affair. Why try to force it into some neat little container or pair of containers that simply disguise its true contours? We must certainly acknowledge the rational element in warrant, but this element must be assigned a suitably measured role, neither deflated nor inflated out of due proportion.

Notes

Thanks to Jim Tomberlin and his colleagues at California State University, Northridge, for very helpful comments and suggestions. Thanks also to Todd Stewart for excellent research assistance and commentary.

1. For a look at contrasting forms of naturalism, both metaphysical and epistemological, see Stroud (1996).

2. For classifications of types of epistemic naturalism, see Maffie (1990) and Goldman (1994).

3. See Rey (1998) for another defense of the compatibility of naturalism and the a priori along lines similar to this one. Rey's paper appeared when the present one was already well underway.

4. If I take this neutral position on abstractness as a condition of a priority, how can I even entertain some restriction concerning necessity? Wouldn't necessity already commit me to abstracta? No, only if one assumes that necessity must be explicated in terms of possible worlds construed as eternal, abstract entities. If this assumption is not made, then one can entertain modal conditions on a priority while preserving metaphysical neutrality. For examples of attempts to develop non-standard approaches to modality, which do not invoke abstracta, see Field (1989); Fine (1985); and Rosen (1990).

5. Also see Plantinga (1993), 110–13.

6. Admittedly, I myself was an early proponent of the sort of trans-mental causal theory Benacerraf was addressing (Goldman 1967), but I subsequently abandoned that kind of theory (Goldman 1976). In any case, that kind of causal theory was only intended as a theory of *knowledge*, not of *justification*, which is the present topic.

7. BonJour recognizes that there are other forms of warrant (like memory and introspection) that make it impossible to identify the a priori in the simple negative fashion that Burge proposes. He proposes to capture the a priori by appeal to its deliverance of putative necessities (BonJour 1998, 8). This prospect will be discussed in the text.

8. The distinction between processes and methods—first introduced in Goldman (1986)—will be explained and examined more fully later.

9. The account offered in Goldman (1992) offers further relevant details that I do not try to present here.

10. [Note added in this edition] What I should have said here is that a belief is "really" justified if (and only if) it meets a correct standard, where a correct standard specifies a process that is genuinely reliable in the actual world. Rigid use of a correct standard would render perceptual beliefs in demon worlds "really" justified.

11. Actually, there is more than one reason offered in Goldman (1979). See that paper for elaboration.

12. Bealer (1996b) rejects contingent reliability in favor of modal reliability, though his discussion concerns basic sources of evidence rather than justification, and his preferred form of modal reliability is slightly different.

13. It is controversial how a proper inductive reasoner should deal with probabilistic relations. One popular approach is that reasoners should have *degrees of belief* which they adjust in the light of new evidence but always so as to conform with the probability calculus. This isn't a perfect fit with the usual presumption of theories of warrant or justification, i.e., the presumption that candidates for warrant or justifiedness are (flat-out) beliefs. So I shall not pursue the degrees-of-belief framework systematically.

14. This issue also concerns Rey (1998), who defends a reliabilist account of a priori knowledge. However, I do not understand exactly what his solution is.

15. On the no-relevant-alternatives requirement see Goldman (1976, 1986) and Dretske (1981).

16. Burge (1998) regards testimony as a potential source of a priori warrant. I do not find this general position convincing; but I am not sure that even Burge would regard the present case as an instance of a priori warrant.

17. The position of extreme domain-specificity (e.g., Manktelow and Evans 1979) says that people rely on memory of specific experiences or content-specific empirical rules to reason about logic tasks. A more moderate position, the pragmatic reasoning schemas approach, says that people use specific experiences to abstract "mid-level" rules, for example, rules that govern permissions of all sorts (Cheng and Holyoak 1985).

18. The importance of this finding is open to interpretation. For example, Rips argues that the subjects, who read a lengthy background story to explain the conditional, may have used this background information to interpret the conditional they were given. It might have "overridden" the literal meaning of this conditional sentence. Thus, relative to the interpretation they gave to the sentence, their responses may have been logically correct (Rips 1994, 333).

19. I do not wish to restrict all concepts to structures associated with natural-language predicates; but insofar as we are interested in philosophical analysis, that is the relevant type of concept.

20. More precisely, I would say that the *process* that leads from a concept to an intuition is a warranter.

21. Philosophers are not very methodologically scrupulous in this matter. They imagine that one can simply *query* other people about their intuitions and get a reliable reading from their answers. However, cognitive and social scientists have learned that the answers one obtains to such queries (and the intuitions that the queries generate) are partly determined by which questions are asked, how they are formulated, and the context in which they are posed. How a question is "framed" and what information is readily accessible or available to the respondent from memory can make an enormous difference to the subject's intuitive response. (For illustrations of these ideas—though not in the precise arena of concept-instantiation—see Shafir and Tversky 1995 and Schwarz 1995.) To the extent that philosophers rely on responses to their queries as evidence, it behooves them to pay more attention to what has been learned about these matters by behavioral scientists.

22. For detailed elaboration, see chapter 4.

23. The contextualism/invariantism distinction is originally due to Unger (1984). For elaboration of the point in the text, see chapter 4.

24. Peacocke also uses the notion of an implicit conception to defend a version of rationalism; but that aspect of his discussion does not so much concern me here.

3

The Unity of the Epistemic Virtues

1. Unitarianism and Its Rivals

One of the central questions about the moral virtues that preoccupied Socrates concerned the unity of the virtues. Are the several virtues aspects of a single virtue or are they entirely distinct and independent? Socrates himself apparently accepted the doctrine of the unity of the virtues. In this chapter I shall explore the tenability of an analogous doctrine for the intellectual, or epistemic, virtues, viz., that the various epistemic virtues are all variations on, or permutations of, a single theme or motif. I am not confident I can make this doctrine stick in full and complete detail, but I want to explore how close one can come in defending its plausibility.

What does one mean by an epistemic virtue and what kind of unity might one hope to find in this territory? Almost everyone agrees that a virtue is an excellence, but which types of things count as excellences? In the Aristotelian tradition, an excellence is some kind of ability, disposition, power, faculty, or habit. Epistemologists like Ernest Sosa and John Greco seem to adopt a heavily Aristotelian conception of excellences in their epistemological uses of virtue theory. They characterize intellectual virtues as mental faculties, powers, or abilities to produce beliefs that are true (Sosa 1988, 1991, chaps. 8, 13; Greco 1992). In my own previous writing from a virtue perspective, I slightly expanded the possible scope of virtues by including mental *processes* (process types) as well as faculties, powers, or competences (Goldman 1992, chap. 9). In this chapter I wish to be more inclusive yet and allow even types of *action* to be subsumed under the epistemic virtues. This would accord with John Locke's usage, who talks of 'virtue' and vice' as applying to actions: "[M]en everywhere ... give the name of virtue to those actions, which

51

amongst them are judged praiseworthy; and call that vice, which they account blamable. . . ." (1959, 1: 476–77).

What kind of unity might we hope to find in the sphere of epistemic virtues? Two strong versions of virtue unitarianism would be (1) an identity theory and (2) an inseparability theory. An identity theory is what Socrates endorsed, the view that all the (moral) virtues are really one and the same.[1] I would not dream of endorsing so strong a theory for the epistemic virtues. Nor am I tempted by an inseparability theory, which would claim that you cannot possess one epistemic virtue without possessing the others. The type of virtue unitarianism I wish to explore is the more modest claim of *thematic* unity: the various epistemic virtues all share, or are derived from, some common unifying theme (or themes). A moderate form of virtue unitarianism would say that all virtues stand in a single relation, for example, a causal relation, to a common value, goal, or desideratum such as true belief. This is roughly the view shared by Sosa, Greco, and myself in earlier writings. A still weaker form of virtue unitarianism would not demand a single relation to a single common end. First, it would permit a plurality of relations to the specified value or desideratum; and second, it might even tolerate a smallish number of intimately related values rather than a single value. (We could not allow too many values, or entirely diverse values, without letting unitarianism collapse into pluralism.) The form of virtue unitarianism I shall try to defend in this chapter is somewhere between a moderate and weak form of unitarianism. The principal relation that epistemic virtues bear to the core epistemic value will be a teleological or consequentialist one. A process, trait, or action is an epistemic virtue to the extent that it tends to produce, generate, or promote (roughly) true belief. But this causal relation is not the only one that will figure in my story.

Some proponents of "high church" virtue epistemology might find elements of teleology or consequentialism anathema to their hopes for a distinctive, virtue-based epistemology. By "high church" virtue epistemology I mean a form of virtue epistemology that models itself closely after virtue ethics, which many theorists view as a rival to ethical consequentialism and deontologism. I think we should resist the temptation to insist that virtue epistemology must conform to the model of ethical theory; in this I depart from some virtue epistemologists such as Linda Zagzebski (1996). Epistemology and ethics are different fields, and it should not be presumed that what holds in one must also hold in the other. Nor is it clear, for that matter, that virtue ethics must eschew consequentialism and deontologism (see Hursthouse 1996; Trianosky 1990).

In the remainder of the chapter, I shall attempt to make a case for the unity of epistemic virtues in which the cardinal value, or underlying motif, is something like true, or accurate, belief. I call this view *veritism* (see Goldman 1999). This position has two types of rivals. The first is pluralism, which denies any thoroughgoing unity among all the epistemic virtues. The second type of rival is any theory that champions an alternative unifying theme, different from truth. Veritistic unitarianism must fend off challenges from both directions.

2. Veritism versus Justificational Value

An obvious challenge to veritistic unitarianism arises from the fact that, on everyone's theory, justified belief is a distinct state of affairs from true belief but a preeminent example of an epistemically meritorious or valuable state of affairs. Unless the admittedly distinct state of justified belief can be shown to have its value in some derivative fashion from the value of true belief, veritistic unitarianism is in trouble. If justificational status has to be posited as a value entirely autonomous and independent of truth, it looks like pluralism wins the day. Or perhaps justifiedness could even replace true belief as the core epistemic value.

The obvious strategy for veritistic unitarianism is to defend a reliabilist theory of justification, or at least some form of truth-linked justification theory. The idea would be that true belief is the ultimate value in the epistemic sphere, and various belief-forming processes, faculties, or mechanisms are licensed as virtuous because they are conducive to true belief. Beliefs are regarded as justified when they are produced by these very truth-conducive processes (or processes thought to be truth-conducive), even on those occasions when the beliefs are false. In other words, justified belief is a separate and independent value from true belief; but beliefs qualify as justified precisely because their provenance is that of truth-promoting processes. So their ultimate source of value remains veritistic.

There are, of course, many alternatives to reliabilism. In the rest of this section I shall examine the chief traditional alternatives: foundationalism and coherentism. There is no space here to try to prove that any viable form of foundationalism or coherentism *must* invoke veritistic value. That would be a book-length project. Instead, I shall mainly content myself with the limited observation that many prominent forms of these approaches *do* invoke veritism. In other words, I shall show how these other approaches are also, quite frequently, steeped in the waters of veritistic value.

Starting with foundationalism, we first note that many foundationalists pledge allegiance to true belief as the prime epistemic desideratum. Chisholm says that it is one's intellectual duty to try his best to bring it about that, for every proposition he considers, he accepts it if and only if it is true (Chisholm 1977, 14). It is also common for foundationalism to provide conditions for basic justification that are linked to truth. In the case of infallibilist foundationalism, a belief is basic if it has some characteristic that necessarily guarantees its truth. In the case of fallibilist foundationalism, beliefs can qualify as basic without necessarily guaranteeing truth, but the status of basicness may nonetheless be conferred by some explicit or implicit form of truth-indicativeness. Beliefs about introspectively accessible subject-matter—one's own current pains or other mental states—may qualify as basic because introspection is highly reliable. Perceptual beliefs may be deemed basic because perceptual appearance states are usually indicative of environmental truths. To be sure, there are accounts of basicness that appeal to such notions as "self-justification," which make no reference to truth. But it is questionable whether a plausible account of self-justification can be given that doesn't tacitly invoke truth-indicativeness. My suggestion, then, is that foundationalism's best prospects for success rest on an appeal to true belief as the fundamental epistemic value in terms of which its distinctive notion of basicness must be defined.

I turn next to coherentism. Some coherentist theories wear their underlying veritism on their sleeves. BonJour's (1985) defense of coherentism makes no attempt to hide the fact that his rationale for a coherence criterion of justifiedness is that coherence is a reliable indicator of truth. BonJour writes:

> The basic role of justification is that of a *means* to truth. . . . If epistemic justification were not conducive to truth . . . , if finding epistemically justified beliefs did not substantially increase the likelihood of finding true ones, then epistemic justification would be irrelevant to our main cognitive goal and of dubious worth. It is only if we have some reason for thinking that epistemic justification constitutes a path to truth that we as cognitive beings have any motive for preferring epistemically justified belief to epistemically unjustified ones. (1985, 7–8)

It would be hard to find a more explicit endorsement of veritism.

Lehrer's form of coherentism also has a rich strain of veritism in it, although it takes a bit of probing to see all of the veritistic themes. First, Lehrer explicitly endorses true belief (or acceptance) as the cardinal epistemic aim involved in justification. He characterizes the "objective of justification" as "accepting something if and only if it is true" (Lehrer 1990, 82). Second, the fundamental doxastic concept in his theory of justification is the concept of "acceptance," defined as a propositional attitude that arises from the purpose of obtaining truth and avoiding error (Lehrer 1974, 1989, 1990). Third, truth is salient in Lehrer's account of "verific justification," which he defines in terms of an acceptance system that is obtained by deleting statements of the form, S accepts that p, when p is false.[2] Fourth, a pivotal role in his theory of justification is played by an ultimate first principle "T," viz., "I am a trustworthy evaluator of truth." Lehrer writes: "What I mean by saying that a person is a trustworthy evaluator of truth and error is that when she accepts something as true . . . , her accepting what she does is a trustworthy guide to truth in the matter" (1989, 143). The fact that it is critical to one's being

justified that one be a trustworthy guide to truth, or at least that one be
justified in believing that one is a trustworthy guide, signals that the fundamental goal of the enterprise is precisely to accept the truth, or at least avoid
error. So veritism really pervades Lehrer's theory. In fact, in one place he
calls himself a sort of reliabilist, just not a *causal* reliabilist. "I agree with
[Goldman] that reliability or probability is central. But it is the state of accepting something that must be a reliable or trustworthy guide to truth rather
than the process that originates or sustains acceptance" (1989, 147).

Are there varieties of coherentism that offer decidedly non-veritistic values? There are certainly authors whose endorsements of coherentism make
no explicit appeal to truth or error avoidance. The question is whether their
theories provide a compelling account of justification if they are sharply dis-
connected from truth. For example, Gilbert Harman's brand of explanatory
coherentism contends that all inductive inference is inference to a total explanatory account. "Induction is an attempt to increase the explanatory coherence of our view, making it more complete, less ad hoc, more plausible"
(Harman 1973, 159). Such an inference is warranted, Harman intimates, if
the resulting total view possesses more explanatory coherence than competing
total views would have. Although Harman does not use the following terminology, he may be taken to imply that explanation and coherence are the
epistemic *values* we seek to maximize, not true belief or error avoidance.

But let us press more deeply. Why do we suppose—granting for the moment that we do—that inferring the view with the greatest explanatory coherence is warranted? I suspect it is because we assume that views which
maximize explanatory coherence are most likely to be *true*. If this is correct,
then the ultimate goal or value associated with warrant is that of true belief.
Isn't this indeed suggested by some of Harman's own language? Isn't a "less
ad hoc" view more likely to be true? Isn't a "more plausible" view more
likely to be true? So it is far from clear that this analysis steers us in a
direction away from veritism.

3. Evidence Proportionalism and Evidence Gathering Virtues

Another possible approach to the theory of justification—which need not be
committed to either foundationalism or coherentism—is what I shall call
deontological evidentialism. Deontological evidentialism, as I conceive of it,
says simply that an agent should assign a degree of belief to a proposition
in proportion to the weight of evidence she possesses. If the weight of her
evidence is strong, her degree of belief should be substantial; if the weight
of her evidence is weak, her degree of conviction should be proportionally
muted. A proponent of this approach would hold that the requirement of

proportioning is a purely deontological one, not derived from any consequentialist consideration, such as the thesis that proportioning leads to truth.
I am not certain which current philosophers, if any, endorse deontological
evidentialism. It might be the position of Richard Feldman and Earl Conee
(1985), and perhaps Richard Jeffrey's (1992) "radical probabilism" is a species of it.[3] A crucial feature of the approach, for present purposes, is that it
would constitute a rival to veritism. It would not rationalize proportionment
as a means to true belief, error avoidance, or any other further end, but would
treat it as an independent principle of "fittingness."

The main problem facing deontological evidentialism is to account for the
virtues of evidence gathering. If proportioning your degree of belief to the
weight of your evidence is the sole basis of epistemic virtue, cognitive
agents can exemplify all virtues without gathering any evidence at all, by
working with the most minimal quantities of evidence. According to deontological evidentialism, it is just as meritorious for an agent to adopt a doxastic attitude of "suspension" when her evidence is indecisive as to adopt a
doxastic attitude of full conviction when her evidence is quite dispositive.
Both are equally good instances of proportioning degree of belief to the
weight of one's evidence. No further epistemic merit or praise can be earned
by investigation, research, or clever experimentation the outcome of which
might discriminate between competing hypotheses. In short, deontological
evidentialism is perfectly content with investigational sloth! This is surely a
major weakness in the theory, because numerous epistemic virtues are to be
found among processes of investigation. When a scientist performs a clever
experiment that selects among otherwise equally plausible hypotheses, she
earns some of her profession's strongest (epistemic) kudos. Good experimental design is at the heart of scientific, and hence epistemic, progress. Deontological evidentialism has no way to accommodate virtues like clever experimentation. Deontological evidentialism implies that a scientific
community's epistemic position is just as satisfactory in the absence of revealing experiments as with them, because scientists can accurately proportion their degrees of belief to their evidence in either case. Without experiments, they can suspend judgment; with experiments, they can favor
experimentally supported hypotheses. In this way, appropriate proportionment is attainable.

Veritism's resources for handling this problem are obviously more promising. The virtue of well-chosen observation or experimentation lies in its
production of experience that tilts in favor of one hypothesis (or perhaps a
family of hypotheses) over others. A cognitive agent who appreciates this
evidence can raise her degree of belief in the favored hypothesis in response
to this evidence; perhaps she will actually accept it. In a favorable case, when
the accepted hypothesis is true, she will achieve an outcome—true belief—
that is the mark of value under veritism. In general, virtues of good inves-

tigation are among the cardinal intellectual virtues. Veritism neatly accounts for such virtues whereas deontological evidentialism draws a blank in trying to rationalize their intellectual merit.

It may be argued that deontological evidentialism is correct as a theory of *justification* but a separate theory is needed as an account of proper *inquiry*. A distinction between these two subject-matters is emphasized by Susan Haack (1993). However, Haack's own conception of the norms of inquiry are distinctly consequentialist and veritistic. She writes: "The goal of inquiry is substantial, significant, illuminating truth" (1993, 203). So her approach does not obviously differ with what I have said above, in terms of its fundamental rationale for the conduct of inquiry.

However, completely different types of rationales for new evidence gathering can be found in the Bayesian literature. To address this question, I. J. Good (1983, chap. 17) produced a proof that making new observations will maximize expected utility. "[*I*]*n expectation*, it pays to take into account further evidence, provided that the cost of collecting and using this evidence . . . can be ignored" (1983, 178, emphasis added). But why should inquiry be directed at increasing *expected* utility? Expected utility is a function of subjective probabilities, and these can be as wild or misguided as you please. As an *aim* of inquiry, expected utility is not well chosen.

This is not to say that new evidence gathering coupled with Bayesian reasoning has no suitable rationale. In fact, if we return to the veritistic perspective, it can be shown that Bayesian reasoning from new experiments yields an *objectively expected* increase in truth-possession—when certain additional conditions are met. Moshe Shaked and I have proved that if an inquirer has conditional probabilities (likelihoods) vis-à-vis a prospective experiment that meet certain conditions, there will be an objectively expected increase in his degree of truth-possession if he performs this experiment and reasons from its observed results in a Bayesian fashion (Goldman and Shaked 1991).[4] This again points to the fact that the most promising way to rationalize the intellectual virtue of designing and performing good experiments lies in the veritistic direction.

I conclude that veritism is the best way to account for the obvious fact that among our chief intellectual virtues—certainly our chief *scientific* virtues—is the clever design and execution of observational or experimental procedures.

4. Monistic versus Dualistic Veritism

I have been touting veritism as a promising unitarian approach, but is it really unitarian? Haven't we been brushing under the rug the fact that veritism really posits, not one, but *two* epistemic values: both true belief and error avoidance. These are distinct values, not reducible to one another, so how can I claim that this pair of values promises to realize the unitarian thesis?

This criticism was already anticipated when I outlined different possible strengths for a unitarian doctrine. Weak unitarianism, I indicated, is a brand of unitarianism that can invoke more than one fundamental epistemic value, as long as the several values have an intuitive homogeneity or integration. That certainly seems to hold for the two values of true belief and error avoidance. However, it is not yet clear that veritism must resign itself to what might be called "dualistic" unitarianism. There is a way to blend the two traditional veritistic values into a single *magnitude* or *quantity* of veritistic value, yielding monistic unitarianism. I have attempted this in *Knowledge in a Social World* (Goldman 1999) and shall further defend it here.

Before turning to the categorical, or binary, concept of belief, let us consider degrees of belief, scaled on the unit interval. Degree of belief 1.0 is the highest degree of belief: subjective certainty. Degree of belief 0 is the highest degree of *dis*belief. This level of disbelief in proposition p is also, equivalently, the highest level of belief in not-p. Degrees of belief at or near 0.50 represent a maximum of subjective *un*certainty; they represent suspension of judgment, or the absence of an opinion. Now, when we try to move from degrees of belief to belief *simpliciter*, it is unclear what the threshold should be. Perhaps any degree of belief in p above 0.80 qualifies as "belief"; or perhaps it is 0.90. It will not matter where, exactly, we set the threshold, but whichever number x we choose as the threshold for belief, we should choose $1.0 - x$ as the threshold for disbelief. If 0.80 and above counts as belief, then 0.20 and below counts as disbelief, or belief in the negation of the proposition.

Let me now turn to values associated with different degrees of belief in true or false propositions. I propose that the highest degree of belief in a *true* proposition counts as the highest degree of "veritistic value" (with respect to the question at hand, e.g., whether p or not-p is the case). In general, a higher degree of belief in a truth counts as more veritistically valuable than a lower degree of belief in that truth (see Goldman 1999, 88–89).

This conception of veritistic value is readily applied to the more traditional but coarse-grained categories of belief, suspension of judgment, and disbelief, as special cases. Whatever the exact threshold for belief may be (greater than 0.50), believing a truth carries more veritistic value than suspension of judgment; and suspension of judgment carries more veritistic value than disbelief. Now, disbelieving proposition p is equivalent to believing proposition not-p. And when p is true, not-p is false. So suspending judgment vis-à-vis a true proposition p has more veritistic value than believing the false proposition not-p. Thus, the intuitive rank-ordering of veritistic value is confirmed: true belief is preferable to suspension of judgment which is preferable to false belief (error).

Various measures of truth-related value seem to presuppose something along the foregoing lines, although these measures don't always exploit all features or details of the foregoing scheme. For example, reliability is a truth-linked measure that gives positive weight to true belief and negative weight to false belief, but it ignores suspensions of judgment. The "power" measure I have proposed elsewhere (Goldman 1986, chap. 6) properly reflects the inferiority of suspension of judgment to true belief, but it wrongly treats suspension of judgment and error as essentially equivalent. Thus, the veritistic value scale proposed above seems preferable, and it has the welcome feature of presenting a *single* magnitude that can serve as the underpinning for a pleasingly *monistic* version of veritistic unitarianism.

Does this scheme of veritistic value accord with commonsense notions about intellectual attainments? I think it does. If a person regularly has a high level of belief in the true propositions she considers or takes an interest in, then she qualifies as "well-informed." Someone with intermediate levels of belief on many such questions, amounting to "no opinion," qualifies as uninformed, or ignorant. And someone who has very low levels of belief for true propositions—or, equivalently, high levels of belief for false propositions—is seriously misinformed. Since the terms "well-informed," "ignorant," and "misinformed" seem to reflect a natural ordering of intellectual attainment, our scheme of veritistic value seems to be on the right track. I think we would also find that many ordinary expressions that designate intellectual virtues refer to processes or traits that promote well-informedness, whereas expressions that designate intellectual vices refer to traits that promote ignorance or error.

5. "Pragmatic" Virtues, Science, and Interest-Responsiveness

Against the veritistic picture I have been painting, there is a panoply of competing cognitive virtues often touted by epistemologists and especially philosophers of science. The latter also offer special reasons for doubting the role of truth in our system of epistemic values. These challenges must now be confronted.

W. V. Quine and Joseph Ullian (1970, chap. 5) list five "virtues" of a hypothesis that count toward the plausibility of a hypothesis. In different terminology, these might be considered "values" for appraising cognitive practices. I'll concentrate on the first three of Quine and Ullian's five. Their first value is *conservatism*. One scientific hypothesis is preferred to another, they say, if it requires scientists to abandon fewer of their previous beliefs. Their second value is *generality*, illustrated by Newton's theory of gravitation. The ability of a hypothesis to explain a wide range and/or variety of phenomena makes it specially worthy of our credence. Their third value is *simplicity*, a widely invoked cognitive value in the philosophy of science literature. Many other epistemologists and philosophers of science echo these themes. In a variant formulation of conservatism, Harman enunciates a principle which says that a person is justified in continuing to accept a prior belief if he lacks a special reason to disbelieve it (Harman 1986, 46). In themes related to generality or explanatory power, we should mention Karl Popper (1962) and Isaac Levi (1980), who in their different ways emphasize the contentfulness or informational value of a potential answer as an important cognitive desideratum. Similarly, Haack (as we have seen) and Philip Kitcher (1993) emphasize that it is not just truth that cognizers seek, but *significant* truth. Since the cited desiderata differ from truth or enlarge upon it, don't they undercut the prospects for epistemic unitarianism?

In response I begin by challenging conservatism, the notion that preserving prior beliefs is a worthy epistemic goal. I don't deny the descriptive thesis that cognitive agents prefer hypotheses or theories that help them retain prior intellectual commitments. But this is simply because they are strongly *attached* to those commitments. They find it hard to be convinced that their old fabric of belief is error-filled, especially in radical ways. It is a philosophical mistake, however, to elevate this descriptive fact into an epistemic value. Furthermore, Harman's conservationist principle of justified belief does not capture any genuine component of the concept of epistemic justification. If someone acquires a belief at one moment by sheer guesswork or wishful thinking, that belief cannot suddenly attain justificational status in the next moment simply because the cognizer has no specific defeater for it.

I turn next to generality and simplicity. The claim I wish to make here, especially about generality, is that this is a *specialized* value peculiar to science, not one that pervades all cognitive inquiry. Science has a distinctive intellectual mission, which includes the attempt to find uniformities of nature and to explain as many phenomena as possible in terms of such uniformities. If more can be explained with less, so much the better. Perhaps the same distinctive mission accounts for the value of simplicity, though this is difficult to say since simplicity means different things to different theorists and no widely accepted analysis of simplicity has yet been found. The main point I wish to make is that epistemologists of science should not be allowed to persuade other epistemologists that distinctive goals and values of science are also goals of cognition and inquiry in general. When it comes to the prosaic purposes of everyday life, or specialties outside of theoretical science, there is no blanket premium on more general or comprehensive truths. We *sometimes* are interested in finding true generalizations, but finding such generalizations is not always more important to us than finding truths about particulars. This simply varies with our interests of the moment.

The moral to be drawn is that *interest* does play a role in evaluating cognitive practices and establishing cognitive virtues. When we are concerned with science, the distinctive interest of science in comprehensive theories therefore comes into play. But generality or simplicity should not be inserted into the pantheon of values for cognition in general. Admittedly, the dimension of interest does complicate our story. We can no longer suggest that higher degrees of truth-possession are all that count in matters of inquiry. But can't we incorporate the element of interest by a slight revision in our theory? Let us just say that the core epistemic value is a high degree of truth-possession *on topics of interest.*[5] Admittedly, this makes the core underlying value a somewhat "compound" or "complex" state of affairs. But, arguably, this is enough to preserve the idea of thematic unity, and thereby preserve unitarianism. A further attractive feature of this approach is that it takes account of the fact that among the intellectual virtues are cognitive processes and practices that promote "interest-responsiveness." The ability to remain diligent, thorough, and persevering in addressing the questions that most interest us are important intellectual virtues (cf. Zagzebski 1996, 114).

Philosophers of science may not be so easily mollified by these maneuvers. There are bigger obstacles, many would contend, to a truth-centered account of epistemic virtue. For example, what can a veritist make of the fact that many so-called scientific laws are not true at all, and known not to be true; yet they continue to be invoked and used in science (Cartwright 1983)? Doesn't this demonstrate that science isn't so interested in truth after all? The same may be said of ordinary conversation and belief, where people are frequently imprecise and hence false in what they say and believe, yet this is blithely tolerated. Maybe *verisimilitude* (closeness to truth) can be substituted as a value in place of truth, but it is doubtful that any adequate concept of verisimilitude has yet been constructed.

My answer to this challenge is to distinguish the laws presented in textbooks and what scientists actually believe. At least in cases where it is known that the "laws" in question are only approximate, practitioners don't believe the contents of the stated laws. What is believed is not the lawlike formula L but instead something of the form, "Approximately, L," or "L holds for such-and-such ranges of application but not outside those ranges." Notice I am not saying that scientists ascribe the property of "approximate truth" to the laws in question. Rather, they have ways of mentally qualifying L to take account of its (known) imprecisions. What they believe (i.e., believe to be *true*) is some suitably hedged proposition. Concerning these hedged propositions, they do aim for truth, and want the contents they accept to be true. No doubt they are still wrong in many of these cases; but we are only talking here of *goals*, not *accomplishments*.

6. The Priority of Truth versus Justification

In this section and the next, I want to return to the matter of justifiedness. The defense of veritistic unitarianism has rested partly on the claim that the value of justifiedness is derivative from the value of truth. This claim might be challenged, however, by finding cases in which justifiedness takes precedence over truth. If such cases could be firmly established, wouldn't that deal a strong prima facie blow to veritistic unitarianism? How could a merely derivative value have priority over a more fundamental one? It would just prove that truth (true belief) isn't really more fundamental.

Before turning to cases, I want to question this style of critique. It is by no means clear that a derivative value could not assume some sort of priority over a more fundamental value. Suppose that a state with fundamental value is, for the most part, only *reachable, realizable*, or *accessible* to human agents via some action or state with derivative value. Moreover, the action or state with derivative value is more directly subject to "guidance" than the state with fundamental value. Then we might place greater weight on achieving or "performing" the more accessible action with merely derivative value. We might even make such an action obligatory. This deontic force or obligatoriness would not necessarily indicate a greater *value* for the accessible action or state. It's just that we can't expect people to achieve the fundamentally valued state but we can expect them to take the best route in its direction. So we may positively *require* agents to take that route without also requiring them to achieve the more fundamental value. This would make it appear as if the required action or state is more important or weighty, and hence not merely derivative. But such an appearance would be deceptive.

Here is an illustration of this idea. In the legal arena jurors are required to vote for a given judgment—guilty vs. innocent, liable vs. non-liable—in light of the *evidence* they have heard at trial. They are not officially invited or required to vote in accordance with the *truth*. It might appear from this as if the legal system prizes evidence or justification above truth, and some might use this as a ground for saying that evidence or justification has priority over truth and is not merely derivative from it. But, as argued above, this would be a mistake. Truth *is* the main institutional goal of adjudication.[6] Since evidential justification is the only reliable route to truth, however, the system imposes an obligation on jurors to judge in accordance with the evidence. This institutional obligation does not negate the claim that truth is the fundamental value at which the adjudication arm of the law aims.

Readers prepared to concede this point for the legal realm might still be unpersuaded of it as a global thesis. Many might still say that the primary responsibility of an epistemic agent is conforming to justificational requirements, not getting the truth. These epistemologists would insist that justified belief, not true belief, is the primary epistemic value. Can this position be rebutted?

It may be illuminating to switch the focus of discussion from doxastic agency to other sectors of intellectual activity. Although traditional epistemology centers on credal acts, we should not forget activities involving speech or communication. When engaged in assertive discourse, people incur duties and responsibilities; they display virtues and vices. The principles governing such speech activities can shed light on the relationship between the twin desiderata of justification and truth.

Norms of assertive discourse are presented by Grice (1989) in the context of a theory of pragmatics; but Grice's norms can equally be seen as principles of social epistemology, which is how I treat them in *Knowledge in a Social World* (Goldman 1999, chap. 5; also see Goldman 1994). Two of Grice's norms—he calls them "maxims"—are the following (see 1989, 27):

(1)   Do not say what you believe to be false,

and

(2)   Do not say that for which you lack adequate evidence.

What is the underlying rationale for these conversational norms? Grice postulates a cooperative venture of a quasi-contractual nature, where the venture's goals include the giving and receiving of information (1989, 29–30). This seems to me exactly right and perfectly fits the veritistic approach, especially when it is understood that "information" entails *truth*. Conversation involves exchanges that can profit hearers because they can acquire true beliefs on the cheap, without being burdened by time-consuming or costly investigation. The posited desideratum—information or truth acquisition—makes excellent sense of the twin norms given above.

Norm (1) is straightforward under this approach. A speaker should not say what he believes to be false because what is so believed stands a serious chance of *being* false, and hearers will be at risk of becoming *mis*informed rather than informed. Norm (2) makes sense for the same reason, if we assume that adequate evidence is generally linked with truth. A proposition for which a speaker lacks adequate evidence stands a good chance of being false, even if the speaker believes it. So assertions unaccompanied by adequate evidence again put the hearer at risk of being misinformed rather than informed.

Can these maxims be rationalized under a different approach, one that gives exclusive or primary weight to justifiedness rather than truth? It might initially appear that this will work, certainly for norm (2) at any rate. How can a hearer acquire justified belief from a speaker's assertion unless the speaker himself has adequate evidence for what he asserts? On reflection, however, we can see that this is wrong. Hearers certainly can acquire justified belief in a proposition even if the speaker who asserts it neither believes it nor has adequate evidence for it. Suppose the hearer has every reason to trust the speaker; then the hearer is justified in believing what the speaker asserts. When a speaker knows that this is the hearer's circumstance, why should he obey either norm, even with the hearer's (epistemic) interest at heart? The hearer will still "profit" from the speaker's asserting something he neither believes nor is justified in believing; at least the hearer will profit in terms of the justificational desideratum, which is what the current approach emphasizes. Consider a second-grade school teacher who considers making various factual statements to his class for which they have no independent evidence one way or the other. The teacher believes all of these statements to be false, and has no justification for any of them. Nonetheless, since his pupils trust him completely, and have adequate reason for so trusting him, his making these statements will make the pupils justified in believing them. Why, then, shouldn't he go ahead and make those statements, according to the current—purely justificational—approach? There is, to be sure, a salient risk of their coming to believe falsehoods rather than truths, but that is irrelevant under the current approach.

A possible reply from the justification-centered camp is to introduce a *transmissional* conception of justification. According to such a conception, a speaker can make a hearer justified in believing a proposition only if the speaker himself *has* justification to *transmit*. Where the speaker lacks such justification, hearers cannot profit justificationally from his assertions. But is such a transmissional conception of justification an appropriate conception for someone who defends a justification-centered approach to epistemic value? I think not. A justification-centered approach is likely to appeal to internalists about justification. After all, externalist conceptions of justification standardly incorporate a link to truth, and are therefore highly congenial to veritistic unitarianism. A justification-centered approach should appeal to internalists who wish to distance the concept of justification from the goal of truth. A transmissional conception of justification, however, is the antithesis of internalism. A hearer cannot tell if he gets justification from a speaker unless he can tell whether the speaker himself is justified, and that is a difficult matter to discern, something to which a hearer has no guaranteed access. Thus, a transmissional conception of justification is unlikely to suit a justification-centered theory; yet without that conception, such a theory cannot rationalize norms (1) and (2).

7. Varieties of Justification

The preceding discussion calls attention to the fact that, according to many writers, there is more than one sense or conception of epistemic justification.[7] If the prospect of multiple senses of justification is accepted, however, won't this undercut the thesis of veritistic unitarianism? Although some of these conceptions of justification—the more externalist ones, in particular—may comport nicely with veritistic unitarianism, other conceptions—especially the more internalist ones—might not comport with it at all. Indeed, the very existence of multiple justificational values seems to pose a challenge to unitarianism.

Now, I have already conceded that *monistic* unitarianism may not be defensible; so it wouldn't close the book on unitarianism if we had to concede more than one conception of justification. The more pressing question is whether all varieties of justification can be traced to the *veritistic* dimension of value. Purely externalist conceptions of justification—at least reliabilist versions of externalism—seem safe in this respect. But what about more internalist conceptions, or even mixed conceptions?

In chapter 1, "Internalism Exposed," I give the example of Sally, who reads about the health benefits of broccoli in a questionable source, e.g., the *National Enquirer*. Despite this notorious source, Sally trusts the story and believes in the benefits of broccoli, though she encounters no further information that either corroborates or conflicts with it. At a subsequent time, Sally finds herself still believing in the health benefits of broccoli, but she no longer recalls where she learned about it. Is Sally's belief justified? I am inclined to say "no" (in this version of the case), because the only possible source of her justifiedness is a wholly unworthy source. Had she acquired her belief from *The New York Times* (another variant of the case I also consider), her belief would be justified. But in the *National Enquirer* version, I don't think the belief is justified. At any rate, it isn't justified in the "epistemizing" sense of justifiedness, in which justifiedness carries one a good distance toward knowledge.

Several readers of this example say that there is *another* sense of justifiedness in which Sally's belief *is* justified. Since Sally thinks she acquired the belief from a reliable source (though she doesn't recall what that source was), the belief seems to be justified *from her current perspective*. And that's all that matters for internalist justifiedness.

I don't want to dispute these readers' intuition that there is such a sense of justifiedness; the question is how to account for it. I offer an account that appeals to the familiar *objective/subjective* distinction. Keeping matters simple, a belief has objective justifiedness if its genesis or sustainment is the result of appropriate processes (e.g., reliable processes). A belief has subjective justifiedness if, *by the agent's own lights*, the belief's genesis or sustainment is the result of appropriate processes. Sally's belief is not objectively justified but it is subjectively justified, because she takes her belief to have resulted from appropriate processes.[8]

The significance of this approach for veritistic unitarianism is as follows. Subjective justifiedness is a secondary concept, derived in an obvious way from objective justifiedness. This is the standard way of understanding subjective Xness for any (objective) concept of Xness (where X could be duty, rightness, etc.). Roughly speaking, the distinction is between how things *are* and how they *appear* from an agent's perspective. In the present case, a belief is objectively justified if it *does* meet certain standards that have a truth-indicative status. A belief is subjectively justified if it appears, from the agent's perspective at the time of belief, to meet those standards.[9]

If, as argued above, the standards for objective justifiedness are deeply rooted in the waters of truth-indicativeness, then subjective justifiedness, by implication, has a derivative element of truth-linkedness. This is not to say that being subjectively justified is a good indicator or means to truth. The relation to truth here is not a straightforwardly instrumental one. But I have not characterized unitarianism as the doctrine that the all concepts of epistemic value or virtue have the *same* relation to a single fundamental desideratum. The possibility of multiple relations was clearly anticipated (though a multiplicity of relations, it was conceded, would mark a weaker form of unitarianism). I am now proposing that subjective justifiedness exemplifies a distinct type of relation to the core veritistic desideratum, not an instrumental relation.

Another conception of internalist justification that differs from the purely subjective one is what I'll call the "higher-level" conception. One example is BonJour's (1985) insistence that justification must meet a "metajustificational" requirement. S's believing p is justified if and only if the belief not only meets some first-order standards of justification but, in addition, S is justified in believing that these standards are adequately truth-indicative (BonJour 1985, 9). Now, I think there is a serious problem about how to formulate the pertinent higher-level condition. But if it embodies a second level of justifiedness, as the term "metajustification" certainly suggests, and if justifiedness itself has a truth-indicative component, it certainly appears as if the higher-level approach to justification is strongly geared toward true belief as a preeminent goal. The relation between the higher-level condition and the truth desideratum may not be straightforwardly instrumental, but I have already argued in the discussion of subjective justifiedness that the relation to truth need not be instrumental to mesh with veritistic unitarianism.

8. Welfare Unitarianism

A completely different alternative to veritistic unitarianism than any considered thus far might center on some generic form of *moral* value, rather than the distinctive value of true belief. A familiar example of such a value is utility or welfare, but the list of relevant possibilities could be expanded to include justice, respect for rights, and so forth. To keep things simple, I shall explore this perspective by reference to welfare as the representative value. The idea would be that welfare underlies and unifies not only the moral virtues, but also the epistemic virtues. In fact, the epistemic virtues may not be distinguishable from the moral ones.

Some such thesis is suggested by Stephen Stich (1990, chap. 6) under the rubric of a "pragmatic" approach to cognitive evaluation. More precisely, Stich talks of cognitive value as residing in whatever people take to be intrinsically valuable. Since he rejects truth as the basis of cognitive evaluation, for a variety of reasons, he sees pragmatic values as a rival approach to veritism. Another example of welfare unitarianism is suggested by Philip Kitcher (1997), in discussing scientific decisions about whether to undertake certain kinds of research, especially research into the biological basis of human behavior. Kitcher presents two candidate decision rules for deciding whether to pursue such research (1997, 285):

(1) Pursue research if and only if the expected utility for the entire population is positive.
(2) Pursue research if and only if the expected utility for the underprivileged is positive.

These are obviously quite different, and Kitcher indicates his preference for (2). For our purposes the important thing to note is the contrast between *both* of these decision rules and veritism. Both rules invoke expected utility, not true belief, as the benchmark for scientific research decisions. To put it in terms of our present theme, utility or welfare would be the benchmark for determining a scientifically "virtuous" course of action.

None of these welfare approaches strikes me as a plausible approach to epistemic value or virtue. In particular, welfarism gives intuitively wrong results if it is applied to the question of *how* research should be conducted, as opposed to what topics should be the objects of research. There will almost certainly be cases in which conducting research in a certain way would pass a suitable welfare criterion though it would generate false beliefs; and conversely, there will almost certainly be cases in which research conducted in a truth-conducive fashion would not pass a welfare criterion. It seems wrong to say, however, that *epistemic* (intellectual) virtue would be exercised by adopting an anti-veritistic method of research in the service of optimizing the appropriate type of welfare.

To say this is not to deny that moral values might sometimes trump epistemic values, so that certain research should be sacrificed. Suppose a clever experiment has been devised that would probably yield extremely interesting data on human emotional responses, as all researchers in the area concede. Unfortunately, it would require infliction of severe pain on human subjects. Every scrupulous scientist will agree that the research should not be done; nor would it get past any human subjects committee. Is this because it lacks epistemic or scientific virtue, as the welfare approach would certainly say? No, there is a better explanation.

Although veritistic value is the fundamental benchmark of epistemic virtue, it is obviously not the *only value*. Nor is it the preeminent value for all purposes of life and action. Epistemological or scientific value sometimes conflicts with moral value, and when they conflict, epistemological value must give way. There is a moral "side-constraint" on scientific research, which is that the conduct of such research should not violate human rights or injure people. The human experiment described above should not be done, but not because it would lack scientific or epistemic value. Rather, it is a case in which the moral disvalue trumps the scientific value. Cases of moral trumping should not be an invitation to confuse scientific value with moral value; the truth desideratum should not be replaced with the welfare desideratum for the sphere of the epistemic.

In rejecting welfare as the benchmark of epistemic value, I do not mean to reject considerations of welfare, or other measures of social significance, as one pertinent criterion in selecting *questions* or *topics* for scientific research. The role of "interest" has already been acknowledged in my own account of core epistemic value, and I do not exclude the notion that one factor that might determine a question's interest is the social significance its answer might have. The crucial thing, from my perspective, is that science is epistemically virtuous to the extent that it promotes a high degree of *truth* possession on questions of interest. What fixes appropriate interests (for science or other arenas of inquiry) is another matter.

The importance of this point is that veritism need not disagree with certain strands of a "value-ladenness" thesis in the philosophy of science, a thesis defended by feminist epistemologists such as Helen Longino (1990) and Elizabeth Anderson (1995a). Veritism need not dispute at least one legitimate role in science for social and contextual values that is stressed by these writers, viz., the role of these values in placing questions on the scientific agenda. Anderson highlights the fact that scientists often judge the significance of questions in medicine, horticulture, and engineering in terms of practical social interests. Similarly, physicists investigate conditions for controlled and uncontrolled nuclear reactions and number theorists study algorithms that can rapidly factor very large numbers because of practical or contextual values (in the latter case the interest concerns the construction and decoding of encrypted messages). Veritism can completely agree with these points. It need not hold that science should always be driven by purely "internal" questions produced by its own puzzle-generating activities. It allows questions to be chosen for scientific research on the basis (at least in part) of practical social interests. Veritism will diverge from the value-ladenness perspective, however, if the latter suggests that the methods of "choosing" theories or fixing beliefs in theories (to answer the selected questions) may properly be guided by considerations that conflict with truth-based considerations. I am not certain what Anderson's or Longino's views are on this matter; but unless they also endorse this last-mentioned thesis, there is no necessary conflict with veritism.[10]

9. Conclusion

I would not claim to have made a thoroughly decisive case for epistemic unitarianism. Nonetheless, veritistic unitarianism has withstood quite a few challenges and passed a number of tests with flying colors. While the specific form of unitarianism developed here is not the purest possible form, its tenability seems more defensible, on reflection, than many might have thought possible.

Notes

Thanks to Todd Stewart for many valuable comments on initial drafts of the chapter, to Julia Annas for instructive discussion of the virtue ethics literature, to Heather Battaly, who raised several useful points in her role as commentator at the Santa Barbara conference, and to Susan Haack, who corrected my misconstrual of her position in an earlier draft.

1. Thus, T. H. Irwin writes: "Socrates believes that each virtue is identical to the very same knowledge of good and evil, and hence that all virtues are really just one virtue" (1992, 973–74).

2. See Lehrer (1990, 134–35, 149).

3. Susan Haack (1993) is an evidentialist but not a deontological evidentialist. She clearly offers truth-conduciveness as the basis for evidentialism: "The goal of inquiry is ... truth; the concept of justification is specifically focused on security, on the likelihood of beliefs being true. Hence my claim that truth-indicative is what criteria of justification need to be to be good" (1993, 203). She defends her own specifically "foundherentist" approach to justification by saying that its criteria offer the best hope for truth-indication that we can have (1993, 220–221).

4. Also see Goldman (1999, chap. 4). The crucial condition is that the agent's subjective likelihoods must *match* the objective likelihoods. The result also assumes

that the agent's priors are neither 0 nor 1.0, and the likelihood ratio is not 1.0 (the likelihoods are not identical). A second theorem is that *larger* expected increases in truth-possession are associated with greater divergences of the likelihood ratio from 1.0. In other words, the more "decisive" an experiment, the greater its objectively expected increase in truth-possession. What are here called "degrees of truth-possession" are discussed in the next section of the text under the label "degrees of veritistic value."

5. The role of interest is acknowledged in *Knowledge in a Social World*, sect. 3.5. The variety of potentially relevant interests discussed there makes for additional complications, but I don't think these are relevant to the present discussion.

6. For defense of this thesis, see Goldman (1999, chap. 9).

7. A particularly strong version of this thesis is advanced by Alston (1993a).

8. The most systematic development of a subjectivist account of justification (or rationality) is found in Foley (1987). In a later book, Foley acknowledges, in agreement with the present proposal, that 'justification' and its cognates "have both an egocentric and an objective side" (1993, 86). My paper "Strong and Weak Justification" (Goldman 1988) comes close to formulating the objective vs. subjective conceptions of justifiedness. But there I conceived of strong and weak justifiedness as "separate but equal," whereas here I want to suggest that subjective justifiedness is a secondary concept, derivative from that of objective justifiedness.

9. "Perspectivalism" is one conception of internalist justification that Alston (1989, chap. 8) considers.

10. Anderson does assign a role to contextual values in theory *choice*, but it is not so clear that the assigned role in any way cuts against truth. She says that contextual values come into play in telling us which *classifications* to use; but the choice of classifications does not obviously have a truth-impeding tendency.

PART II

Intuition, Introspection, and Consciousness

4

Philosophical Theory and Intuitional Evidence

1. Intuitions as Evidence

Philosophers frequently appeal to intuitions in constructing and arguing for philosophical theories. A theory is commonly judged lacking when it fails to "capture" our intuitions and judged acceptable insofar as it captures more of our intuitions than other extant theories. This suggests that philosophers take intuitions to have a kind of evidential value. But what are intuitions, what hypotheses, exactly, do they evidentially support, and why should they have this evidential value? More generally, what is the proper role for intuitions (if any) in the "validation" of a philosophical theory? Many roles philosophers have assigned to intuition do not fall within our purview. For example, we do not examine the role of intuition in the acquisition of mathematical or logical knowledge. Indeed, we restrict our present inquiry to the role of intuitions in philosophical "analysis." This is not to suggest that philosophical analysis exhausts the mission of philosophy, nor that it comprises the most important part of philosophy. It is simply the segment or facet of philosophy where the appeal to intuition seems to us most relevant (not to say unproblematic).

Although different approaches to intuition have different detailed accounts of what intuitions are, we assume, at a minimum, that intuitions are some sort of spontaneous mental judgments. Each intuition, then, is a judgment "that p," for some suitable class of propositions p. An intuitional report is

This chapter was written with Joel Pust.

73

the verbal report of a spontaneous mental judgment. In principle, the verbal report of an intuition can be erroneous, either through imperfect self-knowledge, verbal error, or insincerity. Here we assume, however, that all verbal reports of intuitions are accurate, that is, correctly convey what intuition is experienced. The question facing a philosopher, then, is how and why to treat spontaneous mental judgments, either one's own or those of an informant, as evidence for a philosophical hypothesis.

There seems to be a traditional picture among philosophers of how intuitions might serve as evidence, at least among philosophers favorably disposed toward intuitions as sources of evidence. This picture can be captured with the concept of a *basic evidential source*.[1] Many classes of mental states comprise basic evidential sources, including visual seemings, auditory seemings, memory seemings, and perhaps introspective seemings. In each case, there is a class M of contentful mental states such that being in one of these mental states is prima facie evidence for the truth of its content, at least when the (token) state occurs in favorable M-circumstances. Thus, visual states are a basic evidential source because when a person experiences a state of seeming to see that p and is in favorable visual circumstances, this is prima facie evidence for the truth of p. Auditory states are a basic evidential source because when a person experiences a state of seeming to hear that p and is in favorable auditory circumstances, this is prima facie evidence for the truth of p. Memory is a basic evidential source because when a person has an ostensible memory state of seeming to recall that p and is in favorable mnemonic circumstances, this is prima facie evidence for the truth of p. Introspection might also be a basic evidential source, where introspective states are states having contents of the form. "I now have a conscious mental state of such-and-such type."

Under what conditions, exactly, does a class of states M qualify as a basic evidential source? Minimally, the following condition seems to be required:

(RI)   Mental states of type M constitute a basic evidential source only if M-states are reliable indicators of the truth of their contents (or the truth of closely related contents), at least when the M-states occur in M-favorable circumstances.[2]

The reliable indicatorship requirement is simply the requirement that when M-states occur (in M-favorable circumstances), their contents are *generally true*. When one seems to see that a telephone is on the desk, and when this occurs under circumstances of adequate light, sufficient proximity, and no obstruction, then it is usually true that a telephone is on the (contextually indicated) desk. When one seems to recall that one had cereal for breakfast, and there is no substantial interference from other episodes in memory, it is usually true that one did have cereal for breakfast.

Two other features standardly characterize basic evidential sources: (1) a counterfactual dependence, and (2) a causal medium. The notion of counterfactual dependence is defined by David Lewis as follows:

> Let A_1, A_2, ... be a family of possible propositions, no two of which are compossible; let C_1, C_2, ... be another such family (of equal size). Then if all the counterfactuals $A_1 \square\!\!\rightarrow C_1$, $A_2 \square\!\!\rightarrow C_2$, ... between corresponding propositions in the two families are true, we shall say that the C's *depend counterfactually* on the A's. We can say it like this in ordinary language: whether C_1 or C_2 or ... depends (counterfactually) on whether A_1 or A_2 or ... (1986b, 164–65)

In the standard case of a basic evidential source M, the M-states depend counterfactually on the truth of their contents, at least insofar as M-favorable conditions obtain. For example, in favorable visual conditions, if the object in a person's visual field were red, the person would seem to see that something is red; if the object were yellow, the person would seem to see that something is yellow; and so forth. Similarly for propositions concerning shape: if the object were square, the person would seem to see that something is square; if the object were circular, the person would seem to see that something is circular; and so forth.[3] Note that counterfactual dependences can *explain* reliable indicatorship relations. The fact that an M-state with the content p—that is, M(p)—occurs only if p is true may be explained by the fact that if any contrary state of affairs p* were true, the contrary state M(p*) would occur rather than M(p).

In standard cases of basic evidential sources there is also a distinctive causal route from the family of states of affairs that make the M-contents true or false to the family of M-states. In vision, for instance, the distinctive causal route includes light being reflected from the truth-making state of affairs (or the objects involved in that state of affairs), traveling to the perceiver's retinas, which then send signals or information via the optic nerves to the visual cortex. In many cases of basic evidential sources (e.g., memory), we still lack a firm scientific understanding of what the causal route consists in. Nonetheless, we often have substantial evidence *that there is* such a causal route. Indeed, if we believed that there is no such causal route, there would be grounds for doubting that there are counterfactual dependences of the indicated sort. And if there were no counterfactual dependences of the indicated sort, there would be grounds for doubting that the reliable indicatorship relation obtains. We shall not insist that either a counterfactual dependence or a causal route be present in order to have a basic evidential source. Only the reliable indicatorship relation is proposed as a necessary condition for a basic evidential source. As just indicated, however, if it is known or suspected that there is no relevant causal route or counterfactual dependence, there are grounds for doubting the existence of a reliable indicatorship relation, and hence for doubting the existence of a basic evidential source.

Let us return now to intuitions. A traditional philosophical view of intuition, we believe, is that intuitions constitute a basic evidential source (or perhaps a family of basic evidential sources). For this reason, many traditional philosophers hold that when someone has an intuition with the content p, this is prima facie evidence for the truth of p. In other words, I(p) is prima facie evidence for p. We are tentatively disposed to accept this proposal. That is, *if* intuition is a basic evidential source, I(p) is prima facie evidence for the truth of p. As formula (RI) indicates, however, intuition only qualifies as a basic evidential source if intuitional states (intuitings) are reliable indicators of the truth of their contents (or closely related contents) when they occur in favorable circumstances. It remains to be seen whether intuition indeed satisfies (RI).

Being a basic evidential source is not the only possible way intuitions might qualify as evidence for some sort of philosophical theory or conclusion. Being a basic evidential source is a very special way of providing evidence, and states of all sorts, including mental states, might provide evidence without being tokens of a basic evidential source. A mental state of dizziness, for example, might be evidence that a patient has a certain disease or clinical condition, at least it might be evidence in the hands of a physician or diagnostician with suitable background information. But this does not show that dizziness is a token of a basic evidential source. First, dizziness does not seem to be a *contentful* mental state, which is necessary for being a basic evidential source. Second, even if it were contentful, its content would surely not include the clinical condition inferred by the diagnostician. Like dizziness, intuitions might also be used as evidence without being tokens of a basic evidential source. Most of our discussion, however, will examine intuition as a candidate for a basic evidential source, partly because that is the traditional philosophical approach and partly because, on the view we shall advance, it probably *is* a basic evidential source.

Under standard philosophical methodology (SPM), the content of a typical intuition is a proposition about whether a case or example is an instance of a certain kind, concept, or predicate.[4] In other words, the contents of intuitions are usually singular classificational propositions, to the effect that such-and-such an example is or is not an instance of knowledge, of justice, of personal identity, and so forth. Thus, intuited propositions are standardly of the form, "Example e is (is not) an instance of F," and intuitions are spontaneous mental assentings to such classificational propositions. More fully, the propositional content of a singular intuition might have the form, "Example e is an instance of G (e.g., justified true belief) but not an instance of F (e.g., knowledge)."

Philosophers, of course, do not primarily aim to establish the truth or falsity of singular propositions, at least not of this sort. They usually seek to defend or criticize some general theory, such as, the theory that knowledge is justified true belief, or that personal identity consists in psychological continuity. Establishing or refuting such theories is the main aim of philosophical activity, at least under the mission of philosophical analysis. An adequate reconstruction of philosophical methodology here requires a two-step evidential route. In the first step, the occurrence of an intuition that p, either an intuition of one's own or that of an informant, is taken as (prima facie) evidence for the truth of p (or the truth of a closely related proposition). In the second step, the truth of p is used as positive or negative evidence for the truth of a general theory. The first step is epistemologically central for the topic of intuition, so it will be the main object of our scrutiny. Later, however, we shall also have things to say about the second step.

Without explicit elaboration, philosophers seem to proceed on the assumption that intuitions—at least intuitions of singular classificational propositions—comprise a basic evidential source. That is ostensibly why philosophers regard the first step of the two-step route as warranted. The question that needs to be raised, therefore, is whether intuition really is a basic evidential source, in particular, whether it satisfies condition (RI). Answering this question requires closer attention to the exact content of singular classificational propositions and the exact interpretation of philosophical analysis. As we shall argue, different interpretations of philosophical analysis can offer better or worse prospects for rationalizing the working assumption of SPM that intuition is a basic evidential source.[5]

Before turning to possible interpretations, let us ask what would constitute favorable versus unfavorable circumstances for the working of intuition. What types of circumstances render intuitions unreliable, in something like the way that poor lighting conditions can render visual seemings unreliable, or background noise can render auditory seemings unreliable? There are two plausible candidates in the case of intuitions, and they illuminate how and why careful philosophical practitioners proceed as they do.

If an informant is asked for an intuition about a real live case, but she is ill-informed or misinformed about the case, her intuition as to whether the case is or is not an instance of F may be of little worth. Suppose, for instance, that Sally intuits that Oliver Stone *knows* that the Kennedy assassination was a conspiracy, partly because Sally takes the case to be one in which Stone's belief is *true*. If the latter assumption is mistaken, that is, if the conspiracy hypothesis is false, Sally's intuition that Stone knows is hardly a reliable indicator that he really does know. The possibility of incorrectly representing the facts of the case is a prime reason why philosophers construct hypothetical examples. This gives them the opportunity to stipulate relevant features of an example, so the informant will not be in the dark. Only then can an intuition be a reliable indicator of its content's truth. Things can go wrong even with hypothetical cases, however. The informant may misunderstand the description, or lose track of certain stipulated features of the case. So misinformation and confusion are analogues of poor lighting conditions, or occlusion of the stimulus, which are unfavorable circumstances for the exercise of vision. Just as in the case of vision, however, the fact that unfavorable circumstances can occur does not prevent intuition from qualifying as a basic evidential source. If one seeks to use the source as evidence, however, one wants it to be exercised only in favorable circumstances (insofar as possible).

A second possible source of error is theory contamination. If the person experiencing the intuition is a philosophical analyst who holds an explicit theory about the nature of F, this theory might warp her intuitions about specific cases. So, at any rate, it is widely assumed (and we shall support this assumption in section 2). For this reason, philosophers rightly prefer informants who can provide *pre-theoretical* intuitions about the targets of philosophical analysis, rather than informants who have a theoretical "stake" or "axe to grind." Thus, when intuition is considered as a candidate for a basic evidential source, the condition of having a prior theoretical commitment might be an unfavorable circumstance for its proper (i.e., reliable) exercise.

2. Some Approaches to Philosophical Theory

Let us turn now to possible approaches to philosophical conclusions and ways intuitions might evidentially bear on them. Our taxonomy is intended to provide a small set of simple and perspicuous paradigms rather than a detailed review of the literature. The options we delineate do have some currency among contemporary writers, however, as we shall illustrate.

Broadly speaking, views about philosophical analysis may be divided into those that take the targets of such analysis to be in-the-head psychological entities versus outside-the-head nonpsychological entities. We shall call the first type of position *mentalism* and the second *extra-mentalism*. Both mentalists and extra-mentalists agree that intuitions themselves are conscious psychological states, but they differ on whether the targets of philosophical inquiry—that for which intuitions are supposed to provide evidence—are psychological or nonpsychological. In the case of mentalism, the mental entities in question are not conscious mental entities; otherwise, it would presumably be unnecessary to use indirect inferential techniques to get at them. Rather, they are nonconscious entities or structures to which introspective access is lacking.

We identify three forms of extra-mentalism: (1) the *universals* approach, (2) the *modal equivalence* approach, and (3) the *natural kinds* approach. The first approach says that philosophical analysis aims to elucidate or lay bare the contents of certain abstract, Platonistic entities, namely, certain universals.

The analysis of "S knows that P," for example, is really concerned with identifying the content or structure of a certain universal: knowledge. The second approach says that philosophical analysis aims to provide, for each philosophically interesting predicate, another predicate (or compound predicate) that is modally equivalent to it, that is, has the same intension.[6] For example, in the case of knowledge, analysis tries to find a predicate that applies to the same set of ordered n-tuples in each possible world as "knows" does. The third approach construes philosophy as aiming to provide theories of certain *natural kinds*. Epistemology, for example, tries to provide a theory of the natural kind, knowledge.

As a paradigmatic proponent of the first extra-mentalist approach we need look no further than Plato himself. Plato's forms are classic examples of external entities that are exemplified or instantiated by particulars. They are also depicted as objects of nonperceptual intellectual apprehension, a prototype of how many philosophers construe intuition. Working within a broadly Platonistic tradition, a universals extra-mentalist might say that when someone has an intuition that e is an instance of F, what she has is an intellectual apprehension that a certain universal, F (or Fness), is instantiated by e. On this view, classificational intuitions involve the detection of a relation (instantiation or noninstantiation) between a universal and an actual or possible particular. A twentieth-century philosopher who espoused such a view was Bertrand Russell (1912, chap. 9). Although it is hard to pinpoint contemporary writers who endorse it, strands of it are certainly to be found in the literature. For example, without explicitly invoking universals, Matthias Steup hints at this position when he writes: "when we engage in a philosophical examination of such things as knowledge and justification . . . what we are interested in is not what ideas of knowledge and justification people carry in their heads, but rather what people have in common when they know something, when they are justified in believing something" (1996, 21). Both Alvin Plantinga (1993b, chap. 6) and Jerrold Katz (1981, chap. 6) view intuition as a rational apprehension or "grasping" of extramental entities or states of affairs.

Clearly, the universals approach assumes that intuition is a basic evidential source, a source that gives us access to universals and their relations in roughly the same way as perception gives us access to physical objects and events. But could intuitions meet the RI constraint if their contents are construed as being about universals? How, on this view, might an intuition be a reliable indicator of a singular classificational truth? Let us introduce the notion of an *associated philosophical gloss* of a proposition. If we consider an ordinary classificational proposition like "e is an instance of knowledge," an associated philosophical gloss of it, modulo the universals approach, might be: "The universal KNOWLEDGE is such that e is an instance of it." Presumably, naive informants' judgments do not explicitly refer to universals in this way. Nonetheless, an intuition with the content "e is an instance of F" might be a reliable indicator of the truth of its associated philosophical gloss, namely, that the universal F is such that e is an instance of it. The truth of this classificational fact might in turn provide evidence about the constitution of the universal. Thus, the evidential reconstruction of the role of intuitions on this approach would run as follows. The philosopher obtains informants' singular classificational intuitions and takes them as (prima facie) evidence that the target universal is or is not instantiated by such-and-such examples. This is premised on the assumption that intuition is a basic evidential source. A constructive analytic philosopher would collect the positive and negative instances and frame a hypothesis about the constitution of the target universal. A "destructive" philosopher would use the same positive or negative instances critically: to refute some hypothesis about the constitution of the target universal.

The chief difficulty for this approach comes with the assumption that intuition is a basic evidential source, a source of information about universals. Is there any reason to suppose that intuitions could be reliable indicators of a universal's positive and negative instances (even under favorable circumstances)? The problem is the apparent "distance" or "remoteness" between intuitions, which are dated mental states, and a nonphysical, extra-mental, extra-temporal entity. How could the former be reliable indicators of the properties of the latter? This is similar to the problem Paul Benacerraf (1973) raises about the prospects for mathematical knowledge on any Platonistic view of mathematics. Benacerraf, however, assumes that a causal connection with the object known is necessary for knowledge. We deliberately have not imposed such a requirement for a basic evidential source. Nor have we imposed the requirement of a counterfactual dependence between states of affairs that make an intuition's content true and the occurrence of such intuitions. We have only imposed the reliable indicatorship constraint. However, as mentioned in section 1, wherever it is obscure, as it is here, how a causal relation or counterfactual dependence of the right sort could obtain, there are grounds for serious doubt that the reliable indicatorship relation obtains. Some philosophers (e.g., Plantinga 1993b, 120–21) might reply that abstractness per se does not exclude causal relations. Nonetheless, we certainly lack any convincing or even plausible story of how intuitions could be reliable indicators of facts concerning universals. Thus, the universals approach offers an extremely thin reed on which to base philosophical methodology.

We turn next to the modal equivalence approach. The crucial point here is that the correctness of a philosophical theory depends on the contours of modal space, construed in a fully extra-mentalist, mind-independent fashion. When Edmund Gettier (1963) published his two counterexamples to the justified-true-belief analysis of knowledge, and almost all epistemologists shared the same intuitions about them, the modal equivalence approach interprets these intuitions to show that there are two possible cases in modal space to which the predicate "justified true belief" applies but the predicate "knowledge" does not apply. That these cases in modal space have these properties is evidentially supported by the indicated intuitions, on the supposition that intuition is a basic evidential source. An associated philosophical gloss of the intuitions' contents, modulo this approach, would take the form, "e is a case in the space of possibilities (i.e., in some possible world) that is an instance of G but not F." By getting evidence for such truths, it is demonstrated that "knowledge" and "justified true belief" are not modally equivalent.

The sticking point for this approach is essentially the same as the one facing the Platonistic universals approach. Intuitions are mental occurrences. Why are these mental occurrences with contents about objects in modal space reliable indicators of what is genuinely in modal space? As with the first approach, there appears to be a substantial gap between an intuiting, a type of psychological event, and the contours of objective modal space. It does not matter whether one takes possible worlds to be abstract objects or "concrete," spatio-temporally isolated objects (Lewis 1986a). There is still a substantial gap between the "inhabitants" of such objects and people's actual intuitions. How is this gap supposed to be bridged? To repeat, we are not immediately concerned with either a causal gap or the absence of a counterfactual dependence; we are concerned with a reliable indicator relationship. But given the dim prospects for either a causal connection or a counterfactual dependence, it is hard to see how there could be a reliable indicator relationship. Thus, there would be plenty of grounds to doubt that intuition qualifies as a basic evidential source if its contents were construed in terms of objective modal space.

The third approach, natural kinds extra-mentalism, has been advocated by Hilary Kornblith (1995, 1998) and Michael Devitt (1994). They hold that philosophical inquiry aims to provide a theory about the nature of certain natural kinds. Kornblith, for example, says that "the investigation of knowledge, and philosophical investigation generally" ought to be conducted on the model of the investigation of natural kinds (1998, 134). The proper targets of philosophy are knowledge, meaning, and the good *themselves*, rather than the folk concepts of knowledge, meaning, or the good. Natural kinds theorists are not entirely clear about whether they conceive of natural kinds as a species of universals, but if so, they might construe them as non-Platonistic entities à la David Armstrong (1989).

Natural kinds extra-mentalists endorse a two-step evidential route in philosophical theorizing. The first step is executed by consulting persons thought to be experts about F, and eliciting from them their singular classification intuitions about F. The associated philosophical gloss here seems to be that an intuition provides evidence for truths of the form "e is an instance of natural kind F." The second stage of the method is an empirical investigation of the concrete tokens picked out by the singular intuitions, the aim being to reveal the underlying nature of the property of being an F. This stage may lead to a theory that requires extensive revision of some intuitive judgments, or lead to the conclusion that various folk predicates do not latch onto any legitimate natural kind and should therefore be abandoned.

Our first dissatisfaction with the natural kinds approach stems from our doubt that all targets of philosophical analysis or even most of them, qualify as natural kinds. Presumably something qualifies as a natural kind only if it has a prior essence, nature, or character independent of anybody's thought or conception of it. It is questionable, however, whether such analysanda as knowledge, justification, and justice have essences or natures independent of our conception of them. In our opinion, the lack of natural kind status would not place the topics of knowledge, justification, or justice outside the scope of philosophical analysis. Nor do we think that the corresponding predicates should be abandoned if they fail to pick out natural kinds.

Our second dissatisfaction with the natural kinds approach mirrors our worries about the other forms of extra-mentalism. The problem is: How can intuition get any reliable purchase on the constitutions of both a natural kind and an example so as to decide whether the latter matches the former? We assume here, as before, that the role or task of intuitions is to render (accurate) classification judgments. If the judgments are about natural kinds and their putative instances, a cognizer must first discern the underlying nature of the natural kind, then discern the underlying nature of the example, and then decide whether these match. It is not clear how intuition could contribute to the reliable execution of these tasks. It seems out of the question, then, that intuition could qualify as a basic evidential source under the natural kinds approach. The situation is especially problematic in the case of intuitions about hypothetical examples. Since these are not actual, concrete examples open for empirical inspection, how is intuition supposed to detect their underlying natures to see whether they qualify as instances of the target natural kind? As we have stressed, it is a pervasive feature of SPM that it employs intuitions about hypothetical cases and takes them to be on a par with (or better than) actual cases. The natural kinds approach apparently lacks any way of explaining this feature of SPM.

As indicated earlier, some proponents of the natural kinds approach advocate the use of only *experts'* intuitions. This is at variance, however, with SPM, which regards the intuitions of all people, or all linguistically competent people, as relevant. Furthermore, in the case of real natural kinds, experts are consulted about whether a given specimen is an instance of gold because those experts presumably know best what gold's nature is. But under SPM, nobody is assumed to know beforehand (in any explicit fashion) what F is. The whole purpose of appealing to intuitions is to get information about instances and noninstances of F in order to discover what F is. This seems quite at variance with the procedure advocated under the natural kinds approach.

Natural kinds proponents might concede many of our points. They might cheerfully grant that intuition is not a basic evidential source, and they might agree that their proposed methodology does not precisely match SPM. They might insist, however, that they are not *trying* to provide a rationalization for SPM, because they regard SPM as misguided in certain major or minor respects. If this is indeed their attitude, then their form of extra-mentalism simply does not fulfill the sort of objective with which we started, namely, to show, if possible, how SPM makes proper use of intuitional evidence and how intuition might qualify as a basic evidential source.

It is time to turn to mentalism, our favored approach. Mentalism interprets philosophical analysis as trying to shed light on the *concepts* behind philosophically interesting predicates, where the term "concept" refers to a psychological structure or state that underpins a cognizer's deployment of a natural-language predicate.[7] Thus, Jones's concept of apple is the psychological structure that underlies her deployment of the predicate "apple," and Jones's concept of knowledge is the psychological structure that underlies her deployment of the predicate "knows" (or "has knowledge").[8] (We ignore complications arising from multivocal words in natural languages.) The structures in question presumably include some sorts of mental representations, as well as some kinds of processing routines. The mental representations are assumed to have semantic contents, to which the theorist might appeal. Whether these contents are "narrow" or "wide," that is, determined in an individualist or anti-individualist fashion, is a topic on which we remain neutral.

Unlike the extra-mentalist approaches surveyed earlier, our form of mentalism is very congenial to the notion that intuition might be a basic evidential source. Under mentalism, moreover, its status as a basic evidential source can be sustained in a fully naturalistic framework. To see this, consider first what is the associated philosophical gloss of an intuition's content, according to mentalism. We interpret the gloss to be: "e satisfies my concept that I express through the predicate 'F'." This gloss is not intended to be the precise propositional content of an intuition, which we take to be, "e is an instance of F." But the gloss is certainly a closely related content. Moreover, given criterion (RI), intuition could qualify as a basic evidential source as long as the occurrence of intuitions with the content "e is an instance of F" are reliable indicators of the truth of the associated proposition, namely, "e satisfies my concept that I express through the predicate 'F'." Is it plausible that this reliable indicatorship relation should obtain? Definitely.

It is easy to see that intuitions with the indicated types of contents can be reliable indicators of the truth of their associated glosses. That is because there might well be an appropriate counterfactual dependence between e's satisfaction or nonsatisfaction of the concept expressed through 'F' and what the intuition "says" about e. The concept associated with a predicate 'F' will have many dispositions, but among them are dispositions to give rise to intuitive classificational judgments such as "example e is (is not) an instance of F." Thus, it is not only possible, but almost a matter of *definition*, that if the concept possessor were fully informed about the relevant features of e, then if e satisfied the concept he expresses through 'F', his intuitive response to the question of whether e satisfies this concept would be affirmative; and if e did not satisfy the concept he expresses through 'F', then his intuitive response to the question of whether e satisfies this concept would be negative. In other words, a concept tends to be manifested by intuitions that reflect or express its content. (This is a point made by George Bealer, and the general approach pursued here is similar to that advanced in Bealer 1987, 1996a, and 1998.)[9] The indicated set of dispositions is the relevant counterfactual dependence that underwrites reliability. Moreover, although we do not currently know the precise causal route that connects concept structures with their conscious manifestations, it is extremely plausible, from any reasonable cognitive-science perspective, that there should be such a causal route. Thus, the satisfiability of the reliability condition seems quite safe.

We said a moment ago that it is "almost" a matter of definition that concepts have the indicated dispositions. Why "almost"? The reason, of course, is the possibility of unfavorable circumstances, or interfering conditions. An intuition might be generated or influenced, for example, by an explicit but mistaken *theory* about the concept of 'F' rather than by the concept of 'F' itself. For this reason, there could be a discrepancy between the intuition and the concept. This possibility, however, merely shows that intuitions are not *perfect* indicators of their associated glosses' truth. They can still be quite reliable, however, and, of greater relevance, they can be perfectly reliable *when occurring in favorable circumstances*. Thus, the prospects are excellent that intuitions are a basic evidential source under the mentalist construal.[10]

Some additional remarks about the mentalist interpretation are in order. First, some people might worry about the metalinguistic character of the mentalist approach, which surfaces in the portion of the gloss that alludes to a *predicate* 'F'. Is it really plausible, they might wonder, that the propositional contents of intuitions concern linguistic predicates like 'know' rather than knowledge itself? Our first response is to note that the metalinguistic element in our approach only enters in the *gloss* of the intuition's content, which need not precisely reproduce the sort of content an intuiter herself would choose to report. Second, since SPM typically involves the posing and answering of classificational questions in linguistic terms, it is clear that the process of generating an intuition involves the accessing of concepts via their cognitive relationship with (representations of) linguistic items. Thus, it is entirely appropriate to view an intuition as the manifestation of a psychological structure (viz., a concept) that can be identified by its relation to a predicate of a natural language.

Another question about the mentalist approach takes its point of departure from the assumption that concepts have *contents*. If the mentalist approach traffics in contents, which are ostensibly abstract entities, how different is it, in the end, from the universals approach? Two remarks are relevant here. First, we remain neutral on the ontological status of mental contents, so we are not committed to entities of the same status as Platonistic universals. Second, unlike the universals approach, mentalism has no burden of trying to explain how intuitions could somehow interact with, or reliably reflect, "free-floating" abstract entities. The contents of which mentalism speaks are contents embedded in, or borne by, psychological structures, which are neural or neurally realized states. Interactions between psychological states of these kinds and intuitional events (which are also neural or neurally realized events) are not fundamentally mysterious or problematic in the way that some sort of "apprehension" or "detection" of universals is problematic.

It is worth noting that even if intuitions did not have credentials to qualify as a basic evidential source, they could still have evidential significance for philosophy under the mentalist approach. Just as in the case of dizziness, one might make a justified abductive inference from intuitions as "observed" effects to concepts (with specified contents) as postulated causes. Since the aim of philosophical analysis according to mentalism is to identify the contents of certain concepts, this would be a (complex) one-step inferential route. Furthermore, it would be a straightforward kind of explanatory inference of the kind familiar from the sciences. Thus, using intuition as evidence would not carry any mysterious, nonscientific baggage. That is also true under our defense of intuition as a basic evidential source. Its evidential claims are no more mysterious, from a scientific or naturalistic point of view, than those of perception or memory.

Our exposition of mentalism may suggest that philosophical analysis is concerned with the concepts of single cognizers. More commonly, however, it is concerned with the linguistic or conceptual properties of a community. Can this be accommodated under mentalism? The default assumption of SPM is that competent speakers of a given natural language have roughly the same conceptual contents lying behind their mastery of a particular predicate. That is, the contents of different people's concepts of 'F' are at least roughly the same. The usual aim of philosophical analysis, then, is to identify the one shared content. Information about the concepts of single cognizers is evidentially relevant to the nature of the collectively shared content so long as the chosen informants are suitably typical members of the community, and there is a genuinely shared content. It must be acknowledged, however, that people might have markedly different contents associated with one and the same predicate. In that case, philosophical analysis must be satisfied with using intuitions to get at each person's distinct concept; it must be prepared, if necessary, to abandon the assumption that the content of one person's concept of 'F' can be generalized to others.[11] However, there are notable philosophical examples, such as the Gettier examples, which evoke the same intuitive responses from virtually all hearers who understand them, responses that even fly in the face of (formerly) well-entrenched theories. This strongly suggests that at least some predicates of philosophical interest have robust contents that span a wide spectrum of the linguistic community.

The mentalist approach to philosophical analysis might appear to threaten the *objectivity* of classificational questions. Antecedently one might have thought that whether an entity or state e qualifies as an instance of F is an objective matter of fact. Isn't such objectivity undercut by the mentalist approach to philosophical analysis, with its palpable subjectivity? No, we do not accept this conclusion at all. If the content of a particular concept expressed by 'F' is sufficiently determinate, then it is an objective matter of fact whether or not e is an instance of 'F'. This fact of the matter is fixed by a combination of the content of the concept and the features of e. To be sure, different people may have different conceptual contents associated with the same predicate 'F'. Hence, the question of whether e is an instance of 'F' is in an important sense ambiguous. Once the concept (content) is fixed, however, the correct answer to the question is uniquely determined by the facts concerning e.

Finally, we should add that philosophical theory need not be restricted to the analysis of concepts (or even the analysis of tacit folk theories) as we have depicted it. First, at least certain concepts might have interesting *historical rationales* for their development or evolution, and it may be highly relevant to philosophy to identify those rationales. In fact, some historical rationales may be viewed as a crucial adjunct of the current working concept. An example of this will be given in section 3. Second, philosophical analysis is primarily concerned with elucidating our folk concepts, but philosophy can also prescribe revisions in those concepts. In metaphysics, for example, conceptual analysis tries to lay bare our folk-ontological categories. But there is also room for prescriptive metaphysics, which would seek to improve upon folk ontology through a combination of scientific discovery and broad philosophical reflection (see Goldman 1989a; 1992, chap. 3). However, intuitions are less likely to play so prominent a role in the latter sector of philosophical theory.

3. Philosophical Analysis and the Psychology of Concepts

Mentalism depicts philosophical analysis as trying to pinpoint the contents of certain concepts, in the indicated psychological sense of "concept." But since inferences about these contents are inferences to psychological structures and processes, it would hardly be surprising if the enterprise we have described could benefit from research by psychologists and other cognitive scientists on the subject of concepts and their mental deployment. In this section, we provide a set of examples—all epistemological examples—to illustrate how such benefits might accrue. What we wish to suggest is that the investigation of "conceptual" matters (in the sense here intended) is properly, at least in part, an empirical investigation, in contrast to the traditional philosophical view that sharply opposes the conceptual and the empirical.

The potential benefits from cognitive science that we shall stress enter at the second step of SPM. Having gathered intuitions about a target predicate from one or more informants, a philosopher aims to determine the conceptual content that generates these intuitions. What is the specific content (and perhaps structure) of the informants' concepts that would explain the accumulated intuitions? Although it may be a definitional truth for a given concept that it would generate the actually collected intuitions, that concept need not be the only one with this property. In general, many different concepts—that is, concepts with nonequivalent contents—could give rise to the same (finite) set of intuitions. The philosophical analyst aims to choose from the set of possible concepts the one that best explains the collected intuitions. We shall argue that empirical psychology and linguistics can provide valuable information to assist the philosophical analyst in making a well-motivated choice.

Our first example concerns the impact of context on informants' judgments and intuitions, and the way theorists should take context effects into account in weighing competing analyses of epistemic concepts. We focus here on the concept of knowledge, since a number of recent proposals about knowledge are strongly contextualist (Cohen 1988; DeRose 1992, 1995; Goldman 1976, 1989b; Lewis 1979). A number of different things might be meant in labeling an approach to knowledge "contextualist." Here we have in mind approaches that ascribe a heavy role to the mental "set" of the knowledge *attributor*, a set that can be influenced by various contextual events. One theory that appeals to psychological context is the *relevant alternatives theory* (in some of its variants). According to this approach, the concept of knowledge implies that a subject does not know that p unless she can rule out all relevant alternatives to p. But which alternatives are relevant? According to a contextualist version of the approach, relevance is not fully determined by a rule or criterion embedded in the concept of knowledge and applied to the situation of the subject. Rather, relevance is judged by the sorts of scenarios or possibilities that are mentally "accessible" or "available" to the attributor. If an attributor has never thought of a Cartesian demon alternative, or a brain-in-the-vat alternative, or does not saliently access such an alternative at the time of judgment, he will cheerfully attribute knowledge of p to Jones in favorable circumstances. But if one of these unexcluded possibilities is saliently accessed, the intuitive feeling that Jones does not know will be fairly strong. The plausibility of this approach obviously rests on the plausibility of the idea that what is mentally available or accessible can play a large role in determining an attributor's intuitions, or inclinations, to affirm or withhold knowledge attributions. This is where psychology enters the picture. Psychological research has established that the availability of various alternatives or considerations powerfully influences an evaluator's judgments.

Suppose you are asked the following question, as hundreds of thousands of survey respondents around the world have been asked (see Campbell 1981):

Taking all things together, how would you say things are these days? Would you say you are very happy, pretty happy, not too happy?

As Norbert Schwarz (1995) discusses, you presumably draw on some mental representation of how your life is going these days to answer this question. But do you really "take all things together"? If not, which of the myriad aspects of your life do you draw on? Chances are that you rely on the ones that come to mind most easily at this time. So your answer might be quite different at some other time if other aspects of your life come to mind. This is precisely what is found in a variety of studies.

In one of these studies, Strack, Martin, and Schwarz (1988) explored the influence of dating frequency on college students' general life satisfaction. Previous research had suggested that frequent dating might be an important contributor to general happiness. However, the apparent relevance of dating frequency depended on the order in which questions were asked, and hence on which facts were activated in the subject's mind. When respondents had to answer the general happiness question *before* they were asked a question about their dating frequency (a question that would bring dating to mind), both measures correlated only $r = -.12$. When the general happiness question was asked *after* the dating frequency question, the correlation increased to $r = .66$. Similarly, Strack, Schwarz, and Gschneidinger (1985) instructed some subjects to recall and write down a very negative event in their lives while other subjects were instructed to recall and write down a very positive event. Merely having these events in mind for purposes of comparison strongly influenced their judgment of the current quality of life. Ratings of well-being were higher for those who recalled a past negative event than for those who recalled a past positive event. Similarly, Schwarz and Strack (1991) found that subjects evaluated their own life more favorably when they met a handicapped person and listened to him describe his severe medical condition. The influence of the handicapped confederate was even more pronounced when he was visible to the respondent while the latter filled out the happiness report. Such findings emphasize the role of temporary accessibility in the choice of comparison standards.

How is this pertinent to the analysis of knowledge? If an epistemologist is trying to choose from among competing theories, some of which make heavy appeal to attributor context and some of which do not, these psychological findings are highly relevant. They give greater plausibility to theories assigning a large role to attributor context than those theories would have in the absence of such findings. It is much more plausible to hypothesize that intuitions about knowledge are heavily context driven if other sorts of judgments and evaluations are shown to be so driven.

We turn next to a different theme that bears on epistemic concepts, in this case both knowledge and justified belief. Traditional epistemology spoke of "sources" of knowledge, where the typical sources included perception, memory, reasoning, and introspection. The notion of a source or cause remains in contemporary theories that speak of belief-generating "processes." One question is whether the folk concepts of knowledge and justified belief crucially involve notions of causes or sources. Here it is good to have evidence that might confirm or disconfirm the idea that sources or origins comprise a general category that pervades commonsense thought. Evidence in favor of this notion is in fact found in cognitive science research. The linguists Clark and Carpenter (1989) provide a variety of evidence that supports the primitiveness of the source category. For example, two- and three-year-old children mark sources by using "from" in ways that adults would not. Damon, looking at pieces of a sandwich he had pushed off the edge of his plate, says: *These fall down from me.* Chris, talking about a character in a book, says: *He's really scared from Tommy.* The conceptual origin of the source notion may be that of spatial location, but this is projected onto a variety of nonspatial domains (e.g., Jackendoff 1983; Talmy 1983). Given the wide range of source concepts, it would not be surprising that epistemic concepts like knowledge and justification should also reflect a concern for credal sources. Specifically, a belief qualifies as justified or as knowledge only if it has an appropriate source or combination of sources.

Goldman (1992, chap. 9) advanced this sort of hypothesis earlier, using slightly different terminology. In that earlier terminology, also used by Ernest Sosa (1991), sources are divided into (intellectual) "virtues" and "vices." Virtuous sources are epistemically good ways of forming belief; vicious sources are epistemically bad ways. The proposal of that earlier paper, and of this one as well, is that wielders of predicates like "justified" and "know" represent them not in terms of a rule, criterion, or algorithm for distinguishing virtuous and vicious sources, but rather in terms of a mentally stored list of virtuous and vicious sources. This might strike the innocent philosopher's ear as slightly odd, since philosophers commonly expect concepts to be specified by something like a definition, in particular, a set of necessary and sufficient conditions. This traditional approach is certainly *not excluded* by mentalism. Inspiration for a different approach, however, may be drawn from psychology.

Research on the psychology of concepts has convinced most workers in the field that few common concepts are represented by means of a definition or a set of necessary and sufficient conditions. This so-called "classical" view has been much disparaged (see Smith and Medin 1981). A more listlike approach is found in the exemplar theory, which says that people represent ordinary concepts by means of a stored set of (representations of) previously encountered instances or tokens of the predicate in question (Medin and Schaffer 1978; Hintzman 1986; Estes 1994). For example, "bird" might be mentally represented by the total set or a subset of the birds that the person has previously encountered. When the question is raised whether a new object is or is not a bird, some subset of the stored bird exemplars is retrieved and compared to the target object for similarity. If the similarity reaches a given threshold, the object is classified as a bird. The foregoing is a fairly pure version of the exemplar theory. Other versions would allow more abstraction, involving, for example, representations of *types* of birds. In both cases, however, a similarity-determining operation is a critical facet of the classification procedure. The same holds in our hypothesis about how informants judge whether a target belief is justified or unjustified. The source of the target belief is compared for similarity to the informant's list of virtuous and vicious sources. If the source matches virtues only, the belief is categorized as justified. If the source matches vices, the belief is categorized as unjustified. For example, a perceptually caused belief will intuitively be found to be justified. A belief caused by wishful thinking will be classified as unjustified, at least if the informant has wishful thinking on his or her list of epistemic vices. Of course, actual or hypothetical beliefs might involve antecedently unfamiliar sources. When that occurs, it is the similarity of the posited source to previously stored virtues and vices that critically influences the informant's judgment. Using this approach, a number of troublesome cases in the literature have been handled adequately; that is, the theory predicts the sorts of intuitions that philosophers actually experience (see Goldman 1992, chap. 9).

Epistemologists familiar with the earlier paper might recall that the theory was billed as a new and improved version of reliabilism. But our present formulation of it has not even mentioned considerations of reliability. Where, if at all, does reliability enter the picture? On the present proposal, reliability would enter the picture at the *historical rationale* phase. In other words, we postulate that the linguistic community has identified certain epistemic sources as virtues and other epistemic sources as vices because the community judges the former to be generally reliable (i.e., conducive to truth) and the latter to be generally unreliable. Thus, reliability is the benchmark used for discriminating among approved and disapproved epistemic sources. This benchmark, however, is not represented or utilized by ordinary wielders of the concept of justification. They may only represent the types of sources themselves. Thus, we get a sort of two-stage reliabilism, in which reliability plays a role only in determining virtuous and vicious sources, not in directly deciding which beliefs are justified or unjustified. There is a close parallel here with what we might call descriptive rule utilitarianism. Such a descriptive theory would say that, historically, types of actions like honesty and dishonesty were denominated right and wrong respectively because of their utilitarian consequences. When ordinary agents imbibe moral culture, they need not learn the distinguishing criterion, but only the list of action types that are right or wrong. Newly contemplated courses of action are judged right or wrong by comparing them for similarity with the act-types antecedently stored as moral virtues or vices. Although we do not endorse descriptive rule utilitarianism, we find the two-stage hypothesis very congenial. This same two-stage sort of theory strikes us as attractive in the epistemic domain as well.

The mentalist approach to philosophical analysis is bound to encounter criticism, perhaps the same line of criticism that has been leveled against the epistemological theories outlined above. Certain critics claim, in effect, that the proposals are not genuine epistemological theories because they do not explain the nature of epistemic justification or knowledge. Ernest Sosa (1993) raises this issue when he claims that the "exemplar" approach to justification

> gives us an account of how an evaluator properly goes about evaluating a belief as justified. . . . But it does not tell us . . . what is involved in a belief's being epistemically justified—*not just what is involved in an evaluator's evaluating it as justified, n.b., but what would be involved in its actually being justified* (1993, 61, emphasis in original)

The objection suggested by this passage is developed at greater length by Peter Markie (1996). Markie claims that the mentalist account of our judgments of justification does not offer any explanation of what *makes* a belief justified or a process justification conferring. Instead, it offers us only a psychological hypothesis about how people make epistemic judgments, about how they come to classify beliefs into epistemological categories. For this reason, Markie claims that the mentalist version of the reliability theory of justification is perfectly consistent with positions usually thought opposed to reliabilism. This is, he alleges, because the current proposal is merely a psychological hypothesis about the mechanisms by which people categorize beliefs. It is not, as philosophical theories of justification are, an account of what makes a belief justified. The general position advocated by these critics seems to be that people's beliefs about justification or their concept thereof (in the mentalist's sense of "concept") are an entirely separate matter from the nature of justified belief, what really constitutes justified belief.[12] The claim of these critics, then, is that mentalist theories simply do not answer the *philosophical* question that they ought to answer. Such a theory ought to explain what justification *is*, not how people decide whether something merits the appellation "justified."

Our response is twofold. First, the charge seems, at least on one reading, incorrect. The mentalist does offer an account of what makes a belief justified. The mentalist claims that what makes a belief justified is possession of those properties by virtue of which a deployer of the justification concept, who is aware of all relevant properties of the target belief, would classify it as justified. An account of exactly what those properties are is the very thing that a developed mentalist proposal will provide. If, for example, the concept of justified belief really does consist in a list of belief-producing sources, then what *makes* a belief justified is the fact that it is produced by one or more of those sources (or sufficiently similar ones). In other words, to *be* justified simply *is* to be produced by some such processes.[13]

Second, the charge of philosophical irrelevance is clearly motivated by extramentalism of some kind, for example, the natural kinds approach. The charge rests on a distinction between the real nature of justified belief and our psychological concept of justified belief. Because extra-mentalism claims that the object of philosophical inquiry is a nonpsychological object, it may appeal to such a distinction. Undoubtedly there is a distinction between the psychological concept of water and the real nature of water. Thus, an account of our concept of water would not necessarily be a correct account of the independent entity. But we have argued that the natural kinds approach is an inappropriate account of many of the targets of philosophical analysis. So, while we are aware that some may be dissatisfied with the modesty of the aims of mentalist methodology,[14] it seems to us to be a coherent project with a clear story to tell about how intuitions serve as evidence for the kinds of theories it proposes.[15] Unlike the extra-mentalist approaches we have surveyed, mentalism makes good sense of the standard methodology of philosophical analysis.

Notes

Pust's contribution to this chapter is drawn from his work-in-progress on a doctoral dissertation, "Intuitions as Evidence," at the University of Arizona, subsequently published as Pust (2000). For helpful discussion of earlier drafts, we thank Michael Bergmann, Chris Daly, John Armstrong, and discussants at the Notre Dame conference on intuitions and a University of Arizona colloquium.

1. A clear contemporary proponent of this view is George Bealer. See especially Bealer (1996a).

2. We formulate (RI) as a necessary condition rather than a necessary-and-sufficient condition because, among other things, mere de facto reliability may be insufficient to qualify a class of states as a basic evidential source (cf. Bealer 1996a). We do not wish to try to settle this issue here. Stating (RI) as a necessary condition leaves the question of sufficiency open.

3. In Goldman (1977) perceptual modalities are characterized partly in terms of counterfactual dependences.

4. General principles may also be included among the propositional contents of intuitions, for example, the principle that knowledge is closed under known entailment. We concentrate on singular propositional contents, however, because they are most intensively used in philosophical practice.

5. Our approach obviously takes *intuitings* that p to be (prima facie) evidence, or data, in philosophical methodology. How, then, do we respond to a philosopher like Lycan (1988) who insists that the *intuiteds* (that is, the propositions intuited) not the intuitings, are the philosophical "data"? We find Lycan's approach unconvincing because the intuited propositions per se have no evidential weight. Why should those propositions, rather than the many contrary propositions that are not intuited, have special evidential weight? Clearly, what gives a proposition evidential force is *being intuited*. Evidential force arises from the fact that an intuiting is a sort of mental state that reliably indicates (in favorable circumstances) its content's truth. Thus, it must be the intuiting of p that is the crucial datum, not the intuited proposition p per se.

6. The second predicate must also be "better understood" in some sense. This poses issues about the paradox of analysis that we shall not address here.

7. More generally, the target of philosophical analysis may be a (tacit) folk *scheme* or folk *theory*, not just a folk *concept*; the psychological unit, in other words, may be larger than that of a concept. Our discussion will proceed, however, in terms of concepts.

8. We do not believe that all concepts are so closely tied to language, but those of interest to philosophical analysis are so tied.

9. Our approach also seems to comport with Peacocke (1992).

10. This is not meant to imply that intuition is a basic evidential source for propositions about mathematics, logic, or the like. We remain noncommittal on these domains, especially since their contents may not lend themselves to a mentalist interpretation. Our thesis only concerns the prospects of intuition vis-à-vis singular classificational propositions of the kind illustrated.

11. We shall not speculate about which predicates are likely to have interpersonally shared contents.

12. This objection seems to be a direct descendant of earlier philosophical criticisms of psychological accounts of concepts. Georges Rey (1983, 1985), for example, has charged that many psychological accounts of concepts tend to confuse metaphysical issues with epistemological or psychological ones. Rey notes that the term "categorization" can refer to how things in the world are correctly classified or to how people engage in the process of classification—correctly or incorrectly. An account of the former is the task of the nonpsychological sciences and an account of the latter is the task of psychology. Since the proper account of concepts in the metaphysical sense is provided by the portion of science that deals with the kind in

question, commonsense beliefs or intuitions about X are irrelevant to the nature of X. This distinction and the accompanying division of labor seems to be behind Sosa's and Markie's criticism. It should be noted that this proposed distinction is quite acceptable to most psychologists, even if they profess interest only in the nonmetaphysical issues. Edward Smith (1989), for example, endorses the distinction in language matching Markie's objection when he claims that "a metaphysical categorization considers what *makes* an entity an instance of a particular kind, whereas an epistemological categorization considers *how an agent decides* whether the entity is of a particular kind" (Smith 1989, 57, emphasis added).

13. Where the analyzed concept is revealed to be highly contextualist, however, this straightforward answer to the critic will not be available. But where a concept is highly contextualist, no straightforward answer can reasonably be expected.

14. One of us, Pust, counts himself as not yet fully satisfied.

15. Other critics have conceded the coherence of the mentalist project but found it to be of very little interest. Stephen Stich (1990), for example, asks why anyone genuinely concerned about how they ought to form beliefs should care about the folk concept of justified belief. Our distinction between a concept's content and its rationale may provide some answer to Stich's query. (For another set of answers, see Markie 1997.) Although there is no guarantee that we will reflectively value forming beliefs in the ways deemed justified by the folk, there seems little doubt, pace Stich, that the historical rationale behind the folk concept, namely, true belief formation, retains its power to move us. Even if our current list of sources is an imperfect realization of the historical rationale, there is always room to revise and improve that list in accordance with the historical desideratum, which continues to attract us.

5

Science, Publicity,
and Consciousness

A traditional view is that scientific evidence can be produced only by intersubjective methods that can be used by different investigators and will produce agreement. This intersubjectivity, or publicity, constraint ostensibly excludes introspection. But contemporary cognitive scientists regularly rely on their subjects' introspective reports in many areas, especially in the study of consciousness. So there is a tension between actual scientific practice and the publicity requirement. Which should give way? This chapter argues against the publicity requirement and against a fallback version of it, viz. that evidence-conferring methods must at least have their reliability publicly validated.

1. Publicity in Science

An old but enduring idea is that science is a fundamentally "public" or "intersubjective" enterprise. According to this thesis, the core of scientific methodology is interpersonal rather than private. The publicity thesis was prominent in the positivist era, and although it is less frequently discussed today, I suspect it would still receive a vote of approval, or a nod of assent, from most philosophers of science. The thesis is in tension, however, with certain methodological practices of contemporary cognitive science. If the publicity thesis is correct, those practices are illegitimate, and if they are legitimate, the publicity thesis must be abandoned. After explaining the tension, I shall argue that the publicity thesis should give way.

Even at the advent of modern science, publicity received a prominent role. Boyle insisted that the witnessing of experiments was to be a collective act (Shapin and Schaffer 1985, 56). Intersubjectivity was also assigned a crucial role in the positivist era. Popper held that "the *objectivity* of scientific statements lies in the fact that they can be *inter-subjectively tested*" (1959, 44). Epistemically "basic" statements in science, said Popper, are statements "about whose acceptance or rejection the various investigators are likely to reach agreement" (1959, 104). Hempel followed Popper in requiring that "all statements of empirical science be capable of test by reference to evidence which is public, i.e., which can be secured by different observers and does not depend essentially on the observer" (1952, 22). A more expansive statement of this idea can be found in Feigl (1953):

> The quest for scientific knowledge is . . . regulated by certain standards or criteria. . . . The most important of these regulative ideas are:
> *1. Intersubjective Testability.* This is only a more adequate formulation of what is generally meant by the "objectivity" of science. What is here involved is . . . the requirement that the knowledge claims of science be in principle capable of test . . . on the part of any person properly equipped with intelligence and the technical devices of observation or experimentation. The term *intersubjective* stresses the social nature of the scientific enterprise. If there be any "truths" that are accessible only to privileged individuals, such as mystics or visionaries—that is, knowledge-claims which by their very nature cannot independently be checked by anyone else—then such "truths" are not of the kind that we seek in the sciences. The criterion of intersubjective testability thus delimits the scientific from the nonscientific activities of man. (11)

In recent discussions of scientific objectivity, publicity continues to be one standardly cited strand. For example, Railton characterizes scientific objectivity as involving the thesis that "objective inquiry uses procedures that are intersubjective and independent of particular individuals or circumstances— for example, . . . it makes no essential use of introspective or subjectively privileged evidence in theory assessment" (1985, 815).

Let us look more closely at the publicity thesis. The passages from Popper and Hempel suggest that what is essentially public in science is its basic statements or items of evidence, and what makes these items of evidence public is that they "can be intersubjectively tested" (Popper) or "can be secured by different observers" (Hempel). It is unclear whether Popper and Hempel are referring to statements that *could* qualify as scientific evidence, or statements that *do* qualify as scientific evidence. In the first instance, however, we need an account of when a statement *does* qualify as scientific evidence, i.e., when scientists are warranted in accepting a statement as evidence. The publicity constraint à la Popper and Hempel might then be formulated as follows:

> Statement S qualifies as a piece of scientific evidence only if S is a statement on which scientific observers *could* reach agreement.

I formulate the account in modal terms because both Popper and Hempel use "can" in their formulations. They presumably do not want a statement to be scientifically acceptable as evidence only when more than one scientist has actually observed the state of affairs it describes. It is necessary (to satisfy the intersubjectivity contraint) only that this state of affairs *could* be observed by many scientists, and if they did observe it, they would agree in accepting S.

However, Popper and Hempel presumably do mean to require that at least one person *actually* observes the state of affairs and forms an observation-based belief in S. Unless this requirement is included, the following scenario would establish a statement as a piece of scientific evidence: (1) nobody actually observes S, but (2) if people were to observe the relevant state of affairs, they would form beliefs in S. But surely the mere possibility of observation-based agreement does not confer on S the status of a scientific datum. There must actually be an observational act and a resulting belief in S. The use of observation, moreover, is critical; not just any old method or process of belief-formation will do. If a person forms a belief in S via religious ecstasy, this would not certify S as a scientific datum, even if hypothetical observations would also lead to beliefs in S.

Two important points emerge from these trivial clarifications. First, establishing something as a piece of scientific evidence depends on what *methods* or *procedures* are actually used. Second, observation—and perhaps only observation—is an approved method or procedure for establishing a statement as a piece of scientific evidence. This poses two questions germane to our inquiry. First, what exactly is observation? Does it, for example, include introspection as a species of "inner observation?" Or should introspection be excluded (as the Railton passage suggests)? Second, what are the grounds for treating observation as a privileged class of belief-forming methods, ones that confer scientific evidencehood on a statement? Why do observational methods, and perhaps only observational methods, have this distinctive capacity?

One possible answer to the second question, which invokes the publicity thesis in a slightly new guise, is that observation is a set of methods each of which is capable of producing *agreement* among its users. (This is a new guise because it concerns methods rather than statements.) There are, of course, challenges to the claim that observational methods do generate agreement, challenges from the alleged theory-ladenness of observation. I shall not address this challenge here. The very significance of the challenge, however, may derive from the assumption that the *ostensible* distinguishing characteristic of observation is its agreement-generating ability. When this ability is questioned, its contribution to epistemic warrant is also questioned. Setting the theory-ladenness issue aside, other indications may be found that the question of agreement-production is viewed as crucial. In assessing the inadequacy of Wundt's introspective method, for example, the psychologists Miller and Buckhout write: "His experiments, unlike experiments elsewhere in science, do not ensure agreement among all those who witness them. Introspective observation is essentially private, and disagreements cannot be settled by repeated observations" (1973, 31). Miller and Buckhout apparently subscribe to the thesis that a method incapable of securing agreement among multiple investigators is inappropriate for science. This version of the publicity thesis seems to lie behind their acceptance of perceptual observation and their rejection of Wundtian introspection as candidate methods of evidence-gathering in science. So publicity can be invoked not only to explain why perceptual observation is an evidence-conferring method but also to resolve the first question by excluding introspection from the class of admissible methods.

2. Introspection and Consciousness in Cognitive Science

Although introspection was officially excommunicated from psychology in the behaviorist era, appeals to something akin to introspection are quite widespread in contemporary cognitive science. Newell and Simon's (1972) influential study of problem solving made extensive use of "protocol data," i.e., reports by subjects of what they were thinking during problem-solving tasks. This and similar kinds of research led Estes to write:

> Only in the very last few years have we seen a major release from inhibition and the appearance in the experimental literature on a large scale of studies reporting the introspections of subjects undergoing memory searches, manipulations of images, and the like. (1975, 5)

On reflection, another core domain of psychology, perception research, also tacitly appeals to a subject's introspective knowledge, i.e., knowledge of how a stimulus *appears* to her. If a subject reports that a certain portion of the current stimulus appears as "figure" and another portion as "ground," the researcher typically accepts this report as correct, i.e., as indicating how those respective portions of the stimulus (or the field) *do* appear to the subject. I call this reliance on the subject's introspection.[1]

Another area of research that heavily depends on introspective report is research on "feelings of knowing," or metacognition (Metcalfe and Shimamura 1994; Nelson 1992). Metacognition examines people's ability to predict whether or not they can answer a certain question correctly, i.e., whether they have the answer stored in long-term memory and can retrieve it. One often has a feeling of knowing something although the target item has yet to be retrieved. Psychologists wish to determine how often this feeling is accurate and how the system works that gives rise to such feelings. All such research presupposes that subjects' introspective reports are accurate as to whether or not they currently have a "feeling of knowing." Investigators normally trust a subject's report that she has such a feeling, whether or not the feeling is an accurate predictor of her subsequently finding the sought-after answer.

Psychologists who rely on introspective reports are not committed to the view that *all* such reports are equally reliable or accurate. Ericsson and Simon (1984/1993) devote a lengthy analysis to the question of when, or under what conditions, verbal reports are reliable. (Not everything they call "verbal reports" necessarily qualify as "introspective" reports, however; they themselves avoid the latter phrase.) They distinguish reports issuing from different parts of the subject's cognitive system: sensory stores of very short duration, short-term memory of intermediate duration, and long-term memory. Reports derived from some of these sources are regarded as more accurate than those derived from other sources. Reliability also depends on whether the requisite information was attended to, or heeded. General disavowal of such reports, though, they view as misguided. They criticize Nisbett and Wilson's (1977) apparently broad-gauged critique of introspective reliability. They show that the Nisbett-Wilson critique relies heavily on studies where there was a large time lag between task and probe, so it was unlikely that the relevant information remained in short-term memory at the time of probe. It is hardly surprising that these reports were inaccurate, but that does not undercut *all* such reports. Similarly, some of the studies reviewed by Nisbett and Wilson involved why-questions regarding causes. Correct answers to these questions could only be given if one had access to comparative information with other subjects—the sort of information the investigators themselves obtained through between-subject designs. But subjects could not be expected ever to have had this causal-comparative information in their heads. Hence, their failure to answer such questions correctly hardly betrays a total lack of introspective power.

Now consider the use of introspective reports in the study of consciousness. I focus on the use of such reports to determine whether or not a subject has a conscious state of a specified general type. Three widely discussed domains of consciousness research are blindsight, implicit memory, and prosopagnosia. In all three domains, subjects with neurological deficits are said to lack conscious informational states of a normal sort, but they are also found to possess related information in nonconscious form.[2] Blindsight subjects lack conscious visual experience in a portion of their field of view (their scotoma), but nonetheless show signs of having visually obtained information about objects in the unseen area. Implicit memory is a type of memory that contrasts with explicit memory. Explicit memory involves conscious recollection; implicit memory does not (Schacter 1989). For example, amnesic patients are unable consciously to recall events that they recently experienced, but they show signs of unconsciously remembering these events insofar as their performance at certain tasks benefits from the experience. Profoundly amnesic patients can show normal or near-normal learning of various perceptual and motor skills without any conscious memory for the experiences of learning (Milner et al. 1968; Moscovitch 1982). In prosopagnosia, subjects lack conscious feelings of facial recognition, or familiarity, when seeing even close friends or relatives, but many of these patients demonstrate unconscious recognition in the form of autonomic responses to familiar faces. Bauer (1984) showed a prosopagnosic patient photographs of familiar faces which were presented for 90 seconds, accompanied by five different names, one of which was the correct name. Maximal skin conductance responses to the correct name were found for some 61 percent of trials, a figure well above the chance level of 20 percent. Comparable findings of larger and more frequent skin conductance responses were reported by Tranel and Damasio (1985, 1988).

How do cognitive scientists determine in all these cases that consciousness is present or absent in their subjects' states? The answer is fairly straightforward. Subject to some qualification, consciousness researchers rely on their subjects' introspective reports. To test for a scotoma, as in the case of Weiskrantz's (1986) patient DB, the patient is asked to report what is seen when stimuli are presented to different points in the visual field. DB did not report seeing stimuli falling anywhere in the region to the lower left of the point he was fixating, and for some time he also did not report seeing stimuli in most of the area to the upper left of fixation (for summary, see Young and de Haan 1993). Hence it was concluded that DB lacked conscious vision in those areas. But asked to guess about certain stimuli in those areas, DB's performance revealed some kind of information-bearing state. Since he denied having (visual) information of this sort, however, this state was declared to be nonconscious. Thus, the ability or inability to report a state is taken as a criterion of its being conscious or nonconscious.

A more complete elucidation of the report criterion is provided by Marcel:

> There is really only one criterion for phenomenal experience. This is a person's report, direct or indirect, that they have a sensation of one or another kind, that they are or were conscious in one or another way . . . Direct reports include statements such as 'I have a headache, or an itch', or 'I feel hungry'. Indirect reports include statements such as 'I see a light' or 'I hear a car', where the person is not directly reporting the sensation, but means by the statement that they *consciously* see or hear something. . . . [P]rovided that the person is not lying, there is little reason to doubt the validity of a report *that* there is phenomenal experience. (1988, 131)

As Marcel proceeds to explain, the reports in question need not be *verbal* reports. In many experiments, subjects perform actions such as button-pushing as a way of performing some conventionally arranged speech act, such as asserting that two figures appear equiluminant.[3]

Although I have stressed reports as the criterion in use, it seems quite clear from Marcel's reference to the unlikelihood of lying that there is really a deeper criterion being assumed, viz., the subject's *belief* that a certain conscious state is present or absent. If researchers suspect that a subject's report is insincere, they will not treat the report as evidence for the presence or absence of consciousness. So the underlying criterion is really the subject's (occurrent) belief, not her verbal report.

A subject's report (or belief) about her conscious states is not a perfectly reliable indicator. As Marcel points out (1988, 132), failure to believe that one recently had a certain sensation does not firmly refute the occurrence of such an event. One may forget a conscious state that occurred only a second ago, and very brief episodes of phenomenology may go altogether undetected. But this merely shows that introspection is not infallible, or that it is only reliable within a certain restricted range or scope.

If consciousness researchers systematically rely on introspective reports, how can we explain their approach to the syndrome of anosognosia? Patients who suffer from anosognosia are said to be unaware of their impairments. In Anton's syndrome, blind patients deny their own blindness (Anton 1899; McGlynn and Schacter 1989). If a patient denies that she is blind, she is apparently asserting that she does have conscious vision; so a researcher who claims that the patient is really blind refuses to accept her introspective report. Isn't this incompatible with the report criterion as presented here?

The best explanation of what transpires here is that researchers do not regard the patient's report as the expression of a belief formed by introspection. Introspection is presumably a method that is applied "directly" to one's own mental condition and issues in beliefs about that condition.[4] It presumably contrasts with other ways of forming beliefs about one's mental condition, such as inference from one's own behavior or confabulation. Researchers probably assume that anosognosics' reports stem from confabulation rather than genuine introspection. Perhaps the syndrome even includes selective impairment of the ability to introspect, or perhaps just a refusal to do so. Nothing in my account is committed to the view that introspection is always available or is always applied to one's experiential state. Thus, the way researchers interpret anosognosia does not constitute a problem for the thesis that they standardly rely on subjects' introspections.

Some philosophers of consciousness recommend systematic skepticism about subjects' introspective reports of conscious states. This is the message of Dennett's "heterophenomenological method" for the study of consciousness (1991, 66–98). Heterophenomenology advises the scientist to be neutral vis-à-vis all of a subject's consciousness reports, just as an anthropologist studying a tribe's religion would remain agnostic about the truth of their religious beliefs. Whether this type of advice is well motivated remains to be seen. For the moment, the only claim being made is that most cognitive scientists of consciousness do not practice such skepticism or agnosticism. In fact they rely substantially on subjects' introspective beliefs about their conscious experience (or lack thereof), just as cognitive scientists studying problem solving, perception, and metacognition rely substantially on their subjects' introspective reports.

A critic might argue that in using an introspective report, a cognitive scientist merely relies on her own perceptual powers to detect a public event, viz., the subject's act of reporting. My point, however, is that the scientist does not merely accept the fact that an act of reporting occurs; she also accepts the fact reported, e.g., that the subject experienced a certain figure/ground organization, or a certain feeling of knowing. In accepting the latter type of fact, the scientist relies on the subject's introspective process, which discloses a private, subjective event (see Alston 1973).

Can it be maintained, however, that the introspected event is itself treated as a piece of evidence, or datum, for cognitive science? Is introspection treated as an evidence-conferring method? Yes, I think it is. Consider an analogy from astronomy. Suppose a solitary observer reports seeing a bright flash in the sky. To the extent that astronomers trust the report as sincere and the observation as competent, they may accept that there was such a flash as a datum for astronomy to explain. Similarly, suppose a subject reports experiencing a certain figure/ground organization. To the extent that cognitive scientists trust the subject's quasi-observation to disclose a certain mental fact, they treat this fact as a datum for cognitive science to explain, or as evidence that can be used to confirm or disconfirm hypotheses. Since this is just the sort of thing cognitive scientists frequently do, they appear to rely on introspection as an evidence-conferring method. If reliance on introspection violates a cardinal precept of scientific methodology—i.e., the publicity precept—then there is a tension between this precept and the actual practice of working cognitive scientists. Which ought to give way?

3. Publicity and Agreement

To assist our reflection on this question, let us formulate and examine the traditional publicity requirement more carefully. How exactly is the publicity requirement for methods to be understood? We saw earlier that it has something to do with agreement generation. So we might try the following formulation:

Definition I: Method M is a public (intersubjective) evidence-producing method if and only if all investigators who apply M to the same questions always (or usually) arrive at the same answers (form the same beliefs).

How would this definition work in the case of introspection? Since I cannot introspect your conscious states and you cannot introspect mine, I do not apply introspection to any questions about your states of consciousness and you do not apply introspection to any questions about mine. Introspection is always applied by just one person per question, and never leads two investigators to arrive at different answers to the same question. Hence, introspection vacuously satisfies Definition I, thereby qualifying as a public method. Clearly, this is contrary to virtually everyone's intention.

To remedy this problem, a different definition of method publicity is required, which might run as follows:

Definition II: Method M is a public (intersubjective) evidence-producing method if and only if:
(A) two or more investigators can severally apply M to the same questions, and
(B) if different investigators were to apply M to the same questions, M would always (or usually) generate the same answers (induce the same beliefs) in those investigators.

Introspection clearly fails to meet condition (A), yielding the desired result that it fails to qualify as a public method.

Notice that there remains some ambiguity in Definition II. Specifically, should condition (A) be taken to require that there *actually* exist two or more investigators who can apply M to the same questions? Or does it only mean to require that two or more such investigators *might* exist? These two alternative interpretations should be borne in mind as we proceed.

Given Definition II, our provisional definition of method publicity, let us next ask exactly what role publicity is supposed to play in the requirements for scientific evidence production. Defenders of publicity presumably intend it to constitute at least a necessary condition of scientific evidence production. But perhaps they intend it to serve as a sufficient as well as a necessary condition. Let us begin with this latter, stronger proposal.

(PUB) A statement is an item of scientific evidence if and only if some investigator arrives at a belief in this statement by means of a public method.

This and subsequent proposals should be understood as dealing with *prima facie* scientific evidence. If one investigator uses a legitimate evidential method to arrive at a belief in S, and another investigator later uses the same or another legitimate evidential method to arrive at a belief in not-S, the latter episode tends to defeat or undercut the evidential status of S achieved by the former. But this in no way conflicts with the fact that the first episode conferred *prima facie* evidential status on S.

Is (PUB) an acceptable principle of scientific evidence conferral? Specifically, is (PUB) a sufficient condition for scientific evidence production, given Definition II of method publicity? A moment's reflection reveals that it is far too weak, simply because a tendency toward agreement production is hardly a sufficient condition for evidence production. Suppose that a certain hallucinogenic drug produces vivid belief in any statement S if one takes the drug while asking oneself the question, "Is S true?" Then taking this drug qualifies as a public method according to Definition II. First, more than one person can apply this method to the same question, because method "application" here involves simply taking the drug while querying the statement. Second, if multiple individuals did apply it to the same questions, they would get the same answers (beliefs).

This case shows that the ability to produce agreement is vastly too weak a property of a method to endow it with evidence-conferring power. Its failure suggests that some other type of ingredient must be added (or substituted) for a method to achieve evidence-conferring power. What might this other type of ingredient be? Here we might return to the desideratum of *objectivity*. Commentators on the concept of objectivity often point out that there are at least two senses in which science seeks to be objective, the two senses being *intersubjectivity* and *reliability* (tendency toward truth production). For example, Boyd writes:

> When we think of scientific objectivity, two importantly different features of scientific practice seem to be at issue: *intersubjectivity* (the capacity of scientists to reach a stable consensus about the issues they investigate . . .) and *epistemic reliability* (the capacity of scientists to get it (approximately) right about the things they study). (1985, 48)

So the hitherto missing ingredient might be reliability. This would explain why taking the hallucinogenic drug would not be regarded as an objective, evidence-conferring method. It is obviously not a reliable method, a method that will generally produce true beliefs. Moreover, it would explain why perceptual observation is evidence-conferring, since perceptual observation, at least under favorable conditions, is generally reliable; or at least it is widely thought to be reliable. By adding reliability to intersubjectivity, perhaps we might obtain a set of necessary and sufficient conditions for evidence production. Thus, the following principle may be proposed:

(PUBREL) A statement is an item of scientific evidence if and only if some investigator arrives at a belief in this statement by means of a method that is both public and reliable.

Here the publicity of a method is only a necessary condition for evidence production, not a sufficient condition.

Is publicity appropriate even as a *necessary* condition of evidence production? This is not obvious. To explore the matter, recall that two different interpretations of Definition II were proposed. Under the first interpretation, a method is public (in a certain possible world) only if there exist (in that world) two or more investigators who can severally apply the method to one or more common questions. Is this an appropriate requirement for evidence production? Consider a possible world containing a collection of spatiotemporally isolated inquirers, each in a different spacetime corner of the universe. Each inquirer is outside the spacetime "cone" of every other inquirer. Suppose that each inquirer uses a certain observational method in her scientific repertoire, but this method can only be applied to *local* questions, i.e., questions about the inquirer's own environment. No isolate can apply it to questions about another isolate's environment. According to the current interpretation, this method does not pass scientific muster as a public method. But that seems extremely dubious. Intuitively, such a method seems capable of producing evidential warrant for the beliefs that each inquirer forms about her environment, and it seems possible for each inquirer to proceed *scientifically* on the basis of such evidence. The same holds for a possible world containing just a single person. Can't such a person still conduct her intellectual affairs with scientific warrant?

The second interpretation of Definition II anticipates these problems. It only requires that it be *possible* for multiple inquirers to exist who can apply the same method to the same questions (and if they did, they would get the same answers). In other words, multiple inquirers need not exist in the world of the example, but only in some possible world accessible to it. Notice, however, that this second interpretation threatens to classify as public the paradigmatically private method of introspection. Consider two brain-linked Siamese twins who share a cerebral hemisphere. This looks like a case in which both persons introspect the same (token) conscious states, thereby applying the introspective method to the same question. Now in all real-world cases of introspection where there are no brain-linked Siamese twins, it is nonetheless possible that each individual should have such a twin. Thus, the method of introspection would satisfy the currently considered condition for publicity. Surely this is not what traditional proponents of a publicity constraint intended.

A second doubt about this interpretation concerns its underlying rationale. Proponents of a publicity constraint apparently feel that beliefs formed by public methods have superior epistemic credentials to beliefs formed by nonpublic methods. But why would conformity with the current interpretation ensure higher epistemic status? If no other creature in the world of the example applies the same method to the same question (and gets the same answer), why would the mere possibility that other creatures in an accessible world might apply the same method to the same question confer higher epistemic credentials on a belief? I detect no intuitive plausibility in this idea.

Neither of the two interpretations we have considered, then, yields satisfactory results. Conceivably, there is some other interpretation of publicity-qua-agreement-production that has yet to be considered. But it is more probable, in my opinion, that the publicity constraint itself is the problem. Why must publicity be a necessary condition for evidence production? Since reliability seems so critical to scientific goals, one might account for publicity's allure by reference to reliability. Perhaps the underlying motivation behind the publicity thesis is that intersubjective agreement is a good *indicator* or *sign* of reliability, and that is why it is desirable. In other words, intersubjective agreement is not a separate and independent constraint on scientific methodology, but at most a derivative and instrumental constraint, rationalized by the central desideratum of reliability or truth.

I find this reconstruction entirely plausible, but it leaves the status of the publicity thesis quite precarious. When a method *can* be applied by multiple investigators, its propensity to yield agreement is useful information from the vantage point of truth determination. Although consensus production does not entail reliability (as the hallucinogenic drug example illustrates), it may often be a reasonably trustworthy guide or clue to reliability. However, when there is a method that *cannot* be applied by different investigators to the same questions, the method may still be quite reliable, as reliable (within appropriate scope restrictions) as other approved methods. If reliability is the fundamental desideratum, the intersubjectivity constraint should simply be waived for this kind of method. Why insist on intersubjectivity if the chief goal is reliability or truth? Notice that a reliability constraint alone suffices to disqualify many belief-forming methods that are unsatisfactory from the perspective of scientific evidence-conferral. The methods of guesswork or speculative "insight," for example, can be rejected as evidence-conferring methods because they are plainly unreliable; there is no need to invoke their "privacy" to rationalize their illegitimacy.

4. Publicity as Validation
by Intersubjective Methods

At this juncture a slightly different role for publicity should be considered. Even if it is granted that the nonpublicity of a method should not by itself disqualify it from evidence-conferring power, one might resist the suggestion that reliability alone is sufficient to confer such power. To qualify for scientific acceptability, doesn't a method's reliability have to be certified, established, or validated by wholly public methods? Support for this contention comes from simple analogy with the scientific approach to instrumentation. The readings of a scientific instrument would never be trusted as a source of evidence unless the instrument's reliability were established by standard, i.e., public, procedures. Isn't it similarly necessary that introspection's reliability be established for it to be trusted, and mustn't this reliability also be established by public means? So even if methods can qualify as evidence-conferring without themselves being public, don't they need to have their reliability validated by public procedures? Call this fallback position for the publicity thesis the *public validation constraint.*

There are two possible versions of the public validation (PV) constraint: a *possible*-validation version and an *actual*-validation version. The first would say that a method is evidence-conferring only if it is possible to publicly validate its reliability. The second would say that a method is evidence-conferring only if its reliability has actually been publicly validated. More precisely, it would say that it is appropriate to accept a method as evidence-conferring at time t only if its reliability has been publicly validated as of t. It seems to me that *if* a PV constraint is well-motivated, the second, more stringent, version is the appropriate one. This would preserve the parallel with the treatment of scientific instruments. Clearly, nobody would defend reliance on a scientific instrument at a given time merely on the grounds that it was possible to validate its reliability. Only when its reliability has actually been established is it appropriate for science to rely on it. However, there are several reasons why it is also worth discussing the possibility version. First, one might try to prove the absence of actual public validation (at the present time) by establishing its impossibility. Second, one might want to know whether it may be possible to publicly validate a method's reliability in the future even if it is not publicly validated now.

The fallback position, then, invites us to address two issues in connection with introspection. First, has the reliability of introspection (assuming it is reliable) actually been validated by public procedures (or could it be in the future)? Second, would violation of the public validation constraint really be good grounds for disqualifying introspection as a scientific evidence-conferring method?

Beginning with the first question, let us first ask how cognitive science could go about publicly validating introspection's reliability. Ostensibly, one would have to compare the (presumptively sincere) introspective reports of a subject with the "actual fact" of what is reported, which itself must be determined by procedures that do not involve introspection. Since a cognitive scientist cannot directly observe the mental state of the subject, the actual condition of this mental state must be determined by observation of behavior (or stimuli) plus some sort of theoretical, nomological inference. The basic difficulty is that cognitive scientists lack adequate nomological generalizations that would allow them to draw firm inferences about the sorts of states described in introspective reports, in particular, states of consciousness. Whether or not they could arrive at such generalizations in the future, they seem to lack such generalizations now. This apparently implies that cognitive scientists have not yet validated introspection's reliability by public methods; hence, introspection currently violates the actual-validation version of the PV constraint.

To illustrate the problem, suppose a subject reports having a "feeling of knowing" the answer to a certain question (without yet having retrieved the answer). How is the psychologist supposed to determine whether that feeling really does exist in the subject at the time reported? Psychologists who study metacognition have no nomological principles by which to infer whether such a feeling of knowing does or does not occur at a given time independent of the subject's report. Furthermore, if such principles could be formulated in the future, their verification would presumably require reliance on subjects' introspective reports. This follows from the fact that the report criterion is the fundamental psychological method of determining what a subject's conscious states are.

To take another example, suppose an amnesic patient is set to work on a Tower of Hanoi problem and reports having no conscious recollection of previously having worked on these types of tasks. How is the psychologist supposed to determine whether this introspective report is correct? The psychologist may know that this patient has in fact worked on such problems before and that her current performance shows improvement, suggesting that it has been facilitated by some kind of retention of earlier activities. But this hardly shows that the subject has a *conscious* recollection of the earlier activity; nor that she does not. There seems to be no way to verify independently the subject's report of no conscious recollection. Cognitive scientists might eventually identify neural correlates of consciousness, and these correlates might then be used to determine the current conscious states of a subject. But the initial process of identifying such neural correlates would itself have to rely on introspective reports, so this would be no help to the project of *independent* validation of introspection.

Functionalists, of course, might challenge the claim that reliance on introspective reports is an essential method for determining the presence of absence of conscious states. They contend that consciousness is a functional concept, so there must be some inferential procedure for determining the presence or absence of conscious states via functional laws, without appealing to introspection's reliability.[5] This sort of approach might work for *some* concepts of consciousness, such as Block's (1995) concept of "access consciousness." But it is highly questionable whether all concepts of consciousness, especially the concept of "phenomenal" consciousness, can be given a functionalist reduction. So the problem before us at least encompasses the

domain of phenomenally conscious states. How could introspection's reliability vis-à-vis *these* states be publicly validated?

Pressing further, what kind of functionalist reduction is to be hoped for,
one in terms of commonsense laws or one in terms of scientific laws? The
former is unpromising, because commonsense laws—larded, as they are, with
ceteris paribus clauses—are not precise enough for present purposes. What
about scientific laws? Even if this form of functionalism ("psychofunction-
alism") holds some promise for the future, it is difficult to maintain that any
psychofunctionalist reduction of consciousness has been executed at present.
From the perspective of current information-processing psychology, it is quite
opaque exactly where consciousness fits into the causal picture. As Velmans
(1991) stresses, it is unclear from a psychological standpoint exactly what
tasks or operations require consciousness for their execution. Thus, cognitive
theory alone, without the aid of introspective reports, is in no position to say
exactly when conscious states are or are not present. So cognitive science
currently lacks the wherewithal to validate introspection's reliability independently. Nor is it clear how the situation might improve in the future, since
future understanding of the causal role of consciousness will have to rest
partly on introspection. Thus, when cognitive scientists do rely on introspection, either their reliance is objectionable, in virtue of the PV constraint, or
the PV constraint (especially in its actuality version) is inappropriate.

Chalmers (1996, chap. 6) sketches a scenario under which a set of psychophysical laws involving consciousness may be established. Significantly,
however, his scenario depends on *nonempirical* bridge principles, or "plausibility constraints," including specifically the reliability of introspection.

> The most obvious [of the plausibility constraints] is the principle we rely on
> whenever we take someone's verbal report as an indicator of their conscious
> experience: that people's reports concerning their experiences by and large ac-
> curately reflect the contents of their experiences. *This is not a principle that we
> can prove to be true*, but it is antecedently much more plausible than the alter-
> native. (216–217, emphasis added)

Chalmers' scenario, then, does not help introspection meet the PV constraint,
since the scenario despairs at the outset of any purely observational certifi-
cation of introspective reliability.

Suppose, then, that no independent, public validation of introspection's
reliability has actually been offered, and perhaps none is even possible. Where
does that leave us? Should introspection be abandoned because it violates the
PV constraint? Or should that constraint itself be rejected? I shall argue that
violation of the PV constraint is not such a shocking epistemological situation
for a *basic* or *fundamental* cognitive process like introspection. If introspection is in this epistemic condition, that does not mark it off from other duly
approved basic methods. For a large class of fundamental cognitive processes,

it is impossible to certify their reliability in an independent, i.e., noncircular, fashion. This thesis is defended in detail by Alston (1993b).

Start with memory. Can one establish the reliability of memory without appealing to premises that themselves rely on memory? As Alston argues (1993b:116–117), this is impossible. It might seem as if we can, because there are ways to determine whether Smith's remembered proposition p was indeed the case without oneself remembering p to have happened. To determine whether a TV set was delivered on August 6, 1991, we can look at the delivery slip, consult records at the store, and so on. But the delivery slip is good evidence only if this is the slip that accompanied that TV set; and one has to rely on memory to assure oneself of that, or else appeal to another record, which simply raises the same problem once again. More generally, the reliability of records, traces of past events, and so forth themselves need to be established via memory. Although memory is not a widely discussed method of *science*, only a bit of reflection reveals that scientists constantly rely on memory in their cognitive practice, and science could hardly proceed without it. Even interpreting one's laboratory notes depends on remembering the meaning of the notation. Since memory, like introspection, cannot have its reliability *independently* validated, introspection does not seem to be in such bad company.

Another well-known example is enumerative induction. Since Hume's treatment of induction, it is widely recognized that the reliability of induction cannot be established in any independent, noncircular fashion. Since science also seems to rely on induction (although the exact form of induction is notoriously controversial), introspection again seems to keep respectable company.

What about perceptual observation, which is the principal form of evidence establishment? Alston groups the five senses together and addresses the practice of "sense perception." He argues, quite convincingly, that sense perception is also not suspectible of having its reliability established by any independent practice or method. All attempts to establish the reliability of sense perception must ultimately appeal to sense perception. In the case of sense perception, of course, we have a class of processes with clearly diverse members: vision, audition, touch, and so forth. Each of these sense modalities can have its reliability at least partly established by use of the other modalities. However, as Alston argues, to certify the reliability of the latter modalities, one would ultimately have to turn to the first ones. So there still seems to be an essential form of circularity here. Whether it is as serious as the cases of memory and induction I shall not try to settle.

Although human beings, like most terrestrial creatures, have multiple senses, there could be a creature with just a single sense, e.g., touch. (I presume it is uncontroversial that creatures could have fewer than five senses. But if fewer than five, why not fewer than two?) The sense perception of a single-sensed creature would be no better off than introspection as far as independent validation of reliability is concerned. Yet would we say that such a creature can acquire no evidence at all, in virtue of the fact that its sole observational method violates the independent validation constraint? Surely not.

It is clear, then, that introspection's violation of the independent validation constraint does not put it out of step with most other fundamental methods that are honored as scientifically legitimate. Now since introspection violates the independent validation constraint and it is itself nonpublic, it follows that it violates the *public* validation constraint. But its violation of this constraint is principally due to its sharing a *general* property of fundamental methods (viz., their insusceptibility of independent validation), and the other fundamental methods are accepted as scientifically legitimate. So why should introspection's legitimacy be challenged on these grounds?

It could be argued that introspection deserves epistemic oblivion because it suffers from *two* worrisome epistemic features, not just one. It fails to be public and it fails to be independently validated (or validatable). But the second failure, we have seen, is widespread among fundamental methods. And the first failure, as shown in section 3, is not embarrassing either, because publicity does not deserve to be a *sine qua non* of scientific methods of evidence conferral. So introspection, in my opinion, does not deserve epistemic oblivion on any of these grounds, either singly or jointly.

5. Conclusion

I have not said, it should be noted, that reliability is the only appropriate constraint on the scientific legitimacy of an evidence-conferring method. Minimally, a method should also satisfy a certain "negative" constraint, viz., that there *not* be (undefeated) evidence of its *un*reliability.[6] Thus, even if introspection is reliable, and even if it is not disqualified because its reliability cannot be publicly established, these conditions do not yet get it out of the woods. It would still not deserve scientific reliance if there is (undefeated) evidence of its unreliability.[7]

Is it possible to get evidence for the unreliability of introspection? Yes; unreliability might at least be exposed through internal inconsistencies. If introspection delivers conflicting beliefs (on the very same questions), then in each case of conflict, at least one of the conflicting beliefs must be false. If there is massive conflict of this sort, substantial unreliability would be established.

I do not believe that massive conflict of this sort has materialized, however. Something along these lines seemed to occur in classical introspectionism, but there the matter was more complicated, partly because most of the conflicts occurred *inter*personally rather than *intra*personally. Subjects trained in different laboratories delivered different judgments about their consciousness. This is not technically a contradiction, since each was talking about his or her *own* consciousness. But if we add the (implicit) premise that everyone's consciousness has the same general features, inconsistency follows. This was why introspection was abandoned at that historical juncture; it was a problem, at least an apparent problem, of reliability (not publicity). In that period, however, introspection was asked to reveal details of mental life that no current cognitive scientist expects it to reveal, and subjects were theoretically indoctrinated in ways that corrupted their deliverances.[8] When introspection is confined to a more modest range of questions, as it is today, it has not been shown to be unreliable in such a domain. Everyone nowadays agrees that introspection is an unreliable method for answering questions about the micro-structure of cognition. For example, nobody expects subjects to report reliably whether their thinking involves the manipulation of sentences in a language of thought. But this leaves many other types of questions about which introspection could be reliable.

For all of these reasons, I see no reason to abandon the current cognitive science practice of relying on introspection (with all due caution). In particular, neither the traditional publicity thesis nor the fallback publicity thesis provides grounds for requiring cognitive scientists to abandon their reliance on introspection.

Notes

Some of the research for this chapter was done under the sponsorship of the University of Pittsburgh Center for Philosophy of Science, which I gratefully acknowledge. Various earlier versions of the chapter were presented at the University of Pittsburgh, Southern Methodist University, Bowling Green State University, University of Arizona (Cognitive Science Program), and University of Arkansas. Audience comments at all of these forums were helpful. I am especially indebted to Philip Kitcher, Christopher Hill, Paul Bloom, William Lycan, Gerald Massey, Mary Peterson, Joel Pust, and three anonymous referees for *Philosophy of Science*.

1. Chalmers (1996, 385–86, n. 12) points out that psychophysics also typically relies on introspection.

2. The study of implicit memory is by no means restricted to impaired subjects, but the phenomenon is particularly salient in their case.

3. In more recent work, Marcel (1993) reports differences among modes of report (e.g., button-pushing versus verbal reports). But he does not suggest that this forces any fundamental revision in the report criterion.

4. The exact nature of introspection is a difficult matter (see Shoemaker 1994; Lycan 1996), and no attempt is made here to characterize it fully and precisely.

5. Some functional accounts of consciousness might make verbal report dispositions part of the functional characterization. But this would tend to undercut the picture of introspection as a method that could be contingently reliable or unreliable,

the picture I am assuming here. For a defense of the fallibility of introspective awareness, see Lycan (1996, 17–23).

6. This parallels the sort of "non-undermining" constraint that reliabilists in the theory of justification sometimes propose (see Goldman 1986, 62–63).

7. Does satisfaction of these two constraints (reliability plus no-undefeated-evidence-of-unreliability) suffice for scientific acceptability? I do not wish to commit myself to that positive thesis. The chapter's project is mainly a negative one: that of undercutting the publicity thesis.

8. See Ericsson and Simon (1993, 48–61); Lyons (1986). Notice that although Watson (1913) attacked the analytic methods and results of the classical introspectionists, he acknowledged reliable and robust results to have been obtained by introspection in psychophysics. See Ericsson and Simon (1993, 54, 57).

6

Can Science Know When You're Conscious?

Epistemological Foundations of Consciousness Research

Consciousness researchers standardly rely on their subjects' verbal reports to ascertain which conscious states they are in. What justifies this reliance on verbal reports? Does it comport with the third-person approach characteristic of science, or does it ultimately appeal to first-person knowledge of consciousness? If first-person knowledge is required, does this pass scientific muster? Several attempts to rationalize the reliance on verbal reports are considered, beginning with attempts to define consciousness via the higher-order thought approach and functionalism. These approaches are either (A) problematic in their own right, or (B) ultimately based on a first-person access to consciousness. A third approach assumes that scientists can trust verbal reports because subjects reliably monitor or 'introspect' their conscious states. This raises the question of whether the reliability of introspection (or self-monitoring) can be validated by independent criteria. Merikle's attempts to validate this reliability are shown to involve some unavoidable circularity. It is conjectured that scientists' reliance on their subjects' verbal reports tacitly appeals to their own introspective reliability, which is not independently validatable. Some epistemologists might conclude that this renders scientists' conclusions about conscious states unjustified, but I argue that this does not contravene the constraints of a proper epistemology.

1. Why Rely on Verbal Reports?

Of the many psychological states people occupy, some are conscious and some are not; that is, some involve awareness and some do not. (In what follows, I use the terms "conscious" and "aware" interchangeably.)[1] Scientific research on consciousness seeks to determine which types of states tend to be conscious and why. To answer these questions, consciousness researchers need to ascertain the presence or absence of conscious states within their subjects on specific occasions. How do researchers do that given that their subjects' conscious states are not directly observable? The answer, of course, is that scientists observe their subjects' behaviour, especially their verbal behaviour, and use that behaviour to infer the presence or absence of conscious states. This looks like familiar scientific procedure. By observing public behaviour, consciousness can be studied in an objective, third-person fashion, much like any other topic in cognitive science or neuroscience. This is the standard methodological view, I suspect, among scientific researchers of consciousness. Here I want to ask whether this view is correct. Can consciousness be studied scientifically in a purely third-person fashion, without relying, perhaps tacitly, on first-person knowledge or warrant? If first-person knowledge does turn out to be required, is the methodological respectability of consciousness research thereby threatened? If its epistemological viability is threatened, can this threat be met or overcome?

My discussion focuses on verbal reports. Verbal reports obviously play a central role in most methodologies of consciousness. For example, how do consciousness researchers determine that patients with blindsight lack visual awareness in certain portions of their visual field? Patients report the absence of such awareness, and researchers accept their reports. How do memory researchers determine that certain subjects lack "explicit" memory, i.e. conscious memory, for certain events? Again, the subjects say that they don't remember, researchers construe such sayings as reports to the effect that no conscious memories of the target events are present, and researchers accept these reports as true. Admittedly, reliance on verbal reports is not wholly uncontroversial or unqualified, especially in the case of denials of consciousness. I shall return to the reasons for these qualifications below. In the main, however, researchers rely on their subjects' reports as the fundamental kind of evidence for the presence or absence of conscious states. This is clearly stated by Marcel:

> There is really only one criterion for phenomenal experience. This is a person's report, direct or indirect, that they have a sensation of one or another kind, that they are or were conscious in one or another way. . . . Direct reports include statements such as 'I have a headache, or an itch', or 'I feel hungry'. Indirect reports include statements such as 'I see a light' or 'I hear a car', where the person is not directly reporting the sensation, but means by the statement that they *consciously* see or hear something. . . . [P]rovided that the person is not lying, there is little reason to doubt the validity of a report *that* there is phenomenal experience. (1988, 131)

What warrants consciousness researchers in so relying on verbal reports? Cognitive psychologists and neuropsychologists would not rely, after all, on their subjects' reports about all psychological states or processes. When it comes to the nonconscious sphere of mental processing—the great bulk of what transpires in the mind-brain—scientists would not dream of asking subjects for their opinions. Moreover, if subjects were to offer their views about what happens (at the micro-level) when they parse a sentence or retrieve an episode from memory or reach for a cup, scientists would give no special credence to these views. So what entitles scientists to rely so heavily on subjects' reports when they concern conscious experience?

There are, I suggest, two possible types of interpretation or reconstruction of the epistemic warrant for scientific reliance on verbal reports, a *constitutive* approach and a *non-constitutive* approach.

(1) *Constitutive approach.* The verbal report of a conscious state, or the belief underlying such a report, is wholly or partly constitutive of there being such a state, or of the state's being conscious. For example, part of what it might *mean* for a state to be conscious is that it tends to gives rise to such a report, or to a belief that generates such a report, or the like. So when a scientist observes such a report and infers its underlying belief, this would provide evidence for the presence of the reported conscious state.

(2) *Non-constitutive approach.* Neither the verbal report of a conscious state nor the belief from which it issues is (even partly) constitutive of there being such a state or of its being conscious. However, the report and/or the belief is a *reliable indicator* of the occurrence of such a state. Hence, when a scientist observes such a report and infers its underlying belief, this provides evidence for the presence of the reported conscious state.

To illustrate the difference between the two rationales, consider the meaning of the phrase "run a red light." This phrase means "drive through an intersection while the light is red." Given this meaning, if Jones observes the light to be red while Smith drives through the intersection, then Jones observes something that is *constitutive* evidence for Smith's running a red light. By contrast, if Jones merely hears a witness testify to the effect that the light was red while Smith drove through the intersection, what Jones observes is *non-constitutive* evidence—at best a reliable indicator—that Smith ran a red light. Either observation might provide adequate evidence for the proposition in question, but the evidence is different in the two cases.

Why is there reference to an "underlying belief" in my formulation of the two approaches? As the passage from Marcel indicates, a scientist's trust of a subject's verbal report presumes that the subject is sincere, that she is not lying or idly mouthing the report sentence without genuine conviction. Suppose a scientist suspects that the subject reports a certain state of awareness because a band of science obstructionists offered her a reward to sabotage the study by falsifying her reports. Such a scientist will not trust that subject's reports. In the normal case, of course, consciousness scientists tacitly assume that a subject's reports are sincere, i.e., that she believes what she reports. If a subject *says*, "I am now in conscious state M," then she *believes* that she is now in conscious state M. This presumed belief may play an important evidential role in the scientist's conclusion, either on the constitutive or the non-constitutive approach. In what follows I take for granted that scientists are normally warranted in inferring this kind of underlying belief from a subject's report without examining the basis for such warrant. What interests me is how the scientist can justifiably infer the actual presence or absence of a conscious state from the subject's *belief* in the presence or absence of such a state.

I am not requiring, of course, that either a subject's report or her underlying belief is all the evidence available to the scientist from which to infer a conscious state. A constitutive approach might merely suggest that the report or the belief is *partly* constitutive of being in a conscious state. Let us see whether this approach can work.

2. The HOT Approach

The first example I consider of a constitutive approach is the *higher-order thought* (HOT) theory of consciousness, adapted for the purposes of our current problem. In its simplest form, the HOT theory says that what it consists in for a person's mental state M to be conscious is: (i) the person is in M, and (ii) the same person has a contemporaneous thought, M*, about her being in M, a "higher-order" thought. The leading defender of the HOT theory is Rosenthal (1991, 1997, 2000), and I shall follow his version of it. However, Rosenthal denies that his theory is supposed to provide a "conceptual analysis" (or the meaning) of state-consciousness (Rosenthal 1991, 473). But in the present context, where we are examining the constitutive approach, it is important that the HOT theory be construed as a conceptual thesis, so that is the version I shall examine here. Thus, what I shall discuss and criticize is not quite Rosenthal's view, but a very close relative of it.[2]

A further feature of the HOT approach should be emphasized. The HOT theory does not assert that for a mental state M to be conscious, it must have a *conscious* meta-thought M*; to the contrary, even a non-conscious meta-thought suffices to confer consciousness on M. The notion that a non-conscious meta-thought can confer consciousness on a first-order state is quite counter-intuitive (in my opinion), but the HOT approach is driven to this position by a threat of infinite regress. If a *conscious* meta-thought is required to make a lower-order state conscious, then the existence of a conscious meta-thought implies the existence of a conscious meta-meta-thought, and so on *ad infinitum*. This is an intolerable regress, because although people clearly have conscious states, they do not seem to have infinite hierarchies of embedded conscious states. To avoid such infinite hierarchies, the HOT theory is committed to allowing non-conscious meta-thoughts to turn the trick of conferring consciousness on first-order states. A further reason why the HOT theory needs non-conscious meta-thoughts is that many conscious mental states seem to lack any conscious HOTs. Consider perceptual experiences, which are all or almost all conscious. There is conscious reflection on very few of these states, so if what renders them conscious are HOTs, they must be non-conscious HOTs.[3] True, postulation of these nonconscious meta-thoughts is inherently implausible, because it posits an uneconomical duplication of informational effort. This is a difficulty for the HOT approach, but one I shall not press.

Suppose now that the HOT theory is correct. How could a scientist exploit it to infer a conscious state from a subject's report? The subject reports that she is in M, a report which is assumed to express a belief that she is in M. As long as state M exists, the subject's belief or thought about it would be a higher-order thought (M*), which *entails* that M is conscious. Thus, the scientist can justifiably infer that state M is conscious. Of course, the mere fact that the subject believes she is in state M does not, according to the HOT theory, guarantee that she is. The HOT theory does not assume the infallibility (invariable accuracy) of higher-order beliefs. So there could be a belief that some state M exists (at that time) although no such state does then exist (in the subject). As long as M does exist, though, the HOT theory offers the subject's belief about M as conclusive evidence for M's being conscious. In this fashion, the HOT approach looks promising for the purpose of conferring warrant on a third-person consciousness judgment.

I shall offer two criticisms of the HOT approach. First, it is unsatisfactory as a conceptual analysis of state-consciousness, as I shall show through a single type of problem. Second, it does not cover all the territory that needs to be covered in terms of scientific methodology. Half of what consciousness researchers do with verbal reports cannot be accounted for via the HOT approach.

My critique of the HOT theory as a conceptual analysis focuses on its inability to explain people's distinctive epistemic position vis-à-vis their *own* consciousness. When you are in a conscious state M—at least a salient, nonfringy conscious state—then you automatically have *good evidence* for believing that this state is conscious.[4] If you are consciously thinking about Vienna, for example, that very thinking gives you excellent evidence for the proposition that this thought is conscious. You don't have to believe the proposition, or even reflect on it, to possess this evidence.[5] (If talk of "evidence" strikes the reader as inappropriate, other phrases can be substituted. For example, you have "good reason" to believe the proposition, or you are in a "good epistemic position" to tell that it is true.) This is a traditional philosophical view, and one that I believe is correct. Can it be accommodated by the HOT approach? No, I shall argue.

Recall that the HOT theory is committed to the view that some conscious states are rendered conscious by *non*-conscious HOTs. Let us focus on that class of cases. How does the HOT theory make sense of the fact that one automatically has good evidence for the fact that these states are conscious? Since what *makes* them conscious is the existence of independent, *non*-conscious states, one could only have automatic evidence for the consciousness of the first-order states if one automatically had evidence for the existence of those *non*-conscious HOTs.[6] But why should such evidence automatically be available?

A natural view is that a person has *non-inferential* access to the consciousness of their own conscious states. If this is right, then the HOT theory requires that one have non-inferential access to the existence of a non-conscious HOT—because, in the class of cases under discussion, the existence of such a non-conscious HOT is what makes the first-order state have the property of being conscious. But non-conscious states are precisely ones whose existence can only be detected by inferential routes.

The situation is not much improved if we allow that access to one's own consciousness may be *inferential*. It is still unclear where appropriate inferential evidence might come from, especially in the present class of cases where the HOTs are non-conscious. Whether the person is thinking about Vienna or having a perceptual experience, what enables her to *infer* that she simultaneously has a non-conscious HOT directed at this state? No inferential evidence seems to be standardly available to the subject about the HOT's existence.

Rosenthal might respond here that it is just a brute fact that one does have easy access, whether inferential or non-inferential, to the existence of non-conscious HOTs. This is not very satisfying. As Ned Block points out (personal communication), unconscious Freudian beliefs are not easily accessible; for if they were, why would people pay psychoanalysts large sums of money to uncover them? Similarly, unconscious perceptions are not easily accessible, as is evident in many experiments. So it would be a most mysterious state of affairs if the only non-conscious mental states that *are* easily accessible are the HOTs that make other states conscious.

I turn now to my second criticism of the HOT theory for the purposes at hand, viz., its inadequacy in the role of vindicating scientists' responses to verbal reports. At best the HOT theory does only half the job that needs to be done. Though the theory can explain why a scientist who receives a verbal report of M may legitimately draw the *conditional* conclusion: "*If* the subject is in M, then M is conscious," it offers no explanation of why the scientist is entitled to draw the *un*conditional conclusion: "The subject *is* in M, and M is conscious." The report is assumed to express a HOT, and armed with this HOT the scientist can 'crown' a suitable first-order state with consciousness. But the scientist must first ascertain that there exists a suitable first-order state, and it has not been demonstrated how the HOT theory enables him to do this. Assuredly, scientists regularly *do* make inferences from "she reports she is in M" to "she is in M" (where 'M' is presumed to be conscious); but nothing in the HOT theory offers them a licence to draw such inferences. So, in addition to its intrinsic inadequacy, revealed by its inability to get the first-person epistemology right, the HOT theory does not deliver the epistemological goods that cognitive researchers need.

3. Functionalism and Verbal Reports

The second version of the constitutive approach I shall consider is analytical functionalism. According to analytical functionalism, adapted for present purposes, what it means for a mental state to be conscious is that the state tends to give rise to a report of its content, or to a belief that the state is present. In other words, as a first approximation, the reportability or accessibility of a mental state is part of what it means for such a state to be conscious.[7] If this approach is right, when reports of such states are observed this constitutes (some) evidence that there is a conscious state of the type reported—because that (supposedly) is what it *is* for there to be such a conscious state. Alternatively, if the functional definition is phrased in terms of belief rather than report, then as long as a scientist can infer that an appropriate belief has occurred this provides evidence that there is a conscious state of the type reported—again, because that's what it supposedly *is* for there to be such a conscious state.

Now according to almost every version of functionalism about consciousness, the functional characterization is more complex than the foregoing requirement. Let us call the foregoing requirement, formulated for belief, the "self-intimatingness of conscious states." Self-intimatingness implies that, for any conscious state M, being in M analytically involves a disposition to believe that one is in M (at least for creatures with the conceptual capacity to classify their mental states). No functionalist holds that the self-intimation condition exhausts the meaning of a state's being conscious. At most it would be one conjunct in a larger conjunction of functional characteristics. Since reportability or self-intimatingness is only one conjunct among many, a scientist who observes a report and infers a belief cannot logically deduce from them that the subject has a conscious state of the sort reported. Still, the report would provide helpful evidence which could be combined with other relevant evidence.

I shall present two criticisms of this functionalist approach. First, I shall challenge the adequacy of functionalism as a construal of how scientists use verbal reports. Second, and more significantly, I shall suggest that even if a satisfactory functionalist theory can be identified (a very questionable prospect), discovery of it will rest on an independent, "first-personal," and non-functionalist understanding of consciousness (roughly, "phenomenal" consciousness).

The first criticism parallels my second objection to the HOT approach. Functionalism cannot adequately account for actual research practice in the handling of verbal reports. As noted earlier, functionalism does not authorize a deductive inference from a subject's belief or report that she is in conscious state M to the conclusion that she *is* in conscious state M. The self-intimatingness of conscious states only guarantees that one can make a *forward* inference: from a person's being in conscious state M to her (probably) believing that she is in M. It does not guarantee a *backward* inference from her belief (or report) that she is in M to her actually being in M. But the backward inference is the central sort of inference that scientists make and that we are interested in.

Let me put the matter in another way. According to a functional analysis of consciousness that includes a self-intimation component, a person in conscious state M tends to believe that she is in M.[8] However, this same belief (and report) might equally arise from many alternative states that do not satisfy the full functional analysis of being in conscious state M. Thus, a scientist who knows (on the basis of the subject's report) that she believes she is in M is not warranted by functionalist considerations in inferring that she is in M rather than one of the alternative states that might have given rise to the same belief (and report). Yet it seems that consciousness scientists normally do take such reports as ample warrant for the subject's really being in the reported state.[9]

I turn now to my second criticism. Functionalism is fundamentally a third-person approach to mental states. Functionalism tries to characterize mental states and properties, in this case consciousness, in purely causal terms, i.e., in terms of causal roles that relate psychological states to external stimuli, physical behaviour and other psychological states that are themselves characterized in terms of causal roles. None of this is inherently first-personal.

My own view, by contrast, is that consciousness is a phenomenon we initially understand (in large measure) from a first-person point of view. Any attempt to functionalize the concept of consciousness, then, must try to get as close as possible to this phenomenon. A satisfactory functional concept of consciousness must match the first-person concept either intentionally or at least extensionally. If some functional concept is presented that is alleged to be a species of consciousness but turns out to be intentionally or (especially) extensionally at odds with our first-person concept of consciousness, the proper reaction, I submit, is to dismiss the functional concept as at best a concept of *shmonsciousness*—some sort of related phenomenon—not a concept of consciousness.

Not everybody agrees with this methodological proposal. For example, Block and others contend that there are multiple concepts of consciousness.[10] According to Block (1995), there are at least two bona fide concepts of consciousness, including (1) a purely functional concept, which he calls *access consciousness*, and (2) a non-functional concept, *phenomenal consciousness*. These are intentionally non-equivalent (that is, there are conceptually possible cases in which they diverge) and perhaps extensionally non-equivalent as well (there may be actual cases in which they diverge).

One problem with this approach is that indefinitely many functional concepts might be adduced as candidate consciousness concepts.[11] Should we admit them all as genuine varieties of consciousness, even when they conflict—possibly dramatically—with our first-person conception of consciousness? Shouldn't we rather say, as I urge, that most (if not all) functional concepts are specifications not of *consciousness* but of some related phenomenon (or phenomena): *shmonsciousness*? When a functional concept clashes with our first-person concept of consciousness, we should not conclude that it is a new form of consciousness, e.g. X-consciousness. Rather we should conclude that it isn't a consciousness concept at all. There are passages and arguments in Block (1995) that express this very point of view, but on the whole Block's approach seems rather different, since it aims to legitimize a functional concept of consciousness that diverges at least intentionally, and possibly extensionally, with the first-person concept of consciousness (phenomenal consciousness).

Let me highlight some of these points by looking more closely at Block's account of access consciousness. He presents this concept as follows:

> A state is access-conscious (A-conscious) if, in virtue of one's having the state, a representation of its content is (1) . . . poised for use as a premise in reasoning, (2) poised for rational control of action, and (3) poised for rational control of speech. . . . These three conditions are together sufficient, but not all necessary. (1995, 231)

There are two initial problems with this proposal. First, since Block does not identify any necessary conditions for A-consciousness, the functional specification is importantly incomplete. Second, several of the terms in the definition, especially "poised," "reasoning," and "rational," are open to many interpretations. Thus a large range of rather different functional concepts might fall under this definition. Do all of them express legitimate concepts of consciousness?

Block sometimes deals with this problem in ways quite congenial to my own favored approach. Consider his use of the term "rational" in conditions

(2) and (3). Why is this term inserted into these conditions? Block tells us to rule out the kind of control that obtains in blindsight (Block 1997, 382). Block is saying, in effect, that if we omit the rationality qualifier we shall be left with a functional concept that isn't a good sense of A-consciousness. Why isn't it? Because omission of the qualifier would allow informational states distinctive of blindsight patients (i.e., states that produce only guessing behaviour) to qualify as A-conscious. Why would that be wrong? Presumably because it clashes with our first-person grasp of consciousness. When we imagine ourselves in the position of a blindsight patient, we judge from that "pretend" perspective that there is no conscious awareness of the visual information in question. This threatened mismatch with our first-person conception of consciousness induces Block to avoid a functional definition that omits the rationality proviso. So Block acknowledges the need to bring the functional, or access, concept of consciousness into *alignment* with the first-person, or phenomenal, concept of consciousness. I applaud this move as eminently appropriate; I merely suggest that the same move be made across the board. When a functional concept clashes with the first-person concept of consciousness, the functional concept should be abandoned *as* a concept of consciousness. (Of course, such a functional concept might still have utility in psychological theorizing.)

There are other passages in which Block welcomes this policy. For example, he suggests that the concept of A-consciousness is "in some way parasitic" on the "core" notion of P-consciousness (Block 1995, 274); and he offers the metaphor of a parquet floor that requires another floor beneath it (274). Finally, he writes: "I should welcome attempts to tinker with the definitions of 'P' and 'A' so as to make them coincide better" (277). When he writes these things, he wisely endorses the sort of approach advocated here. But when he urges upon us a functional notion of consciousness that avowedly departs from the first-personal notion, he veers off in a different, and to my mind misguided, direction.

Let us consider two further illustrations of this point. According to the research of Milner and Goodale (1995), there are two types of visual processing systems in the human brain: a dorsal pathway and a ventral pathway. The ventral stream processes visual stimuli for the purpose of recognizing and identifying objects and events and for constructing long-term memories and models of the environment. The events in this processing stream include conscious visual experiences. The dorsal stream, by contrast, is specialized for processing visual input so as to control immediate action; it guides the behaviour of reaching for objects and grasping them. The dorsal system, however, does not involve consciousness. The existence of these two different systems yields, as an upshot, two types of abnormal syndromes. When the ventral system is deprived of visual input after damage to the visual area VI, patients have no conscious visual perception of objects and events in the world. Nonetheless, as long as the dorsal system is spared, these patients can still accurately reach for and grasp objects by visual guidance. Such a patient may grasp an object through visually obtained cues but will report no conscious visual awareness of the object. In the converse syndrome ("optic ataxia"), patients with a preserved ventral pathway but damage to the dorsal pathway can see perfectly well in terms of visual awareness, but they are unable to effectively control reaching and grasping behaviour.

In discussing these cases, Block remarks: "Though there is much disagreement about the specializations of the two systems, it does appear that much of the information in the ventral system is much more closely connected to P-consciousness than that in the dorsal system. . . . So it may actually be possible to damage A-consciousness without P-consciousness and vice versa" (Block 1995, 233). Although he doesn't give details, he apparently thinks that the ventral system is a neural basis of P-consciousness, the dorsal system is a (partial) neural basis of A-consciousness, and there could be one type of consciousness without the other under conditions of damage of the sorts described.

Block's diagnosis strikes me as misguided, however. Why say that the dorsal system involves *any* type of consciousness at all? Block apparently is thinking that damage to the dorsal system constitutes damage to A-consciousness because A-consciousness, by definition, partly involves the control of action. But here he clings to his functional specification of A-consciousness when it ought to be abandoned. Damage to the dorsal system involves no impairment of *consciousness* at all, as Milner and Goodale's own discussion of the case (tacitly) suggests. Milner and Goodale describe patients with optic ataxia as retaining "conscious sight of the objects they are unable to reach towards" (Milner and Goodale 1995, 77). They rightly give no hint that damage to the dorsal system creates any sort of consciousness impairment.

Another case worthy of attention concerns Block's term "poised," which occurs in all three conditions of his definition of A-consciousness. "Poised" is so vague that a wide variety of determinate functional specifications might fall under Block's definition. Which of these does he intend? For example, are unretrieved but retrievable memory states "poised" for use as premises in reasoning? Block explains that by "poised" he means "ready and waiting" (1995, 245), and he evidently intends this to exclude memory states because they are not ready and waiting for use as premises in reasoning. I confess that it isn't clear to me that unretrieved memory states fail to satisfy the phrase "ready and waiting." What is clear, however, is that any remotely acceptable functional specification must exclude memory states. They must be excluded because, *intuitively*, unretrieved memory states are non-conscious states. Moreover, it is the first-personal point of view that makes this classification transparent, not an antecedent grasp on some functional characterization of consciousness. Unretrieved memories simply do not "feel" conscious; there is nothing "it is like" to have unretrieved information stored in memory. Thus any functional specification that classifies them differently would be a bust as a consciousness concept; at best it would be a shmons- ciousness concept. Once again we see how the first-person perspective must guide and constrain any attempt at a functional specification. At root, our epistemic window on consciousness is a first-person window. So, even if a functional specification of consciousness can ultimately be constructed that is usable by consciousness researchers to infer subjects' awareness states from their verbal reports, the vindication of this functional specification must ul- timately rest on a first-person epistemological foundation (Block's underlying floor beneath the parquet floor).[12]

4. The Reliable Indicator Approach

The second general type of approach mentioned in section 1 is the non- constitutive approach. This approach assumes that neither a person's report nor her underlying belief that she is in conscious state M is (even partly) constitutive of her being in M, or of M's being conscious. In fact, unlike the HOT theory and analytical functionalism, this approach offers no particular *analysis* of consciousness. It just maintains that a belief that one is in M is a reliable[13] indicator of actually being in M; at least this is assumed by consciousness researchers. Subjects are regarded as epistemically *competent* to form beliefs about the presence or absence of their conscious states, "com- petent" in the sense that these beliefs are usually accurate.

There are various ways to qualify the claim of competence. If subjects form beliefs about the micro-structure of their conscious states, as they were invited to do in the laboratories of historical introspectionists, such beliefs would not now be regarded as reliable. Current cognitive scientists exercise caution in the sorts of questions they ask their subjects to report about, using only familiar, folk-psychological categories. Nonetheless, experimenters often rely on subjects to follow instructions and make responses about topics with considerable phenomenal complexity. A good example is the work on mental imagery by Kosslyn and colleagues. When it comes to beliefs about the *ab- sence* of conscious states, researchers are particularly cautious. When subjects report no awareness of stimuli close to a sensory threshold, or exposed for only a brief duration, it may be argued that they were nonetheless aware of the stimulus.[14] If we set aside such cases, however, there is a strong tendency to regard reports of, and beliefs about, conscious states as accurate.

One popular model of why (or how) people are competent about their conscious states is the internal monitoring, or inner sense, model.[15] On this view, a person can form accurate beliefs about their conscious states for the same sort of reason that they can form accurate beliefs via the outer senses: they can somehow "scan" or "monitor" these states. Philosophers commonly call such monitoring "introspection." There are two common objections to the inner sense model of self-knowledge:

(1)   Unlike cases of the outer senses, there does not seem to be any physical organ associated with introspection.
(2)   Unlike cases of the outer senses, there does not seem to be any distinctive sensuous character associated with introspection.

The best reply to these objections, I think, is to point out that the inner sense theory suggests only an *analogy*, an admittedly imperfect analogy, between introspection and outer sense. So the existence of disanalogies can certainly be tolerated. Moreover, there might well be an associated physical organ or mechanism, especially if you think that introspection essentially amounts to attention. The physical mechanism would be whatever the mechanism of attention is. Some proponents of the inner sense model use it to *define* consciousness. I do not adduce the model in that vein, but merely as an attempt to explain how introspective beliefs could be reliable indicators of the presence or absence of conscious states. The beliefs are reliable indicators because they are produced by a reliable mechanism or process.

Now, some people might argue that introspection is an infallible procedure—that it *necessarily* yields accurate beliefs. Few contemporary philosophers endorse this once popular view, and I agree with the contemporary consensus. First, it seems as if we sometimes err in characterizing our mental states. In the dentist's chair we might think that we are feeling *pain* when we are actually only feeling *pressure*. Furthermore, as long as there is some temporal gap, however small, between a target mental condition and an introspectively formed judgment about it, there seems to be room for forgetting, which can generate error. Moreover, as long as there is even a tiny temporal gap, the introspective judgment and the target condition must be "distinct existences." If they are distinct existences, how can there be a conceptually or metaphysically necessary connection between them? Finally, as long as an internal monitoring mechanism is conceived of as a physical device, it is presumably open to malfunction and therefore to error (Lycan 1996, 17).[16] Confabulation might be one such malfunction: either confabulating the presence of a conscious state or confabulating its absence.

If introspection were infallible, i.e., necessarily reliable, the epistemological plight of consciousness scientists would be considerably alleviated. But since introspection is at best contingently reliable, as argued above, we face the question of what warrants consciousness researchers in placing considerable trust in introspection's reliability. What reason do they have for thinking that introspection has 80% or 90% reliability, or even reliability greater than chance?

Here is another way of posing the problem. If the present reconstruction is correct (as I think it is), consciousness scientists tacitly rely on their subjects' introspective mechanisms as *instruments* of their science. They rely on these mechanisms in the same way scientists generally rely on instruments and measuring devices. But don't scientists have to *validate* or *calibrate* their instruments before they use them? Don't they need *independent* evidence to establish the accuracy of those instruments? What have consciousness researchers done to validate the reliability of their subjects' introspectors? Because they cannot directly observe their subjects' conscious states, they cannot straightforwardly check up on the accuracy of the subjects' introspective beliefs about these states. How, then, can these beliefs—or the verbal reports in which they issue—legitimately be trusted?

The necessity of validating one's instruments is historically illustrated by Galileo's need to convince his contemporaries of the telescope's reliability. Galileo was convinced that he had discovered four "Medicean planets" (the moons of Jupiter) by means of the telescope. But his opponents, steeped in Aristotelian philosophy, challenged the notion that an instrument constructed from terrestrial materials would be accurate when used to look at the heavens. So Galileo spent several years of hard work trying to demonstrate to these opponents the telescope's reliability (Kitcher 1993, 228–33).

Merikle and his colleagues have worried about the problem of validating the use of subjective reports of awareness. Merikle's primary interest is in the issue of unconscious perception, a topic that has elicited great debates over the proper procedures for distinguishing conscious from unconscious processes. Investigators worry about the proper methodology to use in identifying thresholds of consciousness: at what thresholds do perceived stimuli become conscious? One report criterion used here is to ask a subject how confident she is that she can see a stimulus. The evidence for unawareness is in terms of the subject's report of lack of confidence in her verbal judgment. The trouble with this criterion, as pointed out decades ago by Eriksen (1960), is that it places upon the individual subject the responsibility for establishing the criterion of awareness. "We have no way of objectively knowing when [subject] A says a given judgment was a pure guess and [subject] B makes a judgment and states it was a pure guess that the two [subjects] are talking about the same phenomena or that they are using the same criteria for guessing" (292).

Nonetheless, Cheesman and Merikle (1986) argue that a threshold defined in terms of *claimed* or *reported* awareness is the best way to capture the distinction between conscious and unconscious experiences; better, say, than a threshold of objective chance-level performance of discriminative responding. However, Cheesman and Merikle do not want to leave the subjective threshold unsupported or unvalidated, because critics such as Holender (1986) claim that a purely subjective measure does not rule out the possibility that partial stimulus information was consciously perceived. So Cheesman and Merikle seek to find some converging, or corroborating, operation which validates the subjective report criterion. They pursue this goal by trying to show that the measure of subjective judgments of awareness is correlated with other, non-subjective measures, measures concerning behavioural effects associated with processing perceptual information. This seems to be a search for the sort of independent validation that we were discussing above. Merikle and colleagues successfully identify several objective measures that involve qualitative differences between conscious and unconscious influences as predicted by the subjective measure.

Here are two of these objective measures. It was found that (1) subjects have the ability to initiate a predictive strategy involving a Stroop colour-word priming task when and only when they are consciously aware of the primes (Cheesman and Merikle 1986), and (2) subjects' ability to successfully follow an exclusion instruction reflects greater conscious than unconscious influences (Merikle and Joordens 1997a). The exclusion task, developed by Jacoby (Debner and Jacoby 1994), proceeds as follows. A five-letter word (e.g., "spice") is presented and masked on each trial. Immediately following, a three-letter word stem (e.g., "spi—") is presented and subjects are instructed to complete it with any word *except* the one just presented. Debner and Jacoby (1994) found that subjects were able to follow the instructions to exclude the immediately preceding words from their completions when these words were presented for 150 milliseconds. However, when the words were presented for 50 milliseconds, the subjects had difficulty following the instructions and used many of the immediately preceding words to complete the word stems, despite instructions not to use them. What is the supposed virtue of finding these qualitative differences? As Merikle and Joordens express it:

> Our search for converging evidence followed from previous suggestions that the best way to validate a potential measure of awareness is to demonstrate that the selected measure predicts a qualitative difference in performance across conscious and unconscious perceptual states. . . . Not only can qualitative differences validate a task as a measure of unconscious perception by constraining alternative interpretations, but qualitative differences also serve to move the study of unconscious influences forward by showing how conscious and unconscious processes differ. In fact, it can even be argued that the distinction between conscious and unconscious processes is of questionable value if conscious and unconscious processes do not lead to qualitatively different consequences. (1997b, 115–16)

My problem with these findings of qualitative differences concerns the theoretical conclusions to be drawn. We started out worrying whether subjects' introspective reports about their conscious states are accurate. Merikle's various findings show that subjects' reports are not isolated or random events; rather, they correlate with performance on other tasks. To my mind, this tends to show that the subjects' verbal reports are veridical signs of *something*, of some bona fide psychological events or processes. But why do they show the presence or absence of *consciousness* (or *awareness*)? Unless the objective tasks—initiating a predicting strategy or following an exclusion instruction—are known independently to be good measures of consciousness, the fact that they correlate with subjective reports goes no distance towards showing that the latter are accurate measures of consciousness. But how is it determined independently that the objective tasks are good measures of consciousness vs. unconsciousness?

This problem is tacitly acknowledged by Cheesman and Merikle. They defend the assumption that the ability to initiate a predictive strategy is a good measure of consciousness by saying: "This assumption is consistent with views such as those expressed by both Posner and Snyder . . . and Underwood . . . who equate the attentional processes underlying strategy effects with consciousness" (Cheesman and Merikle 1986, 347–48). This just raises the same problem once again, however! How can researchers have established the relationship between consciousness and attentional processes (defined in some empirical manner) without a prior method of ensuring the presence of consciousness? If the prior method relies on verbal reports, we are moving in a circle. Similarly, how can researchers have demonstrated a relationship between consciousness and an ability to follow an exclusion instruction without a prior method of determining the presence of consciousness? If this prior method relies on verbal reports, we are again caught in a circle.

I would formulate the general theoretical problem as follows. In the case of arbitrary constructs in psychology, one might be interested in whether a given criterion measures *anything* objective of interest. One seeks a converging measure systematically associated with the target measure in order to corroborate the fact that there is some objective phenomenon that both are measuring. But in the present case we have a pre-theoretical phenomenon, consciousness, and we are wondering whether a proposed measure—viz., subjective beliefs or reports—is a good measure of *that* phenomenon. Furthermore, under the non-constitutive approach, we are assuming that it is not a conceptual or definitional truth that verbal reports are reliable indicators of consciousness. Nor is it a definitional truth, presumably, that any objective task performance is a reliable indicator of consciousness. So how are we supposed to identify *any* empirically observable variable that validates verbal reports? Whatever scientific variable, V, is found to correlate with verbal reports, this will not help validate the reports as a measure of consciousness unless V itself is an accurate measure of consciousness. But how can that be ascertained without relying on verbal reports?

5. Starting from the First Person

A first step towards a possible resolution of the problem is to give a fuller reconstruction of what scientists tacitly assume in relying on verbal reports. I conjecture that consciousness researchers, when relying on their subjects' reports, tacitly appeal to their own knowledge of their conscious states. In effect, they appeal to a sort of analogical argument: "I have reliable knowledge of my own states of consciousness; therefore it is reasonable to assume that other people have reliable knowledge of their states of consciousness." Deployment of this sort of analogical argument would be of a piece with a certain theory in the "mind-reading" literature, viz., the *simulation theory* (Goldman 1989c) The simulation theory says that a principal method one uses in attributing mental states to others is to "model" others' mental states by trying to instantiate them, in pretend mode, in oneself. Tacitly, this relies on an assumption that others are like oneself. Although I do not suggest that consciousness scientists always deliberately proceed in this simulationist mode, their study of consciousness may well be founded on some such assumption of similarity-to-self.

Some evidence for this procedural assumption is the fact that cognitive psychologists like to try out experiments on themselves. Occasionally their reliance on personal experience is even made explicit, as in a recent book by Baars (1997). Baars imagines a sceptic who wonders whether science has anything to do with real consciousness. He writes:

> The best reply I can think of is to ask sceptics to try one of the demonstrations in this chapter, and ask, is *this truly your experience?* If yes, an honest sceptic should say that we are indeed dealing with genuine consciousness as a valid topic for exploration. . . .
>
> Could the evidence regarding consciousness just be a clever imitation of the real thing? . . . As an answer, we need only notice that *consciousness as an object of scientific scrutiny fits our personal experience remarkably well.* That is not likely to be a coincidence. (34)

In this passage Baars suggests that the foundation of the scientific study of consciousness rests on first-person "observation."

A serious question still remains, however. Is reliance on first-person observation scientifically legitimate? If first-person observation essentially consists in introspection, aren't we still stuck with the problem of validating introspection's reliability? That was the problem we identified for researchers' reliance on their subjects' introspection. How is the problem in any way alleviated by showing that they rely on their *own* introspections? Isn't the reliability of introspection still in need of independent validation?

Some epistemologists would certainly insist on such validation. For example, BonJour (1985) contends that a necessary condition for a belief to be justified is that the believer have a *metajustification* for that belief. What that amounts to, for present purposes, is that an introspectively formed belief cannot qualify as justified unless the believer has a justification—presumably an independent justification—for believing that introspection is reliable.[17] If an independent metajustification is indeed insisted upon, that is a difficult condition to meet. But is it clear that a proper epistemological theory should impose such a condition? No. Many epistemologists, myself included, think that this independent validability requirement is too restrictive or demanding. In particular, when it comes to one's own *basic cognitive processes*, it would be too much to require that each process be validatable in an independent fashion. Taking such a path leads straight to global scepticism (as I sketch below). This does not mean that independent validation should never be required. It does not mean that it isn't an appropriate requirement for scientific instruments external to our natural cognitive equipment. All it means is that an independent validation requirement should not be imposed "all the way down."[18]

To illustrate the scepticism-inducing potential of such a systematic requirement, consider the case of memory. As Alston (1993b, 116–17) argues convincingly, it is impossible to establish (validate) the reliability of memory without appealing to premises that themselves rest on memory. Non-circular validation might seem possible, because one can check up on whether an ostensibly remembered event really occurred by consulting records or traces of past events. But how can those records be trusted without in turn relying on memory? How can I trust what an old *New York Times* says about the past without relying on memory to support the trustworthiness of the *New York Times* (and without relying on memory to support the belief that the ink-marks on its pages express such-and-such contents)? Though the circle may be large or small, there is no non-circular way of validating memory. Ultimately, memory is our only direct avenue to the past, our only cognitive resource that provides an epistemic window on the past. If we allow memory beliefs to qualify as justified only on the condition that memory's reliability be established in an independent, non-circular fashion, then we will have no justified memory beliefs. The same sort of argument applies to perception. As I argued in chapter 5, an unqualified independent validation requirement would imply that we have no justified perceptual beliefs (see also Alston 1993b). For these reasons, a systematic, unqualified form of such a requirement must be rejected. When we reject this requirement we also free introspection from its yoke. Introspection can yield justified beliefs even if a user cannot perform the impossible feat of giving an independent demonstration of introspection's reliability.

I do not contend that there are no further constraints that should be imposed on the legitimacy or viability of trusting introspection. For example, although it may be impossible to validate or invalidate introspection by entirely independent means, one might demand that introspection pass the test of self-consistency. That is, it should not deliver inconsistent judgments about conscious states, or at least it should not deliver *too many* inconsistent judgments, on pain of proving itself to be highly unreliable. To be sure, passing the test for rampant inconsistency would not establish reliability; but passing such a test could at least be considered an epistemological "plus." If memory frequently delivered inconsistent beliefs, we would be forced to infer that it is not very reliable (even if we couldn't tell *which* memory beliefs were false). It is presumably a favourable epistemic feature of memory that a very large number of memory beliefs cohere with one another. The same would be true for introspection.

We can also demand that introspection should pass the test of not yielding too many false beliefs (as far as we can tell) when combined with other presumptively reliable processes or procedures. Here is an example of how introspection can pass such a test. I now have an introspectively formed belief that I currently *intend* to snap my fingers in the next two minutes. I have a background belief that intentions usually stick around for a while and get acted upon if they are not overridden. I therefore predict that I shall indeed snap my fingers in the next two minutes. If that action is then observed within the specified time interval, this partly "corroborates" the reliability of introspection. That is, it corroborates introspection's reliability in the weak sense of *not defeating* or *not challenging* introspection's reliability. There was a chance that introspection (together with other processes) should have yielded a false belief, but, assuming I can trust my visual observation, this did not occur. So introspection survived a test of sorts. This might be re-described by saying that introspection *coheres*—substantially, at any rate—with other belief-forming methods. Passing such a coherence test might be regarded as a necessary, though not a sufficient, sign of its reliability.[19]

Historically, of course, it was thought that introspection was shown to generate massive contradictions, thereby revealing its substantial unreliability. In that period, however, introspection was expected to reveal details of mental life that current cognitive scientists would not demand of it. Maybe it was proved that introspection isn't reliable on the old, overly ambitious range of questions; but this doesn't establish that it is unreliable when applied to a *narrower* range of questions. I submit that introspection has not been proved to be unreliable with respect to "macroscopic" conscious states, such as whether I now consciously intend to snap my fingers, whether I am now consciously thinking about Vienna, or whether a particular part of a stimulus looks to be figure or ground. To specify more exactly the range or scope of introspection's reliability is a delicate matter. This is not the place to try to embark on such a project. All I am presently arguing is that introspection seems to pass the sorts of tests that one can *reasonably* demand that it pass. This suggests that introspection does not fail any appropriate tests for epistemological admissibility, contrary to the sorts of worries examined earlier.[20]

Thus far I have been addressing the justifiability of regarding one's *own* introspective faculty as reliable. What about the third-person case? Can one legitimately infer the reliability of other people's introspectors from the reliability of one's own? The first point to notice is that one can utilize the same sort of coherence test for other people's introspectors as discussed above for one's own introspector. If someone tells me that she now intends to snap her fingers in the next two minutes, I can do at least a coherence test of this (ostensible) introspective report by seeing whether she does snap her fingers within two minutes. If such introspective reports typically comport with other observable behaviour, this tends to "corroborate" the reliability of her introspector. But why should I regard other people's verbal reports as reports of *consciousness* at all? Isn't that the question we posed originally? In discussing Merikle's work, moreover, we challenged the notion that other tasks people perform (apart from giving verbal reports) can confirm verbal reports as evidence for consciousness. How does the present appeal to other behaviour, however "coherent" it might be with verbal reports, help resolve this issue?

At this juncture I think we need to return to the analogical inference from one's own case. What makes it plausible that other people's verbal reports are expressions of (beliefs about) *conscious* states (or their absence) is, in large measure, the apparent similarity of other people to oneself. This is confirmed by the way we intuitively address questions about the consciousness of animals. We tend to be most confident of the consciousness of animals most similar to ourselves, and less confident as they appear more dissimilar.[21] Moreover, at least a scintilla of doubt remains in many people about even the most similar animals precisely (it would appear) because of their dissimilarity from us.

Even if these remarks support the similarity-to-self idea as the basis for our *intuitive* judgments of consciousness, do they help with the question of the *scientific admissibility* of verbal-report-based research on consciousness? Is there any epistemological legitimacy in such analogical inferences? Philosophers of mind, as a rule, do not take kindly to the argument from analogy to other minds, but I find that other thinkers find this sort of approach congenial. One published endorsement of it is by a noted economist and game theorist, Harsanyi, who discusses it in connection with interpersonal utility comparisons (Harsanyi 1982). Harsanyi says that interpersonal utility comparisons rest on what he calls the "similarity postulate." This is the assumption that, once proper allowances are made for differences in taste, education, etc., between me and another person, it is reasonable for me to assume that our basic psychological patterns are much the same. Harsanyi calls this a nonempirical a priori postulate and contends that such postulates are common in science. He specifically compares it to *a priori*, nonempirical criteria of theory choice such as simplicity, parsimony and preference for the "least arbitrary" hypothesis. We might add to this list the preference in science for theories and models displaying symmetries. Van Fraassen (1989) formulates this preference in the form of the following slogan, which he calls the "symmetry requirement": "Problems which are essentially the same must receive essentially the same solution" (236). He paraphrases this as the principle, "respect the symmetries" (236). If this is an appropriate principle for physical science (from which all of van Fraassen's examples are drawn), why should it not be appropriate for cognitive science? This may be the best strategy for consciousness scientists to take in defending the scientific mettle of their procedures. It may provide an epistemically respectable route from a first-person grasp of consciousness to the third-person study of consciousness.

6. Conclusion

I present the foregoing proposal in a tentative, groping fashion, not as a definitive or fully defended solution to this nest of problems. The entire chapter, in fact, is mainly presented as a reminder that the epistemological dimensions of consciousness research are just as difficult and daunting as the metaphysical ones, on which most of the recent philosophical discussion has focused. I have tried to show that the epistemological credentials of consciousness research cannot be established by trying to put such research on a purely third-person footing; the first-person grasp of consciousness remains fundamental. Nonetheless, this need not abort the prospects for the methodological respectability of consciousness research, as long as one does not succumb to the temptation of placing excessive constraints on epistemic justification.

Notes

Thanks to Ned Block, David Chalmers, David Rosenthal and Holly Smith for very helpful comments on earlier drafts of this chapter, and to the editor and two anonymous referees for constructive suggestions.

1. In this usage I follow many (though not all) practitioners. For example, Weiskrantz titles a paper of his "Some Contributions of Neuropsychology of Vision and Memory to the Problem of Consciousness" (Weiskrantz 1988), but employs the terms "aware" and "awareness" in most of the text. In two papers on prosopagnosia, Tranel and Damasio (1985, 1988) use "awareness" in the title of one of them and "conscious" in the other.

2. Although Rosenthal says that he offers the HOT theory as a "hypothesis" rather than a "definition" (Rosenthal 1999, 6), his various ways of formulating the matter all make it sound rather close to a definition. He presents his account as saying "what

it is *in virtue of which* conscious mental states are conscious" (2, emphasis added); "for a mental state to be conscious is for one to be conscious that one is in that very state" (2); "a mental state's being conscious *consists* not just in one's being conscious of that state, but in one's being conscious of it under some relevant description" (3, emphasis added). Moreover, Rosenthal's own stated view notwithstanding, it seems most natural to understand the HOT theory as a theory about the meaning of state consciousness.

3. Rosenthal explicitly accepted this point when queried about it at the third annual meeting of the Association for the Scientific Study of Consciousness, London, Ontario, 5 June 1999.

4. Also, the fact that a state is conscious implies that it is an easy object of *potential* cognition (by the subject). This must be distinguished, however, from the core thesis of the HOT approach, viz., that a state's being conscious implies that there is some *actual* (contemporaneous) cognition of it.

5. Being in this epistemic position does depend, however, on possession of the *concept* of consciousness. Creatures lacking the concept of consciousness might *be* in certain conscious states without having good reason to believe that they are, simply because they lack the concept.

6. It might be argued that my objection does not cut against Rosenthal's own theory because his is not a semantical-conceptual account of consciousness. If "all Xs are Ys" expresses a semantical truth, as in "all bachelors are unmarried," then indeed one cannot have evidence for something being an X without having evidence for its being a Y. But when "all Xs are Ys" expresses merely a contingent truth, as in (perhaps) "all water is H_2O," one can have evidence for something being an X without having evidence for its being a Y. So my argument does not hold against Rosenthal's own version of the HOT theory. However, if Rosenthal sticks to a non-semantical, non-conceptual version of the HOT theory, he owes us a different theory of the meaning of (state) consciousness, and more of an explanation as to why, given this different *meaning* of "consciousness," it nonetheless turns out that state-consciousness *consists* in having a suitable HOT.

7. Versions of functionalism that express these themes can be found in Putnam (1960), Dennett (1969), and Shoemaker (1988).

8. One might want to build more conditions into this account; for example, her being in M will tend to produce a belief that she is in M only if she first *attends* to the question of whether she is in M. I neglect this type of consideration in the interest of simplicity.

9. It is possible, as Lewis mentions (1980, 214), to build into a functional specification of a mental state the generalization that beliefs about being in that mental state are infallible. But if this stiff condition is imposed, it will no longer be so easy to infer a belief about a mental state from a report, because qualifying as such a belief will require infallibility, and whether anything meets that condition is a dubious matter.

10. This point of view is taken to an extreme in Lycan (1996).

11. Block himself writes: "the word 'consciousness' connotes a number of different concepts and denotes a number of different phenomena" (Block 1995, 227).

12. Chalmers (1996, 225–29) also works at the project of trying to construct a functional concept of consciousness (which he calls "awareness") that would be a perfect correlate of phenomenal consciousness.

13. I use the term "reliable" in the philosopher's sense, in which it corresponds to the psychologist's term "valid."

14. There is also a tricky question about the temporal relation between the stimulus exposure and the response. Subjects might forget they were aware of the stimulus very soon after their awareness.

15. Proponents of the internal monitoring model of self-knowledge include: Locke (1959, bk. 2, ch. 1, sec. 3, p. 123); Kant (1965, A23/B37, 67); Armstrong (1980, 61); Lycan (1996); Pollock (1989); and Baars (1988). For criticisms of this model, see Shoemaker (1996).

16. Some people argue that certain disorders, e.g., schizophrenia, involve an impairment in the self-monitoring system (Frith 1992). In some circles, especially philosophical circles, it is widely thought that Nisbett and Wilson (1977) definitively established that there is *no* capacity for accurate introspection. But the message of that article has been accepted too uncritically in those circles. Ericsson and Simon (1980, 1984) made a systematic critique of the Nisbett and Wilson paper, pointing out that in most of their studies there was a large time lag between task and probe, so that it was unlikely that the information about which subjects were asked to make verbal reports was still in short-term memory. Ericsson and Simon themselves maintain that verbal reports of internal events are likely to be accurate about information that is (i) still in short-term memory and (ii) fully attended. This thesis is not undercut, they claim, by Nisbett and Wilson's findings. Wilson himself concedes this in a later article (Wilson 1985, 16).

17. Views of this type are generally called "internalist" in the epistemological literature. However, that label is liable to cause confusion in the present context, so I shall not adopt it.

18. Thus (in Goldman 1986), I suggest that something like BonJour's meta-justification requirement is appropriate for what I call *methods* (roughly, learned belief-forming procedures), but not appropriate for *processes* (i.e., basic cognitive operations). I offer some changes and improvements in my general account of justifiedness in Goldman (1992, ch. 9).

19. Since I am only adducing coherence as (at most) a *sign* of reliability, I do not regard the present proposal as a way of transforming myself from a reliabilist into a coherentist. Indeed, in earlier writings I also adduced coherence as a useful guide to, or test for, reliability (see Goldman 1986, 100).

20. Some might object that I have not confronted the central objection to introspection as a procedure, viz., its *privacy*. It is commonly maintained that science, at least, should only use *public* methods. I have addressed this point at length in chapter 5. I criticize the publicity assumption by showing, through examples, that methods don't have to be public to qualify as scientific. Admittedly, the examples adduced are mostly hypothetical or "thought-experimental" in nature. But such examples are legitimate when we seek to clarify what is or isn't required by our very conception of science.

21. Of course, much depends on the *respects* of similarity. I am unable to say which respects of similarity loom largest.

PART III

Social Epistemology

7

Experts: Which Ones Should You Trust?

1. Expertise and Testimony

Mainstream epistemology is a highly theoretical and abstract enterprise. Traditional epistemologists rarely present their deliberations as critical to the practical problems of life, unless one supposes—as Hume, for example, did not—that skeptical worries should trouble us in our everyday affairs. But some issues in epistemology are both theoretically interesting and practically quite pressing. That holds of the problem to be discussed here: how laypersons should evaluate the testimony of experts and decide which of two or more rival experts is most credible. It is of practical importance because in a complex, highly specialized world people are constantly confronted with situations in which, as comparative novices (or even ignoramuses), they must turn to putative experts for intellectual guidance or assistance. It is of theoretical interest because the appropriate epistemic considerations are far from transparent; and it is not clear how far the problems lead to insurmountable skeptical quandaries. This chapter does not argue for flat-out skepticism in this domain; nor, on the other hand, does it purport to resolve all pressures in the direction of skepticism. It is an exploratory chapter, which tries to identify problems and examine some possible solutions, not to establish those solutions definitively.

The present topic departs from traditional epistemology and philosophy of science in another respect as well. These fields typically consider the prospects for knowledge acquisition in "ideal" situations. For example, epistemic agents are often examined who have unlimited logical competence and no significant limits on their investigational resources. In the present problem, by contrast, we focus on agents with stipulated epistemic constraints and ask what they might attain while subject to those constraints.

Although the problem of assessing experts is non-traditional in some respects, it is by no means a new problem. It was squarely formulated and addressed by Plato in some of his early dialogues, especially the *Charmides*. In this dialogue Socrates asks whether a man is able to examine another man who claims to know something to see whether he does or not; Socrates wonders whether a man can distinguish someone who pretends to be a doctor from someone who really and truly is one (*Charmides* 170d–e). Plato's term for posing the problem is *techne*, often translated as "knowledge" but perhaps better translated as "expertise" (see Gentzler 1995; LaBarge 1997).[1]

In the recent literature the novice/expert problem is formulated in stark terms by John Hardwig (1985, 1991). When a layperson relies on an expert, that reliance, says Hardwig, is necessarily *blind*.[2] Hardwig is intent on denying full-fledged skepticism; he holds that the receiver of testimony can acquire "knowledge" from a source. But by characterizing the receiver's knowledge as "blind," Hardwig seems to give us a skepticism of sorts. The term "blind" seems to imply that a layperson (or a scientist in a different field) cannot be *rationally justified* in trusting an expert. So his approach would leave us with testimonial skepticism concerning rational justification, if not knowledge.

There are other approaches to the epistemology of testimony that lurk in Hardwig's neighborhood. The authors I have in mind do not explicitly urge any form of skepticism about testimonial belief; like Hardwig, they wish to expel the specter of skepticism from the domain of testimony. Nonetheless, their solution to the problem of testimonial justification appeals to a minimum of *reasons* that a hearer might have in trusting the assertions of a source. Let me explain who and what I mean.

The view in question is represented by Tyler Burge (1993) and Richard Foley (1994), who hold that the bare assertion of a claim by a speaker gives a hearer prima facie reason to accept it, quite independently of anything the hearer might know or justifiably believe about the speaker's abilities, circumstances, or opportunities to have acquired the claimed piece of knowledge. Nor does it depend on empirically acquired evidence by the hearer, for example, evidence that speakers generally make claims only when they are in a position to know whereof they speak. Burge, for example, endorses the following Acceptance Principle: "A person is entitled to accept as true something that is presented as true and that is intelligible to him, unless there are stronger reasons not to do so" (1993, 467). He insists that this principle is not an empirical one; the "justificational force of the entitlement described by this justification is not constituted or enhanced by sense experiences or perceptual beliefs" (1993, 469). Similarly, although Foley does not stress the a priori status of such principles, he agrees that it is reasonable of people to grant *fundamental* authority to the opinions of others, where this means that it is "reasonable for us to be influenced by others even when we have no special information indicating that they are reliable" (1994, 55). Fundamental authority is contrasted with *derivative* authority, where the latter is generated from the hearer's *reasons for thinking* that the source's "information, abilities, or circumstances put [him] in an especially good position" to make an accurate claim (1994, 55). So, on Foley's view, a hearer need not have such reasons about a source to get prima facie grounds for trusting that source. Moreover, a person does not need to acquire empirical reasons for thinking that people generally make claims about a subject only when they are in a position to know about that subject. Foley grants people a fundamental (though prima facie) epistemic right to trust others even in the absence of any such empirical evidence.[3] It is in this sense that Burge's and Foley's views seem to license "blind" trust.

I think that Burge, Foley, and others are driven to these sorts of views in part by the apparent hopelessness of reductionist or inductivist alternatives. Neither adults nor children, it appears, have enough evidence from their personal perceptions and memories to make cogent inductive inferences to the reliability of testimony (cf. Coady 1992). So Burge, Foley, Coady and others propose their "fundamental" principles of testimonial trustworthiness to stem the potential tide of testimonial skepticism. I am not altogether convinced that this move is necessary. A case might be made that children are in a position to get good inductive evidence that people usually make claims about things they are in a position to know about.

A young child's earliest evidence of factual reports is from face-to-face speech. The child usually sees what the speaker is talking about and sees that the speaker also sees what she is talking about, e.g., the furry cat, the toy under the piano, and so forth. Indeed, according to one account of cognitive development (Baron-Cohen 1995), there is a special module or mechanism, the "eye-direction detector," that attends to other people's eyes, detects their direction of gaze, and interprets them as "seeing" whatever is in the line of sight.[4] Since seeing commonly gives rise to knowing, the young child can determine a certain range of phenomena within the ken of speakers. Since the earliest utterances the child encounters are presumably about these *speaker-known* objects or events, the child might easily conclude that speakers usually make assertions about things within their ken. Of course, the child later encounters many utterances where it is unclear to the child whether the matters reported are, or ever were, within the speaker's ken. Nonetheless, a child's early experience is of speakers who talk about what they apparently know about, and this may well be a decisive body of empirical evidence available to the child.

I don't want to press this suggestion very hard.[5] I shall not myself be offering a full-scale theory about the justification of testimonial belief. In particular, I do *not* mean to be advancing a sustained defense of the reductionist or inductivist position. Of greater concern to me is the recognition that a hearer's evidence about a source's reliability or unreliability can often *bolster* or *defeat* the hearer's justifiedness in accepting testimony from that source. This can be illustrated with two examples.

As you pass someone on the street, he assertively utters a sophisticated mathematical proposition, which you understand but have never previously assessed for plausibility. Are you justified in accepting it from this stranger? Surely it depends partly on whether the speaker turns out to be a mathematics professor of your acquaintance or, say, a nine-year-old child. You have prior evidence for thinking that the former is in a position to know such a proposition, whereas the latter is not. Whether or not there is an a priori principle of default entitlement of the sort endorsed by Burge and Foley, your empirical evidence about the identity of the speaker is clearly relevant. I do not claim that Burge and Foley (etc.) cannot handle these cases. They might say that your recognition that the speaker is a math professor *bolsters* your *overall* entitlement to accept the proposition (though not your prima facie entitlement); recognizing that it is a child *defeats* your prima facie entitlement to accept the proposition. My point is, however, that your evidence about the properties of the speaker is crucial evidence for your overall entitlement to accept the speaker's assertion. A similar point holds in the following example. As you relax behind the wheel of your parked car, with your eyes closed, you hear someone nearby describing the make and color of the passing cars. Plausibly, you have prima facie justification in accepting those descriptions as true, whether this prima facie entitlement has an a priori or inductivist basis. But if you then open your eyes and discover that the speaker is himself blindfolded and not even looking in the direction of the passing traffic, this prima facie justification is certainly defeated. So what you empirically determine about a speaker can make a massive difference to your overall justifiedness in accepting his utterances.

The same obviously holds about two putative experts, who make conflicting claims about a given subject-matter. Which claim you should accept (if either) can certainly be massively affected by your empirical discoveries about their respective abilities and opportunities to know the truth of the matter (and to speak sincerely about it). Indeed, in this kind of case, default principles of the sort advanced by Burge and Foley are of no help whatever. Although a hearer may be prima facie entitled to believe each of the speakers, he cannot be entitled, *all things considered*, to believe both of them; for the propositions they assert, we are supposing, are incompatible (and transparently incompatible to the hearer). So the hearer's all-things-considered justifiedness vis-à-vis their claims will depend on what he empirically learns about each speaker, or about the opinions of other speakers. In the rest of this chapter I shall investigate the kinds of empirical evidence that a novice hearer might have or be able to obtain for believing one putative expert rather than her rival. I do not believe that we need to settle the "foundational" issues in the general theory of testimony before addressing this issue. This is the working assumption, at any rate, on which I shall proceed.[6]

2. The Novice/Expert Problem versus the Expert/Expert Problem

There are, of course, degrees of both expertise and novicehood. Some novices might not be so much less knowledgeable than some experts. Moreover, a novice might in principle be able to turn himself into an expert, by improving his epistemic position vis-à-vis the target subject-matter, e.g., by acquiring more formal training in the field. This is not a scenario to be considered in this chapter, however. I assume that some sorts of limiting factors—whether they be time, cost, ability, or what have you—will keep our novices from becoming experts, at least prior to the time by which they need to make their judgment. So the question is: Can novices, while remaining novices, make justified judgments about the relative credibility of rival experts? When and how is this possible?

There is a significant difference between the novice/expert problem and another type of problem, the expert/expert problem. The latter problem is one in which experts seek to appraise the authority or credibility of other experts. Philip Kitcher (1993) addresses this problem in analyzing how scientists ascribe authority to their peers. A crucial segment of such authority ascription involves what Kitcher calls "calibration" (1993, 314–22). In *direct* calibration a scientist uses his own opinions about the subject-matter in question to evaluate a target scientist's degree of authority. In *indirect* calibration, he uses the opinions of still other scientists, whose opinions he has previously evaluated by direct calibration, to evaluate the target's authority. So here too he starts from his own opinions about the subject-matter in question.

By contrast, in what I am calling the novice/expert problem (more specifically, the novice/2-expert problem), the novice is not in a position to evaluate the target experts by using his own opinion; at least he does not think he is in such a position. The novice either has no opinions in the target domain, or does not have enough confidence in his opinions in this domain to use them in adjudicating or evaluating the disagreement between the rival experts. He thinks of the domain as properly requiring a certain expertise, and he does not view himself as possessing this expertise. Thus, he cannot use opinions of his own in the domain of expertise—call it the *E-domain*—to choose between conflicting experts' judgments or reports.

We can clarify the nature of the novice/expert problem by comparing it to the analogous listener/eyewitness problem. (Indeed, if we use the term "expert" loosely, the latter problem may just be a species of the novice/expert problem.) Two putative eyewitnesses claim to have witnessed a certain crime. A listener—for example, a juror—did not himself witness the crime, and has no prior beliefs about who committed it or how it was committed. In other words, he has no personal knowledge of the event. He wants to learn what transpired by listening to the testimonies of the eyewitnesses. The question is how he should adjudicate between their testimonies if and when they conflict. In this case, the E-domain is the domain of propositions concerning the actions and circumstances involved in the crime. This E-domain is what the listener (the "novice") has no prior opinions about, or no opinions to which he feels he can legitimately appeal. (He regards his opinions, if any, as mere speculation, hunch, or what have you.)

It may be possible, at least in principle, for a listener to make a reasonable assessment of which eyewitness is more credible, even without having or appealing to prior opinions of his own concerning the E-domain. For example, he might obtain evidence from others as to whether each putative witness was really present at the crime scene, or, alternatively, known to be elsewhere at the time of the crime. Second, the listener could learn of tests of each witness's visual acuity, which would bear on the accuracy or reliability of their reports. So in this kind of case, the credibility of a putative "expert's" report can be checked by such methods as independent verification of whether he had the opportunity and ability to see what he claims to have seen. Are analogous methods available to someone who seeks to assess the credibility of a "cognitive" expert as opposed to an eyewitness expert?

Before addressing this question, we should say more about the nature of expertise and the sorts of experts we are concerned with here. Some kinds of experts are unusually accomplished at certain skills, including violinists, billiards players, textile designers, and so forth. These are not the kinds of experts with which epistemology is most naturally concerned. For epistemological purposes we shall mainly focus on cognitive or intellectual experts: people who have (or claim to have) a superior quantity or level of knowledge in some domain and an ability to generate new knowledge in answer to questions within the domain. Admittedly, there are elements of skill or know-how in intellectual matters too, so the boundary between skill expertise and cognitive expertise is not a sharp one. Nonetheless, I shall try to work on only one side of this rough divide, the intellectual side.

How shall we define expertise in the cognitive sense? What distinguishes an expert from a layperson, in a given cognitive domain? I'll begin by specifying an objective sense of expertise, what it is to *be* an expert, not what it is to have a reputation for expertise. Once the objective sense is specified, the reputational sense readily follows: a reputational expert is someone widely believed to be an expert (in the objective sense), whether or not he really is one.

Turning to objective expertise, then, I first propose that cognitive expertise be defined in "veritistic" (truth-linked) terms. As a first pass, experts in a given domain (the E-domain) have more beliefs (or high degrees of belief) in true propositions and/or fewer beliefs in false propositions within that domain than most people do (or better: than the vast majority of people do). According to this proposal, expertise is largely a comparative matter. However, I do not think it is wholly comparative. If the vast majority of people are full of false beliefs in a domain and Jones exceeds them slightly by not succumbing to a few falsehoods that are widely shared, that still does not make him an "expert" (from a God's-eye point of view). To qualify as a cognitive expert, a person must possess a substantial body of truths in the target domain. Being an expert is not simply a matter of veritistic superiority to most of the community. Some non-comparative threshold of veritistic attainment must be reached, though there is great vagueness in setting this threshold.

Expertise is not all a matter of possessing accurate information. It includes a capacity or disposition to deploy or exploit this fund of information to form beliefs in true answers to new questions that may be posed in the domain. This arises from some set of skills or techniques that constitute part of what it is to be an expert. An expert has the (cognitive) know-how, when presented with a new question in the domain, to go to the right sectors of his information-bank and perform appropriate operations on this information; or to deploy some external apparatus or data-banks to disclose relevant material. So expertise features a propensity element as well as an element of actual attainment.

A third possible feature of expertise may require a little modification in what we said earlier. To discuss this feature, let us distinguish the *primary* and *secondary* questions in a domain. Primary questions are the principal questions of interest to the researchers or students of the subject-matter. Secondary questions concern the existing evidence or arguments that bear on the primary questions, and the assessments of the evidence made by prominent researchers. In general, an expert in a field is someone who has (comparatively) extensive knowledge (in the weak sense of knowledge, i.e., true belief) of the state of the evidence, and knowledge of the opinions and reactions to that evidence by prominent workers in the field. In the central sense of "expert" (a strong sense), an expert is someone with an unusually extensive body of knowledge on both primary and secondary questions in the domain. However, there may also be a weak sense of "expert," in which it includes someone who merely has extensive knowledge on the secondary questions in the domain. Consider two people with strongly divergent views on the primary questions in the domain, so that one of them is largely right and the other is largely wrong. By the original, strong criterion, the one who is largely wrong would not qualify as an expert. People might disagree with this as the final word on the matter. They might hold that anyone with a thorough knowledge of the existing evidence and the differing views held by the workers in the field deserves to be called an expert. I concede this by acknowledging the weak sense of "expert."

Applying what has been said above, we can say that an expert (in the strong sense) in domain D is someone who possesses an extensive fund of knowledge (true belief) and a set of skills or methods for apt and successful deployment of this knowledge to new questions in the domain. Anyone purporting to be a (cognitive) expert in a given domain will claim to have such a fund and set of methods, and will claim to have true answers to the question(s) under dispute because he has applied his fund and his methods to this question. The task for the layperson who is consulting putative experts, and who hopes thereby to learn a true answer to the target question, is to decide who has superior expertise, or who has better deployed his expertise to the question at hand. The novice/2-experts problem is whether a layperson can *justifiably* choose one putative expert as more credible or trustworthy than the other with respect to the question at hand, and what might be the epistemic basis for such a choice?[7]

3. Argument-Based Evidence

To address these issues, I shall begin by listing five possible sources of evidence that a novice might have, in a novice/2-experts situation, for trusting one putative expert more than another. I'll then explore the prospects for utilizing such sources, depending on their availability and the novice's exact circumstance. The five sources I shall discuss are:

(A)   Arguments presented by the contending experts to support their own views and critique their rivals' views.

(B)   Agreement from additional putative experts on one side or other of the subject in question.

(C)   Appraisals by "meta-experts" of the experts' expertise (including appraisals reflected in formal credentials earned by the experts).

(D)   Evidence of the experts' interests and biases vis-à-vis the question at issue.

(E)   Evidence of the experts' past "track records."

In the remainder of the chapter, I shall examine these five possible sources, beginning, in this section, with source (A).[8]

There are two types of communications that a novice, N might receive from his two experts, E_1 and E_2.[9] First, each expert might baldly state her view (conclusion), without supporting it with any evidence or argument whatever. More commonly, an expert may give detailed support to her view in some public or professional context, but this detailed defense might only appear in a restricted venue (e.g., a professional conference or journal) that does not reach N's attention. So N might not encounter the two experts' defenses, or might encounter only very truncated versions of them. For example, N might hear about the experts' views and their support from a second-hand account in the popular press that does not go into many details. At the opposite end of the communicational spectrum, the two experts might engage in a full-scale debate that N witnesses (or reads a detailed reconstruction of). Each expert might there present fairly developed arguments in support of her view and against that of her opponent. Clearly, only when N somehow encounters the experts' evidence or arguments can he have evidence of type (A). So let us consider this scenario.

We may initially suppose that if N can gain (greater) justification for believing one expert's view as compared with the other by means of their arguments, the novice must at least understand the evidence cited in the experts' arguments. For some domains of expertise and some novices, however, even a mere grasp of the evidence may be out of reach. These are cases where N is an "ignoramus" vis-à-vis the E-domain. This is not the universal plight of novices. Sometimes they can understand the evidence (in some measure) but aren't in a position, from personal knowledge, to give it any credence. Assessing an expert's evidence may be especially difficult when it is disputed by an opposing expert.

Not every statement that appears in an expert's argument need be epistemically inaccessible to the novice. Let us distinguish here between *esoteric* and *exoteric* statements within an expert's discourse. Esoteric statements belong to the relevant sphere of expertise, and their truth-values are inaccessible to N—in terms of his personal knowledge, at any rate. Exoteric statements are outside the domain of expertise; their truth-values may be accessible to N—either at the time of their assertion or later.[10] I presume esoteric statements comprise a hefty portion of the premises and "lemmas" in an expert's argument. That's what makes it difficult for a novice to become justified in believing any expert's view on the basis of arguments per se. Not only are novices commonly unable to assess the truth-values of the esoteric propositions, but they also are ill-placed to assess the support relations between the cited evidence and the proffered conclusion. Of course, the proponent expert will claim that the support relation is strong between her evidence and the conclusion she defends; but her opponent will commonly dispute this. The novice will be ill-placed to assess which expert is in the right.

At this point I wish to distinguish *direct* and *indirect argumentative justification*. In direct argumentative justification, a hearer becomes justified in believing an argument's conclusion by becoming justified in believing the argument's premises and their (strong) support relation to the conclusion. If a speaker's endorsement of an argument helps bring it about that the hearer has such justificational status vis-à-vis its premises and support relation, then the hearer may acquire "direct" justification for the conclusion via that speaker's argument.[11] As we have said, however, it is difficult for an expert's argument to produce direct justification in the hearer in the novice/2-experts situation. Precisely because many of these matters are esoteric, N will have a hard time adjudicating between E_1's and E_2's claims, and will therefore have a hard time becoming justified vis-à-vis either of their conclusions. He will even have a hard time becoming justified in trusting one conclusion *more* than the other.

The idea of indirect argumentative justification arises from the idea that one speaker in a debate may demonstrate dialectical superiority over the other, and this dialectical superiority might be a plausible *indicator*[12] for N of greater expertise, even if it doesn't render N directly justified in believing the superior speaker's conclusion. By dialectical superiority, I do not mean merely greater debating skill. Here is an example of what I do mean.

Whenever expert E_2 offers evidence for her conclusion, expert E_1 presents an ostensible rebuttal or defeater of that evidence. On the other hand, when E_1 offers evidence for her conclusion, E_2 never manages to offer a rebuttal or defeater to E_1's evidence. Now N is not in a position to assess the truth-value of E_1's defeaters against E_2, nor to evaluate the truth-value or strength of support that E_1's (undefeated) evidence gives to E_1's conclusion. For these reasons, E_1's evidence (or arguments) are not directly justificatory for N. Nonetheless, in "formal" dialectical terms, E_1 seems to be doing better in the dispute. Furthermore, I suggest, this dialectical superiority may reasonably be taken as an indicator of E_1's having superior expertise on the question at issue. It is a (non-conclusive) indicator that E_1 has a superior fund of information in the domain, or a superior method for manipulating her information, or both.

Additional signs of superior expertise may come from other aspects of the debate, though these are far more tenuous. For example, the comparative quickness and smoothness with which E_1 responds to E_2's evidence may suggest that E_1 is already well familiar with E_2's "points" and has already thought out counterarguments. If E_2's responsiveness to E_1's arguments displays less quickness and smoothness, that may suggest that E_1's prior mastery of the relevant information and support considerations exceeds that of E_2. Of course, quickness and smoothness are problematic indicators of informational mastery. Skilled debaters and well-coached witnesses can appear better-informed because of their stylistic polish, which is not a true indicator of superior expertise. This makes the proper use of indirect argumentative justification a very delicate matter.[13]

To clarify the direct/indirect distinction being drawn here, consider two different things a hearer might say to articulate these different bases of justification. In the case of direct argumentative justifiedness, he might say: "In light of this expert's argument, that is, in light of the truth of its premises and the support they confer on the conclusion (both of which are epistemically accessible to me), I am now justified in believing the conclusion." In indirect argumentative justifiedness, the hearer might say: "In light of the way this expert has argued—her argumentative *performance*, as it were—I can infer that she has more expertise than her opponent; so I am justified in inferring that her conclusion is probably the correct one."

Here is another way to explain the direct/indirect distinction. Indirect argumentative justification essentially involves an *inference to the best explanation*, an inference that N might make from the performances of the two speakers to their respective level of expertise. From their performances, N makes an inference as to which expert has superior expertise in the target domain. Then he makes an inference from greater expertise to a higher probability of endorsing a true conclusion. Whereas indirect argumentative justification essentially involves inference to the best explanation, direct argumentative justification need involve no such inference. Of course, it *might* involve such inference; but if so, the topic of the explanatory inference will only concern the objects, systems, or states of affairs under dispute, not the relative expertise of the contending experts. By contrast, in indirect argumentative justifiedness, it is precisely the experts' relative expertise that constitutes the target of the inference to the best explanation.

Hardwig (1985) makes much of the fact that in the novice/expert situation, the novice lacks the expert's reasons for believing her conclusion. This is correct. Usually, a novice (1) lacks all or some of the premises from which an expert reasons to her conclusion, (2) is in an inferior position to assess the support relation between the expert's premises and conclusions, and (3) is ignorant of many or most of the defeaters (and "defeater-defeaters") that bear on an expert's arguments. However, although novice N may lack (all or some of) an expert's reasons R for believing a conclusion p, N *might* have reasons R* for believing *that* the expert has good reasons for believing p; and N might have reasons R* for believing that one expert has *better* reasons for believing her conclusion than her opponent has for hers. Indirect argumentative justification is one means by which N might acquire reasons R* without sharing (all or any of) either expert's reasons R.[14] It is this possibility to which Hardwick gives short shrift. I don't say that a novice in a novice/2-experts situation invariably has such reasons R*; nor do I say that it is easy for a novice to acquire such reasons. But it does seem to be possible.

4. Agreement from Other Experts:
The Question of Numbers

An additional possible strategy for the novice is to appeal to further experts. This brings us to categories (B) and (C) on our list. Category (B) invites N to consider whether other experts agree with E_1 or with E_2. What proportion of these experts agree with E_1 and what proportion with E_2? In other words, to the extent that it is feasible, N should consult the numbers, or degree of consensus, among all relevant (putative) experts. Won't N be fully justified in trusting E_1 over E_2 if almost all other experts on the subject agree with E_1, or if even a preponderance of the other experts agree with E_1?

Another possible source of evidence, cited under category (C), also appeals to other experts but in a slightly different vein. Under category (C), N should seek evidence about the two rival experts' relative degrees of expertise by consulting third parties' assessments of their expertise. If "meta-experts" give E_1 higher "ratings" or "scores" than E_2, shouldn't N rely more on E_1 than E_2? Credentials can be viewed as a special case of this same process. Academic degrees, professional accreditations, work experience, and so forth (all from specific institutions with distinct reputations) reflect certifications by other experts of E_1's and E_2's demonstrated training or competence. The relative strengths or weights of these indicators might be utilized by N to distill appropriate levels of trust for E_1 and E_2 respectively.[15]

I treat ratings and credentials as signaling "agreement" by other experts because I assume that established authorities certify trainees as competent when they are satisfied that the latter demonstrate (1) a mastery of the same methods that the certifiers deem fundamental to the field, and (2) knowledge of (or belief in) propositions that certifiers deem to be fundamental facts or laws of the discipline. In this fashion, ratings and conferred credentials ultimately rest on basic agreement with the meta-experts and certifying authorities.

When it comes to evaluating specific experts, there is precedent in the American legal system for inquiring into the degree to which other experts agree with those being evaluated.[16] But precedented or not, just how good is this appeal to consensus? If a putative expert's opinion is joined by the consensual opinions of other putative experts, how much warrant does that give a hearer for trusting the original opinion? How much evidential worth does consensus or agreement deserve in the doxastic decision-making of a hearer?

If one holds that a person's opinion deserves prima facie credence, despite the absence of any evidence of their reliability on the subject, then numbers would seem to be very weighty, at least in the absence of additional evidence. Each new testifier or opinion-holder on one side of the issue should add weight to that side. So a novice who is otherwise in the dark about the reliability of the various opinion-holders would seem driven to agree with the more numerous body of experts. Is that right?

Here are two examples that pose doubts for "using the numbers" to judge the relative credibility of opposing positions. First is the case of a guru with slavish followers. Whatever the guru believes is slavishly believed by his followers. They fix their opinions wholly and exclusively on the basis of their leader's views. Intellectually speaking, they are merely his clones. Or consider a group of followers who are not led by a single leader but by a small elite of opinion-makers. When the opinion-makers agree, the mass of followers concur in their opinion. Shouldn't a novice consider this kind of scenario as a possibility? Perhaps (putative) expert E_1 belongs to a doctrinal community whose members devoutly and uncritically agree with the opinions of some single leader or leadership cabal. Should the numerosity of the community make their opinion more credible than that of a less numerous group of experts? Another example, which also challenges the probity of greater numbers, is the example of rumors. Rumors are stories that are widely circulated and accepted though few of the believers have access to the rumored facts. If someone hears a rumor from one source, is that source's credibility enhanced when the same rumor is repeated by a second, third, and fourth source? Presumably not, especially if the hearer knows (or justifiably believes) that these sources are all uncritical recipients of the same rumor.

It will be objected that additional rumor spreaders do not add credibility to an initial rumor monger because the additional ones have no established reliability. The hearer has no reason to think that any of their opinions is worthy of trust. Furthermore, the rumor case doesn't seem to involve "expert" opinions at all and thereby contrasts with the original case. In the original case the hearer has at least some prior reason to think that each new speaker who concurs with one of the original pair has *some* credibility (reliability). Under that scenario, don't additional concurring experts increase the total believability of the one with whom they agree?

It appears, then, that greater numbers should add further credibility, at least when each added opinion-holder has positive initial credibility. This view is certainly presupposed by some approaches to the subject. In the Lehrer-Wagner (1981) model, for example, each new person to whom a subject assigns "respect" or "weight" will provide an extra vector that should push the subject in the direction of that individual's opinion.[17] Unfortunately, this approach has a problem. If two or more opinion-holders are totally *non-independent* of one another, and if the subject knows or is justified in believing this, then the subject's opinion should not be swayed—even a little—by more than one of these opinion-holders. As in the case of a guru and his blind followers, a follower's opinion does not provide any additional grounds for accepting the guru's view (and a second follower does not provide additional grounds for accepting a first follower's view) even if all followers are precisely as reliable as the guru himself (or as one another)—which followers must be, of course, if they believe exactly the same things as the guru (and one another) on the topics in question. Let me demonstrate this through a Bayesian analysis.

Under a simple Bayesian approach, an agent who receives new evidence should update his degree of belief in a hypothesis H by conditioning on that evidence. This means that he should use the ratio (or quotient) of two likelihoods: the likelihood of the evidence occurring if H is true and the likelihood of the evidence occurring if H is false. In the present case the evidence in question is the belief in H on the part of one or more putative experts. More precisely, we are interested in comparing (A) the result of conditioning on the evidence of a single putative expert's belief with (B) the result of conditioning on the evidence of concurring beliefs by two putative experts. Call the two putative experts X and Y, and let X(H) be X's believing H and Y(H) be Y's believing H. What we wish to compare, then, is the magnitude of the likelihood quotient expressed in (1) with the magnitude of the likelihood quotient expressed in (2).

$$(1) \quad \frac{P(X(H)/H)}{P(X(H)/\sim H)}$$

$$(2) \quad \frac{P(X(H)\&Y(H)/H)}{P(X(H)\&Y(H)/\sim H)}$$

The principle we are interested in is the principle that the likelihood ratio given in (2) is always larger than the likelihood ratio given in (1), so that an agent who learns that X and Y both believe H will always have grounds for a larger upward revision of his degree of belief in H than if he learns only that X believes H. At least this is so when X and Y are each somewhat credible (reliable). More precisely, such comparative revisions are in order if the agent is *justified* in believing these things in the different scenarios. I am going to show that such comparative revisions are not always in order. Sometimes (2) is not larger than (1); so the agent—if he knows or justifiably believes this—is not justified in making a larger upward revision from the evidence of two concurring believers than from one believer.

First let us note that according to the probability calculus, (2) is equivalent to (3).

$$(3) \quad \frac{P(X(H)/H)\ P(Y(H)\ /\ X(H)\ \&\ H)}{P(X(H)/\sim H)\ P(Y(H)\ /\ X(H)\ \&\ \sim H)}$$

While looking at (3), return to the case of blind followers. If Y is a blind follower of X, then anything believed by X (including H) will also be believed by Y. And this will hold whether or not H is true. So,

(4) $P(Y(H)/X(H) \ \& \ H) = 1,$

and

(5) $P(Y(H) \ / \ X(H) \ \& \sim H) = 1.$

Substituting these two values into expression (3), (3) reduces to (1). Thus, in the case of a blind follower, (2) (which is equivalent to (3)) is the same as (1), and no larger revision is warranted in the two-concurring-believers case than in the single-believer case.

Suppose that the second concurring believer, Y, is not a *blind* follower of X. Suppose he would sometimes agree with X but not in all circumstances. Under that scenario, does the addition of Y's concurring belief always provide the agent (who possesses this information) with more grounds for believing H? Again the answer is no. The appropriate question is whether Y is more likely to believe H when X believes H and H is true than when X believes H and H is false. If Y is just as likely to follow X's opinion whether H is true or false, then Y's concurring belief adds nothing to the agent's evidential grounds for H (driven by the likelihood quotient). Let us see why this is so.

If Y is just as likely to follow X's opinion when H is false as when it's true, then (6) holds:

(6) $P(Y(H) \ / \ X(H) \ \& \ H) = P(Y(H) \ / \ X(H) \ \& \sim H)$

But if (6) holds, then (3) again reduces to (1), because the right-hand sides of both numerator and denominator in (3) are equal and cancel each other out. Since (3) reduces to (1), the agent still gets no extra evidential boost from Y's agreement with X concerning H. Here it is not required that Y is certain to follow X's opinion; the likelihood of his following X might only be 0.80, or 0.40, or whatever. As long as Y is just as likely to follow X's opinion when H is true as when it's false, we get the same result.

Let us describe this last case by saying that Y is a *non-discriminating reflector* of X (with respect to H). When Y is a non-discriminating reflector of X, Y's opinion has no extra evidential worth for the agent above and beyond X's opinion. What is necessary for the novice to get an extra evidential boost from Y's belief in H is that he (the novice) be justified in believing (6'):

(6') $P(Y(H) \ / \ X(H) \ \& \ H) > P(Y(H) \ / \ X(H) \ \& \sim H)$

If (6') is satisfied, then Y's belief is at least partly *conditionally independent* of X's belief. Full conditional independence is a situation in which any dependency between X and Y's beliefs is accounted for by the dependency of each upon H. Although full conditional independence is not required to boost N's evidence, *partial* conditional independence is required.[18]

We may now identify the trouble with the (unqualified) numbers principle. The trouble is that a novice cannot automatically count on his putative experts being (even partially) conditionally independent of one another. He cannot automatically count on the truth of (6′). Y may be a non-discriminating reflector of X, or X may be a non-discriminating reflector of Y, or both may be non-discriminating reflectors of some third party or parties. The same point applies no matter how many additional putative experts share an initial expert's opinion. If they are all non-discriminating reflectors of someone whose opinion has already been taken into account, they add no further weight to the novice's evidence.

What type of evidence can the novice have to justify his acceptance of (or high level of credence in) (6′)? N can have reason to believe that Y's *route* to belief in H was such that even in possible cases where X fails to recognize H's falsity (and hence believes it), Y *would* recognize its falsity. There are two types of causal routes to Y's belief of the right sort. First, Y's route to belief in H might entirely *bypass* X's route. This would be exemplified by cases in which X and Y are causally independent eyewitnesses of the occurrence or non-occurrence of H; or by cases in which X and Y base their respective beliefs on independent experiments that bear on H. In the eyewitness scenario X might falsely believe H through misperception of the actual event, whereas Y might perceive the event correctly and avoid belief in H. A second possible route to Y's belief in H might go *partly through X* but not involve uncritical reflection of X's belief. For example, Y might listen to X's reasons for believing H, consider a variety of possible defeaters of these reasons that X never considered, but finally rebut the cogency of these defeaters and concur in accepting H. In either of these scenarios Y's partly "autonomous" causal route made him poised to avoid belief in H even though X believes it (possibly falsely). If N has reason to think that Y used one of these more-or-less autonomous causal routes to belief, rather than a causal route that guarantees agreement with X, then N has reason to accept (6′). In this fashion, N would have good reason to rate Y's belief as increasing his evidence for H even after taking account of X's belief.

Presumably, novices could well be in such an epistemic situation vis-à-vis a group of concurring (putative) experts. Certainly in the case of concurring *scientists*, where a novice might have reason to expect them to be critical of one another's viewpoints, a presumption of partial independence might well be in order. If so, a novice might be warranted in giving greater evidential weight to larger numbers of concurring opinion-holders. According to some theories of scientific opinion formation, however, this warrant could not be sustained. Consider the view that scientists' beliefs are produced entirely by negotiation with other scientists, and in no way reflect reality (or Nature).

This view is apparently held by some social constructionists about science, e.g., Bruno Latour and Steve Woolgar (1979/1986); at least this is Kitcher's (1993, 165–66) interpretation of their view.[19] Now if the social construction-ists are right, as so interpreted, then nobody (at least nobody knowledgeable of this fact) would be warranted in believing anything like (6'). There would never be reason to think that any scientist is more likely to believe a scientific hypothesis H when it's true (and some other scientist believes it) than when it's false (and the other scientist believes it). Since causal routes to scientific belief never reflect "real" facts—they only reflect the opinions, interests, and so forth of the community of scientists—(6') will never be true. Anybody who accepts or inclines toward the indicated social-constructionist thesis would never be justified in believing (6').[20]

Setting such extreme views aside, won't a novice normally have reason to expect that different putative experts will have some causal independence or autonomy from one another in their routes to belief? If so, then if a novice is also justified in believing that each putative expert has some slight level of reliability (greater than chance), then won't he be justified in using the numbers of concurring experts to tilt toward one of two initial rivals as op-posed to the other? This conclusion might be right when *all* or *almost all* supplementary experts agree with one of the two initial rivals. But this is rarely the case. Vastly more common are scenarios in which the numbers are more evenly balanced, though not exactly equal. What can a novice conclude in those circumstances? Can he legitimately let the greater numbers decide the issue?

This would be unwarranted, especially if we continue to apply the Bayesian approach. The appropriate change in the novice's belief in H should be based on two sets of concurring opinions (one in favor of H and one against it), and it should depend on *how reliable* the members of each set are and on *how (conditionally) independent* of one another they are. If the members of the smaller group are more reliable and more (conditionally) independent of one another than the members of the larger group, that might imply that the evidential weight of the smaller group exceeds that of the larger one. More precisely, it depends on what the novice is *justified* in believing about these matters. Since the novice's justifiedness on these matters may be very weak, there will be many situations in which he has no distinct or robust justification for going by the relative numbers of likeminded opinion-holders.

This conclusion seems perfectly in order. Here is an example that, by my own lights, sits well with this conclusion. If scientific creationists are more numerous than evolutionary scientists, that would not incline me to say that a novice is warranted in putting more credence in the views of the former than in the views of the latter (on the core issues on which they disagree). At least I am not so inclined on the assumption that the novice has roughly comparable information as most philosophers currently have about the methods of belief formation by evolutionists and creationists, respectively.[21] Certainly the numbers do not *necessarily* outweigh considerations of individual reliability and mutual conditional independence. The latter factors seem more probative, in the present case, than the weight of sheer numbers.[22]

5. Evidence from Interests and Biases

I turn now to the fourth source of possible evidence on our original list: evidence of distorting interests and biases that might lie behind a putative expert's claims. If N has excellent evidence for such bias in one expert and no evidence for such bias in her rival, and if N has no other basis for preferential trust, then N is justified in placing greater trust in the unbiased expert. This proposal comes directly from common sense and experience. If two people give contradictory reports, and exactly one of them has a reason to lie, the relative credibility of the latter is seriously compromised.

Lying, of course, is not the only way that interests and biases can reduce an expert's trustworthiness. Interests and biases can exert more subtle distorting influences on experts' opinions, so that their opinions are less likely to be accurate even if sincere. Someone who is regularly hired as an expert witness for the defense in certain types of civil suits has an economic interest in delivering strong testimony in any current trial, because her reputation as a defense witness depends on her present performance.

As a test of expert performance in situations of conflict of interest, consider the results of a study published in the *Journal of the American Medical Association* (Friedberg et al., 1999). The study explored the relationship between published research reports on new oncology drugs that had been sponsored by pharmaceutical companies versus those that had been sponsored by nonprofit organizations. It found a statistically significant relationship between the funding source and the qualitative conclusions in the reports. Unfavorable conclusions were reached by 38% of nonprofit-sponsored studies but by only 5% of pharmaceutical company–sponsored studies.

From a practical point of view, information bearing on an expert's interests is often one of the more accessible pieces of relevant information that a novice can glean about an expert. Of course, it often transpires that *both* members of a pair of testifying experts have interests that compromise their credibility. But when there is a non-negligible difference on this dimension, it is certainly legitimate information for a novice to employ.

Pecuniary interests are familiar types of potential distorters of an individual's claims or opinions. Of greater significance, partly because of its greater opacity to the novice, is a bias that might infect a whole discipline, subdiscipline, or research group. If all or most members of a given field are infected by the same bias, the novice will have a difficult time telling the real worth of corroborating testimony from other experts and meta-experts. This makes the numbers game, discussed in the previous section, even trickier for the novice to negotiate.

One class of biases emphasized by feminist epistemologists involves the exclusion or underrepresentation of certain viewpoints or standpoints within a discipline or expert community. This might result in the failure of a community to gather or appreciate the significance of certain types of relevant evidence. A second type of community-wide bias arises from the economics or politics of a sub-discipline, or research community. To advance its funding prospects, practitioners might habitually exaggerate the probativeness of the evidence that allegedly supports their findings, especially to outsiders. In competition with neighboring sciences and research enterprises for both resources and recognition, a given research community might apply comparatively lax standards in reporting its results. Novices will have a difficult time detecting this, or weighing the merit of such an allegation by rival experts outside the field.[23]

6. Using Past Track Records

The final category in our list may provide the novice's best source of evidence for making credibility choices. This is the use of putative experts' past track records of cognitive success to assess the likelihoods of their having correct answers to the current question. But how can a novice assess past track records? There are several theoretical problems here, harking back to matters discussed earlier.

First, doesn't using past track records amount to using the method of (direct) "calibration" to assess a candidate expert's expertise? Using a past track record means looking at the candidate's past success rate for previous questions in the E-domain to which she offered answers. But in our earlier discussion (section 2), I said that it's in the nature of a novice that he has no opinions, or no confidence in his own opinions, about matters falling within the E-domain. So how can the novice have any (usable) beliefs about past answers in the E-domain by which to assess the candidate's expertise? In other words, how can a novice, *qua* novice, have any opinions at all about past track records of candidate experts?

A possible response to this problem is to revisit the distinction between *esoteric* and *exoteric* statements. Perhaps not every statement in the E-domain is esoteric. There may also be a body of exoteric statements in the E-domain, and they are the statements for which a novice might assess a candidate's expertise. But does this really make sense? If a statement is an exoteric statement, i.e., one that is epistemically accessible to novices, then why should it even be included in the E-domain? One would have thought that the E-domain is precisely the domain of propositions accessible only to experts.

The solution to the problem begins by sharpening our esoteric/exoteric distinction. It is natural to think that statements are categorically either esoteric or exoteric, but that is a mistake. A given (timeless) statement is esoteric or exoteric only *relative* to an epistemic standpoint or position. It might be esoteric relative to one epistemic position but exoteric relative to a different position. For example, consider the statement, "There will be an eclipse of the sun on April 22, 2130, in Santa Fe, New Mexico." Relative to the present epistemic standpoint, i.e., the standpoint of people living in the year 2000, this is an esoteric statement. Ordinary people in the year 2000 will not be able to answer this question correctly, except by guessing. On the other hand, on the very day in question, April 22, 2130, ordinary people on the street in Santa Fe, New Mexico, will easily be able to answer the question correctly. In that different epistemic position, the question will be an exoteric one, not an esoteric one.[24] You won't need specialized training or knowledge to determine the answer to the question. In this way, the epistemic status of a statement can change from one time to another.

There is a significant application of this simple fact to the expert/novice problem. A novice might easily be able to determine the truth-value of a statement at a time when it has become exoteric. He might be able to tell *then* that it is indeed true. Moreover, he might learn that at an earlier time, when the statement was esoteric for the likes of him, another individual managed to believe it and say that it would be true. Furthermore, the same individual might repeatedly display the capacity to assert statements that are esoteric at the time but become exoteric later, and she might repeatedly turn out to have been right, as determined under the now exoteric circumstances. When this transpires, novices can infer that this unusual knower must possess some special manner of knowing—some distinctive expertise—that is not available to them. They presumably will not know exactly what this distinctive manner of knowing involves, but presumably it involves some proprietary fund of information and some methodology for deploying that information. In this fashion, a novice can verify somebody else's expertise in a certain domain by verifying their impressive track record within that domain. And this can be done without the novice himself somehow being transformed into an expert.

The astronomical example is just one of many, which are easily proliferated. If an automobile, an air-conditioning system, or an organic system is suffering some malfunction or impairment, untrained people will often be unable to specify any true proposition of the form, "If you apply treatment X to system Y, the malfunction or impairment will be cured, repaired, or restored to proper functioning." However, there may be people who can repeatedly specify true propositions precisely of this sort.[25] Moreover, that these propositions are true can be verified by novices, because novices might be able to "watch" the treatment being applied to the malfunctioning system and see that the system returns to proper functioning (faster than untreated systems do). Although the truth of the proposition is an exoteric matter once the treatment works, it was an esoteric matter before the treatment was applied. In such a case the expert has knowledge, and can be determined to have had knowledge, at a time when it was esoteric.[26]

It should be emphasized that many questions to which experts provide answers, at times when they are esoteric, are not merely yes/no questions that might be answered correctly by lucky guesses. Many of them are questions that admit of innumerable possible answers, sometimes indefinitely many answers. Simplifying for purposes of illustration, we might say that when a patient with an ailment sees a doctor, he is asking her the question, "Which medicine, among the tens of thousands of available medicines, will cure or alleviate this ailment?" Such a question is unlikely to be answered correctly by mere guesswork. Similarly, when rocket scientists were first trying to land a spaceship on the moon, there were indefinitely many possible answers to the question, "Which series of steps will succeed in landing this (or some) spaceship on the moon?" Choosing a correct answer from among the infinite list of possible answers is unlikely to have been a lucky guess. It is feats like this, often involving technological applications, that rightly persuade novices that the people who get the correct answers have a special fund of information and a special methodology for deploying it that jointly yield a superior capacity to get right answers. In this fashion, novices can indeed determine that others are experts in a domain in which they themselves are not experts.

Of course, this does not provide an algorithm by which novices can resolve all their two-expert problems. Only occasionally will a novice know, or be able to determine, the track records of the putative experts that dispute an issue before him. A juror in a civil trial has no opportunity to run out and obtain track record information about rival expert witnesses who testify before him. Nonetheless, the fact that novices can verify track records and use them to test a candidate's claims to expertise, at least in principle and in some cases, goes some distance toward dispelling utter skepticism for the novice/2-experts situation. Moreover, the possibility of "directly" determining the expertise of a few experts makes it possible to draw plausible inferences about a much wider class of candidate experts. If certain individuals are shown, by the methods presented above, to have substantial expertise, and if those individuals train others, then it is a plausible inference that the trainees will themselves have comparable funds of information and methodologies, of the same sort that yielded cognitive success for the original experts.[27] Furthermore, to the extent that the verified experts are then consulted as "meta-experts" about the expertise of others (even if they didn't train or credential them), the latter can again be inferred to have comparable expertise. Thus, some of the earlier skepticism engendered by the novice/2-experts problem might be mitigated once the foundation of expert verification provided in this section has been established.

7. Conclusion

My story's ending is decidedly mixed, a cause for neither elation nor gloom. Skeptical clouds loom over many a novice's epistemic horizons when confronted with rival experts bearing competing messages. There are a few silver linings, however. Establishing experts' track records is not beyond the pale of possibility, or even feasibility. This in turn can bolster the credibility of a wider class of experts, thereby laying the foundation for a legitimate use of numbers when trying to choose between experts. There is no denying, however, that the epistemic situations facing novices are often daunting. There are interesting theoretical questions in the analysis of such situations, and they pose interesting practical challenges for "applied" social epistemology. What kinds of education, for example, could substantially improve the ability of novices to appraise expertise, and what kinds of communicational intermediaries might help make the novice-expert relationship more one of justified credence than blind trust?

Notes

For helpful comments on earlier drafts, I am indebted to Holly Smith, Don Fallis, Peter Graham, Patrick Rysiew, Alison Wylie, and numerous participants at the 2000 Rutgers Epistemology Conference, the philosophy of social science roundtable in St. Louis, and my 2000 NEH Summer Seminar on "Philosophical Foundations of Social Epistemology."

1. Thanks to Scott LaBarge for calling Plato's treatment of this subject to my attention.

2. In his 1991 paper, Hardwig at first says that trust must be "at least partially blind" (693). He then proceeds to talk about knowledge resting on trust and therefore being blind (693, 699) without using the qualifier "partially."

3. However, there is some question whether Foley can consistently call the epistemic right he posits a "fundamental" one, since he also says that it rests on (A) my justified *self*-trust, and (B) the *similarity* of others to me—presumably the *evidence* I have of their similarity to me (see 63–64). Another question for Foley is how the fundamentality thesis fits with his view that in cases of conflict I have more reason (prima facie) to trust myself than to trust someone else (see 66). If my justified trust in others is really fundamental, why does it take a back seat to self-trust?

4. Moreover, according to Baron-Cohen, there is a separate module called the "shared attention mechanism," which seeks to determine when another person is attending to the same object as the self is attending to.

5. For one thing, it may be argued that babies' interpretations of what people say is, in the first instance, constrained by the assumption that the contents concern matters within the speakers' perceptual ken. This is not an empirical finding, it might be argued, but an a priori posit that is used to fix speakers' meanings.

6. Some theorists of testimony, Burge included, maintain that a hearer's justificational status vis-à-vis a claim received from a source depends partly on the justificational status of the source's own belief in that claim. This is a *transpersonal, preservationist,* or *transmissional* conception of justifiedness, under which a recipient is not justified in believing p unless the speaker has a justification and entitlement that he *transmits* to the hearer. For purposes of this chapter, however, I shall not consider this transmissional conception of justification. First, Burge himself recognizes that there is such a thing as the recipient's "proprietary" justification for believing an interlocutor's claim, justification localized "in" the recipient, which isn't affected by the source's justification (1993, 485–86).

I think it is appropriate to concentrate on this "proprietary" justification (of the recipient) for present purposes. When a hearer is trying to "choose" between the conflicting claims of rival speakers, he cannot appeal to any inaccessible justification lodged in the heads of the speakers. He can only appeal to his *own* justificational resources. (Of course, these might include things *said* by the two speakers by way of defense of their contentions, things which also are relevant to *their own* justifications.) For other types of (plausible) objections to Burge's preservationism about testimony, see Bezuidenhout (1998).

7. In posing the question of justifiedness, I mean to stay as neutral as possible between different approaches to the concept of justifiedness, for example, between internalist versus externalist approaches to justifiedness. Notice, moreover, that I am not merely asking whether and how the novice can justifiably decide to accept one (candidate) expert's view *outright*, but whether and how he can justifiably decide to give *greater* credence to one than to the other.

8. I do not mean to be committed to the exhaustiveness of this list. The list just includes some salient categories.

9. In what follows I shall for brevity speak about two experts, but I shall normally mean two *putative* experts, because from the novice's epistemic perspective it is problematic whether each, or either, of the self-proclaimed experts really is one.

10. It might be helpful to distinguish *semantically* esoteric statements and *epistemically* esoteric statements. (Thanks to Carol Caraway for this suggestion.) Semantically esoteric statements are ones that a novice cannot assess because he does not even *understand* them; typically, they utilize a technical vocabulary he has not mastered. Epistemically esoteric statements are statements the novice understands but still cannot assess for truth-value.

11. By "direct" justification I do not, of course, mean anything having to do with the basicness of the conclusion in question, in the foundationalist sense of basicness. The distinction I am after is entirely different, as will shortly emerge.

12. Edward Craig (1990, 135) similarly speaks of "indicator properties" as what an inquirer seeks to identify in an informant as a guide to truth-telling ability.

13. Scott Brewer (1998) discusses many of the same issues about novices and experts canvassed here. He treats the present topic under the heading of novices' using experts' "demeanor" to assess their expertise. Demeanor is an especially untrustworthy guide, he points out, where there is a lucrative "market" for demeanor itself—where

demeanor is "traded" at high prices (1998, 1622). This practice was prominent in the days of the sophists and is a robust business in adversarial legal systems.

14. Of course, in indirect argumentative justification the novice must at least *hear* some of the expert's premises—or intermediate steps between "ultimate" premises and conclusion. But the novice will not share the expert's *justifiedness* in believing those premises.

15. These items fall under Kitcher's category of "unearned authority" (1993, 315).

16. Appealing to other experts to validate or underwrite a putative expert's opinion—or, more precisely, the *basis* for his opinion—has a precedent in the legal system's procedures for deciding the admissibility of scientific expert testimony. Under the governing test for admitting or excluding such testimony that was applicable from 1923 to 1993, the scientific principle (or methodology) on which a preferred piece of testimony is based must have "gained general acceptance in the particular field in which it belongs" (*Frye v. United States*, 292 F. 1013 D.C. Cir. 1923). In other words, appeal was made to the scientific community's opinion to decide whether the basis of an expert's testimony is sound enough to allow that testimony into court. This test has been superseded as the uniquely appropriate test in a more recent decision of the Supreme Court (*Daubert v. Merrell Dow Pharmaceuticals*, 509 U.S. 579 [1993]); but the latter decision also appeals to the opinions of other experts. It recommends that judges use a combination of four criteria (none of them necessary or sufficient) in deciding whether proffered scientific expert testimony is admissible. One criterion is the old general acceptance criterion and another is whether the proffered evidence has been subjected to peer review and publication. Peer review, obviously, also introduces the opinions of other experts. Of course, the admissibility of a piece of expert testimony is not the same question as how heavily a hearer—e.g., a juror—should trust such testimony if he hears it. But the two are closely intertwined, since courts make admissibility decisions on the assumption that jurors are likely to be influenced by any expert testimony they hear. Courts do not wish to admit scientific evidence unless it is quite trustworthy. Thus, the idea of ultimately going to the opinions of other experts to assess the trustworthiness of a given expert's proffered testimony is certainly a well-precedented procedure for trying to validate an expert's trustworthiness.

17. Lehrer and Wagner say (1981, 20) that one should assign somebody else a positive weight if one does not regard his opinion as "worthless" on the topic in question—that is, if one regards him as better than a random device. So it looks as if every clone of a leader should be given positive weight—arguably, the same weight as the leader himself, since their beliefs always coincide—as long as the leader receives positive weight. In the Lehrer-Wagner model, then, each clone will exert a positive force over one's own revisions of opinion just as a leader's opinion will exert such force; and the more clones there are, the more force in the direction of their collective opinion will be exerted.

18. I am indebted here to Richard Jeffrey (1992, 109–10). He points out that it is only conditional independence that is relevant in these kinds of cases, not "simple independence" defined by the condition: $P\,(Y(H)\,/\,X(H)\,) = P\,(Y(H))$. If X and Y are even slightly reliable independent sources of information about H, they won't satisfy this latter condition.

19. I myself interpret Latour and Woolgar as holding a more radical view, namely, that there is no reality that could causally interact, even indirectly, with scientists' beliefs.

20. This is equally so under the more radical view that there are no truths at all (of a scientific sort) about reality or Nature.

21. More specifically, I am assuming that believers in creation science have greater (conditional) dependence on the opinion leaders of their general viewpoint than do believers in evolutionary theory.

22. John Pollock (in a personal communication) suggests a way to bolster support for the use of "the numbers." He says that if one can argue that $P(X(H)/Y(H) \& H) = P(X(H)/H)$, then one can cumulate testimony on each side of an issue by counting experts. He further suggests that, in the absence of countervailing evidence, we should believe that $P(X(H)/Y(H) \& H) = P(X(H)/H)$. He proposes a general principle of probabilistic reasoning, which he calls "the principle of nonclassical direct inference," to the effect that we are defeasibly justified in regarding additional factors about which we know nothing to be irrelevant to the probabilities. In Pollock 2000 (see also Pollock 1990) he formulates the idea as follows. If factor C is irrelevant (presumably he means *probabilistically* irrelevant) to the causal relation between properties B and A, then conjoining C to B should not affect the probability of something's being A. Thus, if we have no reason to think that C is relevant, we can assume defeasibly that $P(Ax/Bx \& Cx) = P(Ax/Bx)$. This principle can be applied, he suggests, to the case of a concurring (putative) expert. But, I ask, is it generally reasonable for us—or for a novice—to assume that the opinion of one expert is probabilistically irrelevant to another expert's holding the same view? I would argue in the negative. Even if neither expert directly influences the opinion of the other, it is extremely common for two people who work in the same intellectual domain to be influenced, directly or indirectly, by some common third expert or group of experts. Interdependence of this sort is widespread, and could be justifiably believed by novices. Thus, probabilistic irrelevance of the sort Pollock postulates as the default case is highly questionable.

23. In a devastating critique of the mental health profession, Robyn Dawes (1994) shows that the real expertise of such professionals is, scientifically, very much in doubt, despite the high level of credentialism in that professional community.

24. In the present discussion only *epistemic* esotericness, not *semantic* esotericness, is in question (see note 10).

25. They can not only recognize such propositions as true when others offer them; they can also produce such propositions on their own when asked the question, "What can be done to repair this system?"

26. I have discussed such cases in earlier writings (Goldman 1991; Goldman 1999, 269).

27. Of course, some experts may be better than others at transmitting their expertise. Some may devote more effort to it, be more skilled at it, or exercise stricter standards in credentialing their trainees. This is why good information about training programs is certainly relevant to judgments of expertise.

8

Social Routes to Belief and Knowledge

Doxology versus Epistemology

Many of the cognitive and social sciences deal with the question of how beliefs or belief-like states are produced and transmitted to others. Let us call any account or theory of belief-formation and propagation a *doxology*. I don't use that term, of course, in the religious or theological sense. Rather, I borrow the Greek term "doxa" for belief or opinion, and use "doxology" to mean the study or theory of belief-forming processes. How is doxology related to *epistemology*? Epistemology is the theory of knowledge, and according to standard accounts (setting aside issues posed by Gettier 1963) knowledge is justified true belief. Since knowledge entails belief, doxology would seem to be intimately related to epistemology. How can we say what produces knowledge unless we can say what produces belief? Of course, many epistemologists are not so interested in what *produces* knowledge. They are interested in specifying the conditions *definitive* of knowing. We need not be so restrictive, however, about epistemology's scope. Historically, epistemology was concerned with the sources or methods of knowing: which methods of belief-formation, which routes to belief, augur well not only for belief production but for the production of knowledge? Which routes to belief offer good prospects (or the best prospects) for yielding *true, justified* belief?

In the discussion that follows, I am going to downplay the justification component in the standard concept of knowledge. I shall work on the assumption that, in addition to this standard concept, there is also a weaker sense or concept of knowing in which it simply consists of having true belief (see Goldman 1999). In different terminology, to know that p is to possess the information that p, where "information" is used in a truth-entailing (but

164

not justification-entailing) sense. John Hawthorne (2000) defends this simple information-possession sense of knowing with the following example. If we are asked who in the room knows that Vienna is the capital of Austria, we would want to include anyone in the room who believes or possesses the information that Vienna is the capital of Austria, even if he acquired the information in an unjustified fashion. For example, even if his only source for this fact was somebody he knew full well was untrustworthy (but he believed him anyway), he should still be counted as knowing that Vienna is the capital of Austria. This seems, intuitively, exactly right—at least for *one* sense of the term "know."

Information possession is a valuable resource. If I plan to open a restaurant and I am deciding where it should be located, it will be extremely useful to have the information that the only popular restaurant in a certain prime area is about to go out of business. A *true* belief to this effect will greatly facilitate my business venture; a *false* belief to the same effect could prove to be a debacle. So belief *per se* is not valuable, and certainly it should not be confused with knowing. For related reasons, the proper aim of educational institutions, including universities, is not merely the production and dissemination of *beliefs* (or propositions offered as belief-worthy), but the production and dissemination of *knowledge*, in the foregoing sense of genuine (true) information (Goldman 1999, chap. 11).

For all these reasons, one would not want to conflate the mission of epistemology with the mission of doxology. Still, epistemology can get help from doxology. Since knowledge entails belief, a study of the most effective or powerful routes to knowledge must take into account the available routes to belief. Nobody can attain knowledge without attaining belief. Now it is abundantly clear that a vast number of human beliefs are produced by *social* routes. While some beliefs may be formed by purely personal observations, recollections, and/or inferences, a greater preponderance of beliefs are vectored into the brain by means of communications from others. So doxology must look intensively at social, i.e., interpersonal, pathways. Similarly, epistemology must take an interest—more than a mere passing interest—in these social routes to belief. Which of them are most effective in terms of knowledge-production, and which are more dubious and tenuous? At least this is what the social branch of epistemology (as I conceive it) should do.

In this chapter I shall examine the prospects for certain general approaches to the social causation or propagation of belief. I'll examine them partly with an eye to their descriptive or empirical adequacy and partly with an eye to their potential utility in helping epistemologists distinguish truth-producing from falsehood-producing routes to belief.

Memetics and the Epidemiology of Belief

A general approach to social doxology that has garnered a certain following is called "memetics." According to memetics, thoughts and ideas are items in one mind that can be copied to, or replicated in, other minds. *Memes* are the posited units of thought, and more generally the units of culture. Like genes, from which the idea of memes takes its inspiration and its name, memes are propagated from one carrier to another. The term "meme" was coined by Richard Dawkins, in his book *The Selfish Gene* (1976). Dawkins distinguished between "replicators" and their "vehicles." A replicator is anything of which copies are made, and their vehicles are things that carry the replicators around inside them. The most familiar replicator is DNA. At the end of his book, however, Dawkins argued that there are other replicators, viz., cultural replicators that are transmitted by imitation. The Greek word for imitation is "mimeme," which Dawkins shortened to "meme," in part to rhyme with "gene." As examples he suggested tunes, ideas, catch-phrases, clothes fashions, and ways of making pots and of building arches. For present purposes I shall focus attention on the ideational or intellectual form of memes, which meshes with an interest in applying memetics to epistemology.

The application of evolutionary models to cultures or cultural entities is quite old, at least as old as Darwin (Blackmore 1999, chap. 3). Darwin himself likened languages to species, arguing that pairs of languages often contain homologies that are best explained as arising from a community of descent (Darwin 1859). Like species, he pointed out, languages that become extinct never re-appear. Similar themes are echoed and elaborated by contemporary comparative linguists, such as Pinker (1994). In the nineteenth and early twentieth centuries, many thinkers advanced evolutionary theories of societies and civilizations, including Herbert Spencer, Lloyd Morgan, and James Baldwin. In recent decades, evolutionary models of culture have been advanced by Boyd and Richerson (1985) and by Cavalli-Sforza and Feldman (1981). Studies of the diffusion of inventions and technologies, based on the evolutionary concepts of variation and imitation, have been published by Diamond (1997), Tudge (1995), and Basalla (1988). Dawkins's version of the evolutionary model of culture has been taken up by Blackmore (1999), Hull (1982), Dennett (1991, 1995), and others.

An epidemiological variant of the evolutionary paradigm compares thoughts to viruses or other disease agents that are passed from host to host. Several books and articles on memetics adopt the language of epidemiology, moving almost silently from the biological to the disease metaphor. Works on memetics often bear epidemiological titles such as *Thought Contagion: How Belief Spreads Through Society* (Lynch 1996), and *Virus of the Mind: The New Science of the Meme* (Brodie 1996). Other works embrace the epidemiological paradigm without discussing the memetic one, e.g., Sperber's "The Epidemiology of Beliefs" (1990).

It is standard among evolutionary approaches—or *selectionist* approaches, as they are also called—to identify three core elements in an evolutionary model. Such a model posits types of elements that are subject to (1) random variation, (2) replication, or copying, and (3) differential retention through some sort of "fitness." Selection by "fitness" implies that the number of copies of an element depends on interactions between features of that element and features of the environment in which it persists, where the environment includes other elements with which it competes (cf. Dennett 1991, 200). This kind of model has been proposed for the development of science, often called "evolutionary epistemology" (though it hasn't usually focused, as I wish to do, on the issue of truth-values). Karl Popper (1972) made some initial proposals toward an evolutionary epistemology, and similar ideas were vigorously pursued by Donald Campbell (1960, 1974). Campbell specifically argued that the development of science features the blind variation of ideas and hypotheses, some of which are retained and others discarded under selectional forces, especially empirical tests.

Evolutionary epistemology of science has come under substantial fire. Here is a sample of criticisms from Paul Thagard (1980; also see Skagestad 1978). Thagard first addresses the thesis that the generation of scientific concepts, hypotheses and theories is "blind" in Campbell's sense that they occur independently of their environmental conditions. Thagard argues, to the contrary, that conceptual variation *is* dependent on environmental conditions. Scientific innovations are designed by their creators to solve recognized problems, which are part of their "environment." Specifically, Thagard points to the scientific practice of abductive reasoning, a form of non-deductive reasoning that generates an explanatory hypothesis as a conclusion. Originally formulated by Charles Peirce, a modern formulation of abductive reasoning is given by Norwood Russell Hanson (1961):

Phenomenon P is puzzling.
  Similar phenomena have been explained by hypotheses of kind K.
  Therefore, it is likely that the hypothesis we need to explain P will be of kind K.

By using abductive inference, scientists narrow their search to certain kinds of hypotheses, which is not a blind process at all.

Thagard's second criticism of the biology/science analogy is that in biological evolution the selection criterion, "fitness," is extremely variable. What determines fitness for a given organism or species varies dramatically from environment to environment. In science, by contrast, the selection standards, such as accuracy of prediction, simplicity, and so forth, are quite invariant.

Third, Thagard faults evolutionary epistemology for the poor analogy between biological replication and scientific propagation. Replication in biology is by inheritance, he points out, whereas replication in science is by publication and pedagogy. The former is very slow, whereas the latter can be very fast.

While these are serious disanalogies, they may not be entirely crushing. Positive analogies may be fruitful even when they are accompanied by disanalogies. Perhaps ideational evolution can do without the assumption of *blind* or *random* variation; and surely evolutionary epistemologists can concede without embarrassment that the forms of replication in the two domains are quite different. So Thagard's criticisms do not totally undercut evolutionary epistemology. Still, it remains to be shown that the application of an evolutionary paradigm to the sphere of science is genuinely fruitful.

The prospects for memetics seem stronger in cultural arenas outside of science, in more informal and unreflective venues. This is especially true if we fasten on *imitation* as the sole mechanism of memetic replication. Imitation seems to be (at most) a facet of rather primitive human cognition and behavior, unsuited for an account of the sophisticated, highly reflective operations of scientific thought. By contrast, imitation seems more promising as a mechanism for the propagation of everyday beliefs and folk-culture.

Imitation and Cultural Diffusion

Imitation is a key component in the theory of memetics, which identifies imitation as the unique mechanism responsible for meme replication.[1] But the centrality of imitation in cultural diffusion is problematic in both directions. First, some socially produced replication does not involve imitation. Second, not all imitation involves replication (exact copying). To illustrate the first problem, consider a youngster learning to extract food from a food source. In both animals and humans, the adult might not directly model or instruct the youngster in the appropriate behavior. Instead the adult might simply expose the stimulus to the youngster, or draw her attention to it, and let the youngster learn or explore on its own (Tomasello, Kruger, and Ratner 1993). For example, a chimpanzee mother might draw a youngster's attention to a rock-hammer and an open nut, both left on a hard surface necessary for successful cracking. Such a situation might enable the child to learn to perform actions *just like those of the mother*, so that behavioral replication takes place, but it is not transmitted by imitation because the learned behavior is not displayed by the adult facilitator.

The second problem is whether imitation always yields replication. To the contrary, there seem to be many cases in which imitation generates a piece of behavior or an artifact that bears some resemblance to an original but is hardly a copy of it. For one thing, what is intended as imitation does not always exactly reproduce the originating source. Sociologists studying rumors find that they change quite a lot as they diffuse. Similarly, Tomasello et al. (1993) describe how infant imitation often involves the reproduction of an adult's goal but not the adult's method of execution; Wood (1989) calls this "emulation." Dawkins himself is aware of this general point: "The copying process [in the case of memes] is probably much less precise than in the case of genes; there may be a certain 'mutational' element in every copying event. . . ." (1993, 112).

However, memeticists have a plausible response to this problem. As Richard Byrne points out, behavioral sequences have a hierarchical organization and can be described at several levels (Byrne 1993; Byrne and Russon 1998). A low level description of a manual task might specify the muscle groups that operate to move hands or fingers. At a higher level there might only be a description of some intermediate stages of the behavior, such as opening a hatch or pulling a lever. At the very highest level, the behavior might be coded in terms of a single achieved goal. Imitation could take place at any one of these levels or any combination of them. An imitator might fail to duplicate the lower levels of a model's behavior but might nonetheless duplicate the highest level. At the highest level of coding, there would be true replication or copying, even though there would not be copying at every level. Memeticists are not obliged to say that whenever there is copying, every feature is copied. One would, of course, like a theory about which features *do* get copied, or what *determines* which features get copied. Thus far memeticists have little to say about this.

A more fundamental challenge to memetics is presented by Dan Sperber (1996). Sperber contends that there are relatively few cases of genuine cultural replication First, he distinguishes between cultural items that are mental representations and cultural items that are public productions, such as pots, texts, songs, and so on. He agrees that some public productions involve replication. Some people copy chain-letters; medieval monks copied manuscripts; and pots are copied by potters. Under modern technologies, such as broadcasting, printing, and e-mail forwarding, massive replication can occur (although many of these copies have little cultural significance). However, if an individual cultural token is a genuine copy, there should be a specific token that is its parent, or model. However, Sperber argues, in most cases a token is not a replica of one parent token, but of an indefinite number of tokens some of which play a more "influential" role than others. When you sing "Yankee Doodle," you are not trying to reproduce any one past performance. Indeed, many past performances you have heard probably influence your version. The paradigm of influence, says Sperber, should be contrasted with that of genic replication. Influence is much more a matter of degree. If a pottery pupil has several teachers, her style might be influenced to different degrees by the styles of her several teachers. The meme model might be seen as a limiting case of the influence model, i.e., where descendants are either perfect replicas or complete mutations. Cultural transmission, argues Sperber, is much more like influence than like the meme model.

Sperber does not accept the influence model either, however. Both the meme model and the influence model, he says, place too much weight on the inputs accepted or chosen by the receiving organism. Not much of culture is transmitted by simple imitation or averaging from observed inputs. Human brains use all the information they are presented with as evidence with which to construct representations of their own, utilizing much background information (in the case of grammar, information contained in a language acquisition device). Thus, Sperber concludes, most cultural descendants are *transformations* rather than replicas.

A principal conclusion of Sperber's story, then, is that "there is much greater slack between descent and similarity in the case of cultural transmission than there is in the biological case" (1996, 108). However, Sperber agrees that resemblance among cultural items is greater than one would expect if all one knew is that cultural transmissions occur by transformation rather than imitation (or influence). His hypothesis is that transformations can be biased in the direction of certain "attractors." Though descent is rarely by exact duplication, certain transformations may be more probable than others. As he shows with diagrammatic illustrations, descendants might be heavily centered near a certain point in a region even if these descendants are not produced by exact replication. An "attractor" is a point in a region around which descendants tend to cluster.

The language of "attractors," Sperber emphasizes, is just a way of talking about patterns of transformation probabilities. An attractor is not a material thing. "To say that there is an attractor is not to give a causal explanation; it is to put in a certain light what is to be causally explained: namely, a distribution of items and its evolution, and to suggest the kind of causal explanation to be sought: namely, the identification of genuine causal factors that bias micro-transformations" (1996, 112).

That's fine as far as it goes. What remains to be supplied, however, is precisely the types of causal factors that are at work, either in general or in particular contexts. To put the point slightly differently, what are the psychological or cognitive factors that are responsible for transformations? Why does an agent who observed a given cultural token T (or a set of such tokens) proceed to produce another cultural token T', which bears some sort of resemblance to T? If imitation is not a good characterization of the psychological mechanism, as Sperber implies, what would be a preferable (detailed) characterization? These are not easy questions to answer. But the development of a full-fledged social doxology and epistemology seems to require such answers.

Imitation and Belief

Not all cognitive scientists regard imitation as a significant factor in human behavior. But recent research, especially by Andrew Meltzoff, requires a more serious respect for the role of imitation in human life, especially at early stages (for a review, see Metlzoff 1999). Meltzoff and Moore (1983) established that infants as young as forty-two minutes old successfully imitate adult facial gestures, such as tongue protrusion and mouth opening. Older infants engage in behavioral imitation games with adults and evidently take much pleasure in them. Infants apparently use behavioral imitation to sort out the identity of people (Meltzoff and Moore 1998). Aspects of language development also appear to depend on imitation. Vocal imitation is a principal vehicle for infants' learning of the phonetic inventory and prosodic structure of their native language (Kuhl and Meltzoff 1996). So imitation plays a salient role in early human life.

Behavioral imitation is not a mere reflex. It is a voluntary or intentional act, which can be delayed and controlled over a period of time, not a response that only works in temporal proximity to a stimulus. In one study (Meltzoff 1995b) infants were shown a series of acts on novel objects that they themselves were not allowed to touch. After a delay of hours or even weeks, infants from six to fifteen months of age performed deferred imitation. Other experiments show that young infants *try* to imitate certain tongue movements even when they have physical disabilities that prevent them from doing so. They exhibit obvious frustration at their inability to imitate. Do young children always imitate, or try to imitate, exactly the behavior they observe? No. A study by Meltzoff (1995a) shows that even eighteen-month-olds often imitate what an observed adult *tries* to do, not what he or she actually does. Thus, imitation may be directed at the goals of someone else's behavior, not at the behavior per se.

All of the immediately preceding discussion focuses on the imitation of *behavior* or attempted behavior. The principal topic of this chapter, however, is the propagation of *belief* across individuals. Is there evidence that imitation also applies to belief? An important reason for being skeptical of imitation's role in belief propagation is that, as we have seen, behavioral imitation is *intentional* or *voluntary*, but it is doubtful that belief formation is a voluntary activity.[2] It might be replied that public memes such as tunes, pots, and clothing also aren't intentional in themselves and yet they are the products of imitation. Why shouldn't the same thing hold of beliefs? In reply, I grant that these objects are not themselves intentional, but clearly they are the *products* of intentional activity. For each such token (or almost every one) there was an intentional act of producing it. The same cannot be said for beliefs. One does not, in general, decide to believe (endorse, assent to) a given proposition and then execute that decision. Belief isn't a matter of deliberate choice. One can choose whether to communicate a belief, but a hearer doesn't (generally) choose whether to adopt a belief that has been proffered in such a communication.

A Contagion Model of Belief Transmission

I have criticized an imitation-based account of belief transmission—more precisely, of the formation of belief—because of the voluntariness of imitation and the non-voluntariness of belief formation.[3] I now wish to offer tentative and qualified support for an epidemiological conception of belief transmission, i.e., a "contagion" account. At least some *primitive* cases of belief transmission might be understood on a contagion model. Memeticists, of course, often conflate imitation and contagion. I propose to distinguish between them, because the relevant parts of contagion operations are automatic or semi-automatic, as contrasted with the voluntary and purposeful character of imitation.

Although I use the language of "contagion," I don't mean to model belief transmission specifically on the transmission of disease. Belief transmission might helpfully be compared to *emotional* contagion, which also involves psychological processes. Like disease contagion, emotional contagion can be decomposed into two parts. First, the carrier exposes his condition to a potential receiver, and second, the receiver "catches" or contracts the condition. In emotional states (at least the so-called basic emotions), an emotion is expressed or "exposed" by means of observable facial and musculoskeletal changes. The contraction or "catching" part occurs when the potential receiver acquires the same condition. The contraction part itself can be decomposed into two steps. First, when the potential receiver observes the facial expressions (etc.) of the carrier, his own face involuntarily mimics that of the sender. Next these facial events trigger resonant emotions in the observer. Thus, there is a multi-step process by which one person's emotion is communicated to, or re-created in, another. In an interesting further demonstration, Dimberg et al. (2000) found that facial contagion can be elicited even when the observer is only *unconsciously* exposed to happy or angry facial expressions.

We can conceptualize belief transmission as a similar multiple-step process. In normal humans beliefs give rise to natural public expressions, viz., verbal communications. (The conditions under which such public expressions occur will be explored later.) Second, when a belief is expressed in the mental environment of a potential receiver, there is a natural tendency for the receiver not only to receive the proposition communicated (i.e., grasp it) but to accept or believe it. This doesn't happen invariably, of course. As in the disease analogue, there may be "antibodies"—i.e., contrary evidence possessed by the receiver—that repel or reject the "invading" proposition. But acceptance of a proffered proposition may well be the default reaction. (The conditions of acceptance will be explored later.) Unlike the imitation model, there is no assumption that acceptance versus non-acceptance is a matter of voluntary choice. However, a sender's act of communicating a belief certainly is a voluntary act. In this respect, belief communication contrasts with emotional contagion.

Let us now turn to two questions: (1) Under what circumstances are beliefs expressed (and "directed" toward this or that receiver)? and (2) under what circumstances does a receiver accept proffered beliefs? Since the latter topic has been addressed by philosophers of testimony, let us start there (though for now I am still focusing on doxological rather than epistemological matters).

Acceptance Dispositions

When a hearer receives a report or expression of (ostensible) belief, what tendency does he have to accept it? Two Scottish philosophers, David Hume and Thomas Reid, offered accounts that lie at opposite ends of a spectrum. Hume held that trust in testimony must be supported by a receiver's own observational evidence of the testifier's reliability (Hume 1972, 111). If we transform this into a piece of developmental psychology, Hume would claim that a young child would not believe a report without personal observational evidence of the testifier's reliability (on the subject in question). At the other extreme, Reid ascribed to children an initial trait of total (default) credulity, a disposition to believe any speaker without personal evidence of that speaker's reliability:

> [An] original principle implanted in us by the Supreme Being, is a disposition to confide in the veracity of others, and to believe what they tell us. . . . [W]e shall call this the *principle of credulity*. It is unlimited in children, until they meet with instances of deceit and falsehood; and it retains a very considerable degree of strength through life. (1970, 240)

Presumably Reid did not mean that the mere apprehension of an intelligible proposition uttered by a speaker is enough to tempt or induce belief. Presumably, the principle applies only to communications that (seem to) express genuine conviction. Without signs of speaker conviction, a hearer has no natural belief predilection. If Reid is right, then at least for young children it would seem appropriate to speak of belief contagion. It is very easy for a child to "catch" a belief from somebody else. Of course, the language of contagion need not be restricted to cases where a transmitted belief is acquired with little background inference by the receiver. But the language of contagion seems particularly apt here.

As Reid states it, the default disposition for credal trust is directed at everyone. It draws no distinction between parents, kinfolk, and strangers. I wonder if this is right. An alternative hypothesis is that credal trust, in the first instance, is only vouchsafed to those with whom there is a prior social bond or affective rapport. The young child will of course trust its mother and father, and others who have displayed attitudes of care and emotional resonance. These affective interactions may play a causal role in producing credal trust. Of course, such trust can be extended to a much wider class of humanity later. Initially, however, young children may be disposed to trust those who have shown caring or bonding behavior toward them. As the child matures, the causal influence of bonding or affective resonance may ebb. Alternatively, it may continue to play a more modulated role.

To corroborate the bonding-based hypothesis, consider adolescence, a period in which children abruptly increase their propensity to reject beliefs of their elders, especially parents. Adolescence is noteworthy as a period in which large-scale changes occur in bonding relationships. Emotional ties with parents and other members of the older generation are weakened and new ties with age-mates are initiated or greatly strengthened. Teenagers spend enormous amounts of time talking on the telephone with their friends, they reduce the time spent socializing with elders, and engage in other large-scale changes in socializing patterns. Arguably, this bonding-pattern change is responsible for teenagers' dramatically reduced propensities to accept beliefs of the older generation.

Another way to think of this relationship is in social contract terms. Many evolutionary psychologists contend that a keen awareness of social contracts is wired into the social part of our brains (Cosmides 1989; Cosmides and Tooby 1992). I suggest that believing or accepting what your mates tell you is part of a tacit social contract. (This may not apply to young children, whose sense of a social contract may not yet be in place.) If you are offered information, principles of social exchange require you to show respect by accepting the proffered information (unless you have clear evidence to the contrary). To accept the proffered information is to "cooperate" in the social exchange; to reject it is to "defect." Thus, among people in a bonding relationship, e.g., the group with whom you share games, gossip, or drinks, it is expected that hearers will trust what speakers report. (None of this applies to academics, of course, who constitute a peculiar subgroup that prizes disagreement.) This idea might fit with Robin Dunbar's (1996) hypothesis that language evolved from grooming, which is itself a practice dedicated to social bonding and the maintenance of social order.

Let us explore the bonding approach to belief-acceptability (either in its pure form or in its social contract variant). I label this hypothesis "BABA,"

the acronym for "bonding and belief acceptability." BABA is a possible specification of the second stage of belief-contagion, the receiver stage. It contrasts with Reid's hypothesis because the latter postulates early belief sus-
ceptibility vis-à-vis all speakers, i.e., undiscriminating credulity. As one item
of evidence in support of BABA, consider the "social referencing" phenomenon among twelve-month-olds. Toddlers look back at their care-giver to
decide how to react to a novel stimulus. This is evidence for a discriminating
stance toward specific adults and preferential trust for adults with whom there
is bonding.

We are now almost ready to frame epistemological questions. If BABA is
the acceptance heuristic people actually use, how effective is it in veritistic
(truth-conducive) terms? How would it compare veritistically to the acceptance heuristic posited by Reid? These questions cannot be answered without
making some assumptions about the reporting habits of speakers. The knowledge benefits or costs that would accrue to hearers from these possible practices depend also on the practices of speakers. Perfectly truthful speakers, for
example, offer different knowledge benefits than perfectly deceitful or incom-
petent speakers (Goldman 1999, chap. 4). So let us consider possible speaker
practices before returning to the epistemological issues. What factors determine, or at least influence, the frequency and choice of speakers' communications?

Speech Dispositions

Theorists enamored of the rational choice tradition might ask: Where's the
problem? The rational choice model can account for speech behavior just as
it accounts for other types of voluntary, intentional behavior. However, even
if one accepts rational choice as a universal model of intentional behavior,
this will not fully resolve the issue. To explain behavior in rational choice
terms one must identify the goals, values or preferences that figure in people's
choices. Evolutionary psychology may find evidence of certain values and
valuational orderings that would not be obvious for most rational choice
theorists.

Here again we should consider a hypothesis of Reid, a principle of testimonial speech that complements his principle of testimonial belief discussed
earlier. Reid postulated a natural propensity for people to speak the truth.
"[E]ven in the greatest of liars . . . where they lie once, they speak truth a
hundred times. Truth is always uppermost, and is the natural issue of the
mind. It requires no art or training, no inducement or temptation, but only
that we yield to natural impulse" (1970, 239). Reid presumably does not
mean that people naturally speak what is in fact true. He must mean that they
naturally speak what they *believe* to be true, i.e., what they believe. Now

such a natural impulse is obviously not dictated by rational choice theory, because it isn't obvious that saying what one believes is the best route to maximizing expected utility. This could be accommodated, though, by assuming that people assign high utility to speaking the truth, i.e., speaking sincerely. Thus, Reid's default sincerity principle could be subsumed under rational choice theory, but whether one chooses this option or not does not matter for present purposes.

Looking at Reid's principle of default sincerity more closely, what exactly does it imply? As I interpret it, it means that when people choose to make reports, they have a natural impulse to report what they honestly believe. This leaves open the question, however, of how often and in what contexts people choose to make reports. The default sincerity principle is compatible with communicational miserliness, with people choosing to communicate only rarely. It says that when people *do* communicate, their communications are normally sincere. But this offers pretty lean prospects for widespread diffusion of beliefs through society. Large-scale diffusion, however, is precisely what memeticists and sociologists commonly observe, or claim to observe. So some additional psychological processes (or perhaps cultural processes) must evidently be at work.

To fill this gap, I am inclined to postulate a principle of default disclosure. People with normal speech capacities are not inclined to keep their beliefs to themselves; they are disposed toward their avowal or transmission, subject to certain important constraints. First, they are mainly inclined to disgorge their knowledge or belief when they think that their potential hearers are (1) *interested in* those pieces of knowledge and (2) *do not already possess, or share that knowledge.* In other words, there is a speech principle of informativeness or newsworthiness: "Don't go around repeating things that others already know, or may be presumed to know." In accordance with this principle, people don't go around intoning elementary arithmetical truths or the order of the letters in their alphabet (unless they are teaching these things to young children, for whom these items are indeed news). Second, people are particularly prone to disclose their beliefs to people with whom they have bonded, to whom they have special loyalties and obligations, with whom they have a tacit "social contract" for information sharing.

The second principle is obviously subject to some exceptions. People in various communication "businesses," including teachers, town callers, newscasters, and the like, have special communication responsibilities to anonymous audiences, audiences with whom they have no bonding relationship. Other special commitments, arguably, are constructed on the fly. If a stranger on the street asks you for directions, a temporary contract is established that commits you to information disclosure. However, the two principles introduced above go some distance toward identifying the *root* practices of speech and communication, practices that have something to do, I suspect, with the evolution of communication (though the details, to be sure, are controversial).

These hypotheses have elements in common with Dunbar's (1996) account of language evolution, which strikes me as quite intriguing if not totally compelling. According to Dunbar language arose as an extension of the primate practice of mutual grooming, which is a form of social "networking." He views language, at least in its origins, as another form of social networking. In a different vein from Dunbar, human language can be seen as a sophisticated development of animal communication, a prominent strain of which involves warning calls. Warning calls are descriptions of the current environment that are "newsworthy" for conspecifics. They call attention to events or facts with the twin properties mentioned above: they are of presumptive interest to the intended audience, and they are facts of which this audience is not already apprised.

Evidence of a natural propensity to disclose the newsworthy items one believes is readily identified. If I narrowly escaped an automobile accident this afternoon, I have a strong disposition to relate this event to others, especially those closest to me. I presume that this fact will interest them and that it will be news. I won't, however, relate it to every random person on the street. One feels a spontaneous urge to share with (bonded) others things that strike one as significant. Even when people are deterred by potential repercussions from sharing their thoughts or knowledge, the thoughts frequently well up anyway and find non-standard outlets. Criminals confess their crimes to their buddies; travelers unburden their life stories to fellow passengers who are total strangers.

I have been emphasizing certain belief-disclosing dispositions that are, I think, largely independent of the personal advantages to the speaker (except insofar as being a cooperative participant in a social contract yields personal advantages). However, speech acts can also arise from calculated personal advantage, and these need to be treated separately from the ("spontaneous") kinds of speech dispositions I have been discussing. Thus, people often say what they believe—or what they do not believe—because they hope to obtain some private gain by so saying (e.g., by getting other people to act in desired ways). Such "strategic" speech dispositions are somewhat different, I think, from spontaneous dispositions to express what you believe, especially to members of your bonded community. Nonetheless, these strategic speech dispositions are unquestionably part of the informational environment with which hearers must contend.

Communication Dispositions and
Prospects for Truth

Finally, let us turn to the question of truth. How do the various communication dispositions I have sketched bear on the likelihood of diffusing knowledge through society (where knowledge, again, is true belief). First, consider the acceptance disposition described by Reid: default credulity with no distinction among speakers. This disposition makes it very easy to diffuse beliefs, and potentially to diffuse knowledge, across persons. There will be little resistance, at any rate, at the hearer stage. So long as the hearer harbors no suspicion of speaker deception or incompetence, the Reidian disposition creates a smooth transition from speaker assertion to hearer acceptance. If speakers regularly do speak the truth, then what hearers receive at the other end will equally be true; and their knowledge will thereby increase. (An "increase" occurs, of course, only if the propositions transmitted are not previously believed by the hearers.) By the same token, if speakers assert many falsehoods, whether through insincerity or incompetence, the Reidian acceptance disposition will breed lots of erroneous beliefs, not knowledge. Hearers will be duped or deceived into believing falsehoods. To be sure, the Reidian acceptance disposition is not unqualified. Hearers who learn of speaker fallibility or deceptiveness will be on the alert, and they may thenceforth decline to accept statements from questionable sources. Reid's principle isn't specific enough about hearers' doxastic dispositions, however, to make further inferences about their ability to discriminate true from false pieces of reportage. If they are poor at identifying dubious sources, however, they run a high risk of socially produced false beliefs.

Next let us turn to BABA, an acceptance disposition more qualified than Reid's universal default credulity. Users of BABA are less risk-prone because their default procedure only licenses trust in testifiers with whom they have a bonding relationship. If testifiers in this category are less prone to insincerity (deception), then that should have a payoff in hearer veritistic terms. There will be fewer cases in which testifiers of this sort will speak falsehoods, and hence fewer occasions when the beliefs hearers inherit from testimony are false. Of course, sincerity does not guarantee truth; a speaker's belief may be false for innocent reasons, i.e., ordinary fallibility. But sincerity offers a boost in the veritistic direction. It blocks one possible route to socially induced error.

Nothing in BABA implies that testimonial acceptance is *restricted* to speakers with whom the hearer has close social ties. BABA is merely a hypothesized foundation for testimonial acceptance. Hearers presumably learn to trust other people as well, perhaps others who are identified as trustworthy by members of their bonding group. These details will vary somewhat from culture to culture and from individual case to individual case.

Thus far I have focused on hearers and their acceptance dispositions. Also I have implicitly focused on the risk of error and the degree to which the various dispositions would expose a hearer to error. The general question of knowledge diffusion, however, should not be restricted to error avoidance. More social knowledge can be attained if more true beliefs are transmitted and (freshly) accepted.[4] So, from the vantage point of a community's total knowledge state, we should be concerned with how often truths are disseminated. This depends on speaker dispositions as well as hearer dispositions. A more "expansive" disposition to communicate truths—at least truths that will be credible—holds greater prospects for a community's advance in knowledge.

The belief-disclosure heuristic described in the previous section is pretty expansive insofar as it disposes speakers to transmit beliefs to anyone in their own bonding group. At the same time, that heuristic is selective. By requiring newsworthiness as a condition of communicability, it keeps speakers from sending messages that are redundant for hearers. Without such a constraint, a cacophony of messages might fill the air, too much for hearers to assimilate or filter (a problem that already exists with the Internet). The constraint on transmission to bonding-group members does limit the number of potential beneficiaries. But the kind of heuristic I am thinking of, a psychologically primitive heuristic, might have evolved among tribes that were small enough to coincide with the bonding group. In any case, if BABA is the acceptance disposition at work among hearers, only people in your own bonding group have an initial inclination to accept your statements, so that is the main group for which belief communication would be effective anyway.

Can Truth Be an Attractor?

In this final section I return to Sperber's notion of an "attractor" for beliefs. To say that a point in belief possibility space is an attractor is to say that something biases belief creation so as to cluster a community's beliefs at or around that propositional point. Now many propositions might serve as attractors for belief without any linkage to truth. Cultural forces often make certain religious theses attractors for belief, though by many people's lights this would be unconnected to truth. More generally, propositions that are difficult to falsify but have somehow acquired widespread assent in a culture become attractors for further beliefs in that culture. An existing consensus creates attractor status for a proposition if it isn't readily testable by non-social evidence, i.e., from personal observation. For centuries physicians believed in therapeutically worthless techniques (as judged by current lights) because it was difficult to test causal hypotheses, or at least they didn't know how to test them properly.

From an epistemological point of view, it would be advantageous if a proposition's truth were a "force" that makes it into an attractor. Could the truth of a proposition ever have such a property, the property of sucking minds toward it like a magnet attracts iron filings or a black hole attracts light? Are there social or cultural conditions that promote the attractional force of truth over falsehood? Let us specify what conditions would be required, or at least helpful, for this to obtain.

First, to be socially attractional, a truth must be detected by *somebody* in some fashion other than belief transmission. It must be detected by perception, memory, inference, or some combination of the above. If nobody ever detects the ozone hole over the Antarctic by non-transmissional means, then the existence of the ozone hole will never become widely recognized.

Second, among those who detect the truth in question, at least some must be adequately motivated to disseminate it. If scientists detect the ozone hole but don't give a hoot whether anybody else learns about it, they might keep this fact to themselves (not a likely scenario, of course). There are indeed innumerable truths that get detected by somebody but never make it onto the nightly news. Typically this is because detectors of these truths realize that they are merely of private or local interest, and they make no attempt to disseminate them.

Third, at least some knowers of the truth must have good opportunities for belief dissemination; motivation is not enough. There must be some knowers who have both motivation and opportunity for dissemination. Here is an interesting historical example in which motivation was presumably adequate but not opportunity. In 1601 an English sea captain, James Lancaster, conducted a controlled experiment to assess the ability of lemon juice to prevent scurvy (Rogers 1983, pp. 7–8). Lancaster commanded four ships en route to India. He served three teaspoonfuls of lemon juice per day to the sailors on the largest of these ships, and they mostly stayed healthy. On the three other ships the sailors received no lemon juice, and by the halfway point of the journey 110 out of 278 had died of scurvy. One would have thought that the British Navy would have wanted to disseminate Lancaster's discovery that lemon juice prevents scurvy. Clearly, the Navy had the institutional clout to disseminate this truth widely, but they didn't use it (perhaps for a complex of reasons). Without the support of the British Navy, Lancaster himself lacked the opportunity to disseminate what he believed (and knew). Thus, it was not until 1795, almost 200 years later, that the truth of this proposition became widely known. In general, belief dissemination often depends on institutions, on gatekeepers of information, on technologies of communication, and the like. Contrary to the image purveyed by memeticists, not many beliefs spread by word of mouth without amplification from powerful or well-positioned disseminators.

Fourth, it is not enough for messages to be put out by well-motivated and well-positioned speakers and amplifiers. The sources must be credible to the receiving audience or they will not be believed. A dictator who controls his country's media may publish and broadcast what he wants the citizenry to believe, but if they generally distrust the media, that won't suffice. Distrust may keep them from believing even truths that happen to get published.

An intriguing question in this territory is the conditions under which a truth is able to win widespread assent even when its competitors start with an initial advantage, viz., substantial community acceptance. This is the kind of topic, of course, that interests social epistemologists and philosophers of science. Memetics can prove its mettle if it can say something instructive about this type of problem, or related problems. At present it hasn't developed the kinds of analytical tools that might enable it to do so. Whether it will in the future remains to be seen.

Notes

1. Blackmore makes it a definitional truth that memes are transmitted by imitation: "[M]emes depend on being transmitted from one person to another and, *by definition*, this is done by imitation" (1999, 58, emphasis added).

2. For a representative critique of "doxastic voluntarism," see Alston (1989, chap. 5).

3. In one place Blackmore proposes to understand imitation "in the broad sense." "Imitation includes any kind of copying of ideas and behaviours from one person to another" (1999, 43). But this proposal threatens to reduce the program of memetics to a trivial definitional truth. If memes are defined as things transmitted by imitation (see note 1 above), and imitation is defined as what is responsible for transmission, i.e., copying, then we are left with a trivial tautology. Memetics as a scientific hypothesis would seem to disappear. So I assume that imitation should not be defined in the way Blackmore proposes but rather as a phenomenon of human nature susceptible of independent characterization. Included in that characterization, I have suggested, is the intentionality or voluntariness of imitation.

4. For a more quantitative approach, which proposes a schema for balancing truth acquisition and error avoidance, see Goldman (1999, chap. 3).

9

What Is Social Epistemology?
A Smorgasbord of Projects

Philosophers and academics in other disciplines increasingly talk about "social epistemology," under that label or kindred labels. What is the mission and scope of this subject? How does social epistemology relate to epistemology in general? Is it merely one branch of epistemology, or does it mean to swallow up all of epistemology? How is social epistemology related to classical epistemology? Does it tackle the same problems in a more "socialized" form, or is its agenda quite different from that of classical epistemology? Does it aim to succeed or replace traditional epistemology on the assumption of the latter's demise? What is "social" about social epistemology? Do social factors fit into traditional epistemology, and if so how? How is social epistemology related to other "social-isms" of our times? Is it a comrade-in-arms of social constructivism, for example, or should it proceed independently from—perhaps even in opposition to—the main tenets of social constructivism? How is social epistemology related to the sociology of knowledge and the social studies of science? If the latter fields are purely descriptive, as most of their practitioners would presumably claim, does this mean that social epistemology is also a descriptive subject? If, on the contrary, social epistemology is some sort of normative subject, what are the norms with which it deals, and what are the foundations or grounds of these norms?

At this point, there is no unanimity on any of these questions. Many individual writers and groups of writers have sharply divergent views on what social epistemology is or should be. In this chapter I lay out some of the contrasting perspectives on the field, and situate my own approach (or combination of approaches) within this larger range of options.

Epistemology as the Study of "Knowledge": Strict and Loose Conceptions

Some common ground might perhaps be found in the suggestion that social epistemology is the study of *knowledge*, a study that emphasizes the social dimensions of knowledge. Perhaps all contributors to social epistemology would agree on this much. What is knowledge, however, or how is the term "knowledge" to be employed? One source of the multiple conceptions of social epistemology, I submit, is the multiple uses of the term "knowledge," some strict and some loose. By a "strict" use I mean one that conforms to some standard, ordinary sense of the term in colloquial English (as judged by what epistemologists who attend to ordinary usage have identified as such). By a "loose" use I mean an extended, technical use that departs from the standard, colloquial senses. I do not mean, necessarily, to criticize writers who use "knowledge" in a nonstandard, noncolloquial, sense; I initially point out these differences only for descriptive or classificatory purposes. Using this classification, I propose to distinguish four uses of the term "knowledge" that are found in the literature of social epistemology or its neighborhood:

(1)   Knowledge = belief
(2)   Knowledge = institutionalized belief
(3)   Knowledge = true belief
(4)   Knowledge = justified true belief (plus)

Uses (1) and (2) are loose senses of "knowledge," employed by sociologists of knowledge and a variety of other researchers (including cognitive scientists, for example) who do not aim to conform to standard usage. Uses (3) and (4) are strict senses of "knowledge," typically advanced by one or more philosophers. Philosophers propose many different variants of (4), but these differences will not loom large here, so I shall tend to ignore them.

Under sense (1), "knowledge" would apply to any item of belief, whether true or false, rational or irrational, agreed to or not agreed to by other members of the believer's community. The totality of an individual's knowledge, in sense (1), is the totality of his or her beliefs, and the totality of a society's or community's knowledge is the totality of what its members believe, or perhaps what they concur in believing, whether these beliefs are true or false. Sociology of knowledge, science and technology studies, cultural anthropology, intellectual history, and many other disciplines typically study knowledge in this sense, focusing on the generation or transformation of belief via social or cultural processes. Such disciplines deliberately abstract from, or ignore, the question of whether the beliefs studied are true or false, rational or irrational. Nonetheless, practitioners of these disciplines commonly describe themselves as studying "knowledge," so they might wish to say that what they do is part of social epistemology.

I call sense (1) a loose sense because I agree with mainstream philosophical epistemologists that the standard, colloquial sense of "knowledge" (at least propositional knowledge) entails truth. A person does not know a proposition, strictly speaking, unless it is true. For example, it is incorrect to say that anybody ever knew that the earth is flat, assuming that it isn't true that the earth is flat. An ordinary speaker (who assumes that the earth is round) will resist saying that ancient people who believed in a flat earth *knew* that the earth is flat. They might be willing to say this in a scare-quoted way, to indicate that the believers in question *thought* they knew that the earth is flat, or would have *claimed* to know this. But this scare-quoted usage would typically be signaled by an appropriate intonation, calling attention to the nonstandardness of the speaker's utterance (given the assumed fact). It is not necessarily a fatal blunder for sociologists, anthropologists, historians, or other social scientists to use the term "knowledge" in a nonstandard, non-truth-entailing sense. I shall discuss the ramifications of this decision below. For now I merely mean to keep this fact in focus in trying to understand how and why different researchers might have very different conceptions of epistemology in general and social epistemology in particular. Even if everyone verbally agrees that epistemology is the study of knowledge, and that social epistemology studies the social dimensions of knowledge, this ostensibly shared starting point is an illusion if some people intend one thing by the term "knowledge" and others intend something entirely different.

Not all loose uses of "knowledge" equate it with belief pure and simple. Many writers place additional constraints on knowledge though not the constraint of truth. This is brings us to sense (2), a sense of "knowledge" employed by many sociologists of science. Consider the following passages from David Bloor, in *Knowledge and Social Imagery* (1976/1991).

> [T]here are many intuitive connections between knowledge and society. Knowledge has to be gathered, organized, sustained, transmitted and distributed. These are all processes visibly connected with established institutions: the laboratory, the workplace, the university, the church, the school. (53)

> The strong programme [Bloor's own position] says that the social component is always present and always constitutive of knowledge. (166)

On Bloor's understanding of "knowledge," we don't have knowledge unless individual believers belong to a community that has a way of bringing order to cognitive affairs. Knowledge is presented as a "collective representation of the world [that] is constituted out of individual representations. This shared conception of the world . . . will be held by the group as a convention, not as an atomized set of individual dispositions" (1976/1991, 169). Thus, only *institutionalized* belief, it appears, qualifies as knowledge under Bloor's conception.

A similar approach is found in Steven Shapin's *A Social History of Truth* (1994), here applied partially to "truth" rather than "knowledge," though the two are not carefully distinguished:

> What counts for any community as true knowledge is a collective good and a collective accomplishment. That good is always in others' hands, and the fate of any particular claim that something "is the case" is never determined by the individual making the claim. This is a sense in which one may say that truth is a matter of collective judgment and that it is stabilized by the collective actions which use it as a standard for judging other claims. In short, truth is a social institution and is, therefore, a fit and proper topic for the sociologist's investigation. (5–6)

This "institutional" characterization of truth and knowledge makes it obvious, of course, why epistemology, as the study of knowledge, must be social. For present purposes, however, the point I am stressing is that this is still a loose sense of "knowledge." Although truth is nominally brought into Shapin's account of knowledge, truth for him is just a matter of other people's judgments or beliefs. So knowledge reduces to a matter of shared beliefs—not at all what orthodox ("realist") epistemologists have in mind by truth as a condition of knowing.

I turn now to the two "strict" senses of knowledge on my list, and I start with (4). Mainstream philosophical epistemologists (going back to Plato) almost unanimously hold that mere belief or opinion is not sufficient for knowledge, that knowledge also requires truth. Furthermore, they almost all concur that true belief does not qualify as knowledge unless it is justified, warranted, or acquired in some suitable fashion (e.g., by reliable methods). In brief, justified true belief is necessary for knowing. The argument for the justification condition on knowledge is based on linguistic intuitions about selected cases. Suppose that a Chinese philosopher who is acquainted with American epistemologists suddenly forms the belief that Alvin Goldman awoke at 7:00 that morning. Although this philosopher has no perceptual or testimonial evidence about the matter, his belief happens to be true. Wouldn't we be disinclined to say that this person "knows" that Goldman awoke at that hour? This kind of case motivates a justification or warrant condition for knowledge, because justification is what seems to be lacking here. Edmund Gettier (1963) went on to show that knowledge requires even more than justified true belief, though the nature of that extra ingredient is controversial.

Although I don't dispute the existence of one sense of "knowledge" that corresponds roughly to (4), I think there is also a second, weaker sense of "knowledge" captured by (3). In this weaker sense, to know that p is simply to possess the information that p, where "information" entails truth but "possession" merely entails belief, not necessarily justified or warranted belief.

This sense of "knowledge" is proposed in Goldman (1999), and John Haw-thorne (2000) offers the following example to support it. Suppose a teacher wonders which of her students know that Vienna is the capital of Austria. She would surely count a pupil as knowing this fact if the pupil believes (and is disposed to answer) that Vienna is the capital of Austria, even if the student's belief is based on very poor evidence. The teacher would classify the pupil as one of those who "know" without inquiring into the basis of his/her belief, and even in the face of evidence that it was a poor basis. So there seems to be a sense of "know" that corresponds to sense (3).

What conceptions of social epistemology are naturally associated with the disparate uses of "knowledge" we have identified? If knowledge is belief, as in sense (1), then the study of knowledge is the study of belief, and presumably this means a study of the *causes* of belief. This is the mission of the social science disciplines I identified above. Now if knowledge is merely belief, and if epistemology as the study of knowledge is the study of all sorts of causes of belief, there should be a part of epistemology that isn't social. After all, aren't there psychological mechanisms of belief-causation that involve no social or interpersonal ingredients? I have in mind biologically endowed equipment such as perceptual mechanisms, memory mechanisms, counting mechanisms, and rudimentary inference mechanisms. Using innate perceptual equipment, infants form perceptual beliefs about nonsocial stimuli, for example, beliefs about the shapes and locations of objects. Explaining these beliefs would not seem to require any appeal to social factors. To pinpoint the junctures at which social factors enter the story is, no doubt, quite a delicate matter, but there seem to be some extrasocial factors at work (in any reasonable sense of "social" that might be chosen). So epistemology, construed as the study of the causes of belief, would not study only the *social* causes of belief, it would have nonsocial parts as well.

Sense (2) of "knowledge" presents a slightly different picture. If knowledge is institutionalized belief, then perhaps all epistemology would be social epistemology, because all the factors responsible for belief institutionalization are (arguably) social factors. This is certainly maintained by the Edinburgh School, and by many other practitioners in the social studies of science (or science and technology studies). All explanations of scientific knowledge are held to be social explanations. First, social bodies are responsible for the specific practices that comprise the distinctive matrix and methods of science. Second, groups of individuals, working in tandem or in disputatious interchange, comprise the actors that determine or prosecute the course of science. Members of the Edinburgh School, and of other movements in the social studies of science, often mean by "social factors" something more specific and restricted than the foregoing suggests, as will be discussed later. For now, however, we can admit that if "knowledge" is restricted to institutionalized belief, it is plausible to expect epistemology to be social through and through.

This perspective helps explain why Barnes and Bloor (1982) urged their "symmetry" or "equivalence" postulate, according to which all beliefs are on a par with one another with respect to the causes of their credibility. If one ignores differences among beliefs such as their truth-values and their justification statuses, and if one focuses on them purely as the outputs of an institutional network or set of conventions, then all scientific beliefs might have similar causes—at least causes of *certain* types. However, although beliefs in different categories may share *certain* types of causes, they may also have contrasting causes of *other* types. As James Robert Brown points out, it depends on the chosen level of generality (1989, 39). While the same principles of physics apply to both standing bridges and collapsing bridges, different specific explanatory factors will have to be cited to explain why one bridge collapsed and why another is still standing. An earthquake would explain the former but not the latter.

When we turn to the strict senses of "knowledge," (3) and (4), the picture of epistemology in general and social epistemology in particular changes fairly dramatically. Even if we stick to a causal-explanatory conception of the epistemological mission (a conception to be mooted later), there are likely to be significant differences. Starting with sense (3), epistemology would study the distinctive causes of true beliefs; it would try to explain why true beliefs are acquired in some scenarios and false beliefs (or no beliefs at all) in others. This yields a rather different set of questions than the ones posed when trying to explain beliefs per se, or institutionalized beliefs. Admittedly, in trying to explain a true belief, it might be possible to construct a "bifurcated conjunctive explanation," an explanation that combines an explanation of the belief with a wholly separate explanation of the fact that makes this belief true. When these component explanations are combined, there is a conjunctive explanation of the belief and of its being true. However, this is not the kind of explanation of true belief that is likely to interest an epistemologist, even a descriptive-explanatory epistemologist. Rather, an epistemologist would like to explain not just the occurrence of single beliefs that happen to be true; he or she would like to explain patterns of truth alignment for various sets of beliefs. If some beliefs are regularly aligned with the truth, how does that transpire? What features of the methods or practices used in forming these beliefs account for this result? If another set of beliefs are not so well aligned with the truth, what features of the belief-forming methods or practices produce this result? An interest in the causal production of belief persists here, but it focuses on the pattern of truth values among the beliefs and seeks an understanding of these patterns. Nothing resembling this interest arises from senses (1) or (2) of "knowledge."

Now it could turn out that although something explains a pattern of truth versus falsehood in a given set of beliefs, nothing *social* accounts for this pattern. Suppose that the pattern is one of 60% accuracy or reliability, and this is explained by the fact that 60% of the time believers use rational methods of inference and 40% of the time they do not. (Moreover, suppose that no social factor is responsible for this incidence of rational inference.) Assuming these rational inferential methods are purely individualistic, there would be no *social* explanation for the pattern of truth versus falsity. If this story were typical, this would cast doubt on social epistemology's prospects for contributing to the study of knowledge construed as true belief. Social factors might explain the repertoire of concepts out of which belief contents are created, but social factors would not tilt beliefs toward truth rather than falsehood. However, several social epistemologists—for example, Philip Kitcher, Hilary Kornblith, and I—have ventured the hypothesis that social factors *do* make systematic differences to truth-value outcomes (Goldman 1987, 1999; Kitcher 1993, 1994; Kornblith 1994). This yields a "veritistic" conception of social epistemology of the sort developed at length in Goldman 1999.

Suppose now that knowledge is *justified* true belief, and for simplicity ignore the extra factors needed to accommodate the Gettier problem. Can there be a social epistemology of knowledge so construed? Proceeding in parallel with the foregoing discussion, this would seem to depend on whether there are social factors that tilt not only toward true as contrasted with false belief but toward justified as contrasted with unjustified belief. Is this a plausible idea, and how could it work in detail? One possibility is that justificational status can depend on social factors that figure in a belief's formation. A second possibility is that, although justificational status depends wholly on the psychological processes of the believer, the selection or choice of these psychological processes is influenced by social factors. In other words, in this second scenario, social factors tilt individual cognizers toward deployment or failure to deploy the kinds of psychological processes that yield justifiedness. Since either of these scenarios would suffice for the viability of social epistemology under the fourth construal of "knowledge," its prospects for viability may be robust. However, the exact role of social factors in a justification-oriented epistemology will receive more attention later.

Inclusiveness versus Exclusiveness

In the foregoing discussion I have tentatively adopted a relatively ecumenical or inclusive posture toward the varied conceptions of social epistemology on offer. But not everybody adopts this posture, and it isn't one that I have always adopted, so several comments are in order. Proponents of more radical approaches to social epistemology rarely defend their approach by terminological preference, by appeal to a loose sense of "knowledge." Vindication of their approach is more typically accompanied by a rejection of the very possibility of traditional approaches to epistemology, for example, truth-oriented or justification-oriented approaches. So their stance or posture is the opposite of inclusive or ecumenical. Social epistemology is frequently viewed as a *replacement* or *successor* subject, one that should supplant classical epistemology once the latter's demise is acknowledged. Under this conception social epistemology presupposes the "death" of classical epistemology.

Reports of epistemology's death, however, are greatly exaggerated. What are the alleged causes of death? At least two themes pervade Richard Rorty's *Philosophy and the Mirror of Nature* (1979), which proclaimed this death. First, there is no legitimate conception of truth as mirroring, or correspondence. Second, the traditional, foundationalist notion of epistemic justification is bankrupt, because (as Dewey, Quine, and others have shown) there are no "certain" propositions to serve as foundations. Neither of these themes is at all convincing, however, as an argument for classical epistemology's death.

Starting with truth, many respectable epistemologists have recently defended a correspondence theory, or at least a closely related "realist" theory (Alston 1996; David 1994; Kitcher 1993; Schmitt 1995). Second, and more importantly, a correspondence theory of truth is probably not a precondition for a truth-oriented epistemology. Even if some form of deflationism, for example, provides the best way to define or characterize the use of the term "true," there are still differences in truth-values among propositions: some are true and others are false. This is all that is needed to defend the integrity and significance of the traditional epistemological project of trying to identify better and worse methods of forming beliefs, that is, methods that are better or worse at getting the truth and avoiding falsehood (cf. Goldman 1999, 66–68).

Rorty's attack on foundationalist justification is equally inconclusive and misguided. Although foundationalism of a Cartesian flavor—foundationalism predicated on infallible foundations—is indeed largely moribund, weaker forms of foundationalism continue to flourish in epistemology. These weaker forms hold that certain beliefs are foundational in the sense that they acquire prima facie justification from some source other than inference, but these foundational beliefs are not infallible or immune to revision. Justification requires no such immunity under weak or moderate foundationalism. In addition to this non-Cartesian form of foundationalism, other options in justification-theory abound, including coherentism and reliabilism. So even if the report of foundationalism's collapse were correct, it would not be the death knell of justification-centered epistemology.

In the social studies of science Thomas Kuhn's remarks against (correspondence) truth are probably more influential than Rorty's. Kuhn disparaged the idea of salvaging any notion of a theory "matching" nature: "[T]he notion of a match between the ontology of a theory and its 'real' counterpart in nature now seems to me illusive in principle" (1962/1970, 206). As Philip

Kitcher (1993, 130) points out, however,—Kuhn confines his strictures on truth to its application to "whole theories." He is comfortable with the idea that progress occurs in science in the form of improvements in "puzzle solutions" and "concrete predictions." Kuhn writes : "I do not doubt, for example, that Newton's mechanics improves on Aristotle's and that Einstein's improves on Newton's as instruments for puzzle-solving" (1962/1970, 206). Yet how can good sense be made of progress in puzzle solutions and concrete predictions without recourse to the notion of truth?

But perhaps Kuhn and his followers are worried by the fact that there is no Archimedean point from which one can have access to both a theory and nature to see whether there is a match. We have no theory-independent way of *knowing* when a match between theory and nature occurs. In reply, the first point to make is that the objection shifts the question from whether there *is* such a thing as a match between theory and nature to the different question of whether we can *know* about such a match in a theory-independent way. Second, a truth critic who argues in this fashion invokes the very notion of "knowledge" that is currently under dispute. This critic relies on a notion of (objective) justification in virtue of which it is allegedly impossible to be justified in believing that a match between theory and nature obtains. Such a point could not be sustained if there were no bona fide notion of justification, the obtaining of which is precluded in the present instance. (If knowledge were equated with mere belief, for example, there would be no problem about "knowing" that a theory matches nature; for it is certainly possible for someone to *believe* that there is such a match.)

The foregoing are some of the grounds—quite insufficient grounds, by my lights—on which radical social epistemologists reject traditional conceptions of epistemology rooted in definitions (3) or (4) of "knowledge." Later I shall review another such challenge from social constructivism. Meanwhile, what should we say about classical epistemologists who reject definitions (1) and (2), and dismiss conceptions of (social) epistemology associated with them? Are these dismissals legitimate; or do they merely reflect an obtuse rigidity rooted in terminological obsession?

I myself often emphasize the distinction between belief and knowledge, as well as the distinction between the study of the former and the study of the latter (see the distinction between "doxology" and "epistemology" in Goldman 2001a, reprinted here as chapter 8). This emphasis stems from more than a terminological obsession. It obviously doesn't matter which *words* are used to mark the concepts of true belief, justified belief, and the like, so long as these concepts are retained in our theoretical tool kit. There would be no substantive loss if the term "knowledge" were ceded to cognitive scientists, sociologists of knowledge, or intellectual historians who wish to use it to designate belief. Few traditional epistemologists would object to any of these fields as legitimate empirical subjects. But what would be gained by ceding

the terms "knowledge" or "epistemology" to these disciplines? Other perfectly good terms are already available both for the disciplines themselves
and for the subject matter they share, namely, states of belief. On the other
hand, a change in terminology that shifts the meaning of "knowledge" away
from its strict meaning(s) does pose a danger. The danger is not the change
in terminology per se. The serious threat is the potential loss of concepts
traditionally marked by the strict sense(s) of "knowledge," and the attendant
loss of inquiries that concern themselves with knowledge in this (these) strict
sense(s). Of course, if a robust case were made that the concepts of truth,
justification, and their ilk have no legitimate use or viability, then the anticipated losses would not matter. But despite the efforts of radical social epistemologists or death-of-epistemology purveyors, no good case of this kind
has been mounted (though many people have been wrongly persuaded that
it has). Against this background, it is inadvisable to abandon the strict uses
of "knowledge" and "epistemology" in favor of new, loose uses that would
simply obscure important types of inquiries.

In resisting conceptions of social epistemology based on loose senses of
"knowledge," I do not mean to reject all aspects of radical social epistemologies. For example, some styles of radical social epistemology seem bent on
showing by historical examples how science is riddled through and through
with social causes *and* that these causes undermine the truth-status or justificational status of scientifically accepted beliefs. I would cheerfully recognize
these claims as legitimate forms of social epistemology (which is not to say
that I would accept all such claims), precisely because they bear on questions
of truth or justification. What I reject are attempts to defend radical social
epistemologies by appeal to premature and poorly argued dismissals of the
key elements of classical epistemology: knowledge (in one of its strict
senses), truth, and justification.

What Is the "Social" in Social Epistemology?

When writers call their preferred brand of epistemology "social," what do
they mean to say about it? In what sense of "social" is social epistemology
social? Different projects for social epistemology fasten on different conceptions of the social. In early formulations of the sociology of knowledge,
"social factors" referred primarily to various types of "interests": class interests, political interests, or anything else having to do with the "real" or "existential" world of power and politics. Early proponents of sociology of
knowledge and sociology of science such as Karl Mannheim (1936) and
Robert Merton (1973) exempted natural science from the influence of societal
or "existential" factors of the types that influence other categories of belief.
Science was viewed as a society unto itself, largely autonomous from the rest

of society. But later sociologists of science have declined to offer the same exemption. It is a cardinal point of the Edinburgh school, or the "Strong Programme" in the sociology of science, that even physical science is contaminated by social factors. In both cases, however, "social factors" refers to interests or proclivities linked to class, politics, or other societal movements with no intrinsic relation to the scientific matter at hand. Historical cases studies of science within the Strong Programme have sought to show how scientists were swayed by considerations "external" to the scientific issues and evidence before them. Paul Forman (1971) tried to show how scientists of the Weimar Republic endorsed antideterministic views in physics because of public pressure and an intellectual milieu that emphasized the importance of "spiritual values" and "the mystery of things," and which found fault with the principle of causality. Steven Shapin (1975) argued that phrenology, a theory of mental faculties, was powerfully supported in Edinburgh in the early nineteenth century because it became associated with a social reformist movement. According to Shapin, the debates over phrenology in Edinburgh were heavily influenced by class affiliations. Phrenology was supported by the middle and working classes, whose institutions regularly offered courses on the subject and gave it pride of place. At the Edinburgh University, by contrast, phrenology was never taught. Shapin's social account of the matter is disputed by G. N. Cantor (1975), but here I am not interested in assessing the merits of their dispute. The present point is that all parties to the dispute agree that "social factors" refers to factors lying outside the evidential or epistemic realm. "Social" factors contrast with "rational" factors. With this usage of "social" in mind, Larry Laudan proposed his "arationality principle": "the sociology of knowledge may step in to explain beliefs if and only if those beliefs cannot be explained in terms of their rational merits" (Laudan 1977, 202). This dichotomizing principle makes sense if sociology deals with social factors and if social factors are extra-epistemic or extra-rational states of affairs.

If one adopts the foregoing conception of "social factors," a call for the total "socialization" of the epistemology of science would naturally be associated with a conviction than science is not driven by "rational" factors; and this is indeed the conviction of Strong Programmers. A different conception of the "social," however, might situate social factors squarely within the realm of the rational and the epistemic. This perspective is shared by such social epistemologists of science as Helen Longino and Philip Kitcher, who are otherwise quite different.

Longino is quite explicit in her desire to transcend the dichotomizing of the social and the cognitive (1993, 260). She advocates a brand of contextualism about scientific inquiry that emphasizes the social context in which scientific work takes place but sees this context as an integral part of the epistemic nature of science. The epistemic normativity of science is rooted in this social context. "[T]he rules or norms of justification that distinguish knowledge (as justified hypothesis acceptance) from opinion must operate at the level of social as opposed to individual cognitive processes" (1993, 260). The main norm of science, on Longino's view, is that of objectivity, where "objectivity" refers to the avoidance of individual subjectivity and bias. She regards objectivity as a characteristic of a community's practice of science rather than a characteristic of an individual scientist. Crucial to objectivity is the use of critical discourse, so it is essential to a scientific community to have four features: recognized avenues for criticism, responsiveness of beliefs to critical discussion, shared standards of responsiveness to criticism, and equality of intellectual authority. Longino regards these features as conducive to epistemic justifiedness: "To say that a theory or hypothesis was accepted on the basis of objective methods does not guarantee that it is true, but it does—if anything does—justify us in asserting that it is true, for it reflects the critically achieved consensus of the scientific community" (1993, 268).

Kitcher similarly locates the social within the epistemic, not in opposition to it. Two of the main ingredients in Kitcher's (1993) sophisticated analysis of the epistemic advancement of science are social in nature: (1) consensus practices, and (2) the organization of cognitive labor. Kitcher's idea of a consensus practice is built up from the idea of an individual scientist's practice. An individual practice is a multidimensional entity that features the following components: (i) a scientific language, (ii) a set of questions identified as significant, (iii) a set of statements in the field that he accepts, (iv) a set of explanatory texts that he accepts, (v) a set of informants he regards as credible, (vi) some paradigms of experimentation and observation, and (vii) a methodology of scientific reasoning (1993, 74). From this notion of an individual practice, Kitcher constructs the notion of a consensus practice. A consensus practice is made up of the same elements as an individual practice, but it is associated with a scientific community. A *core consensus practice* consists in the elements of individual practice common to all members of the community. A *virtual consensus practice* is a practice generated by taking into account the statements, methodologies, and so on that all members accept "indirectly" by consensually deferring to other scientists as authorities or experts (1993, 88). Kitcher then proceeds to construct a notion, or family of notions, of scientific "progress." These focus on the progress of consensus practices and characterize progress in terms of improvements in getting significant truth and achieving explanatory success (1993, chap. 4). Thus, the cognitive achievements of science are located squarely at the social level, the level of consensus practices.

A second major social element in Kitcher's analysis concerns the division of cognitive labor (Kitcher 1990, 1993, chap. 8). The progress of science is optimized, he says, when there is an optimal distribution of effort within scientific communities. It may be better for a scientific community to attack a given problem by encouraging some members to pursue one strategy and others to pursue a different strategy. It may also be better for science if workers trust and rely on the work of others—at least selected others—rather than do everything by themselves. (Integrating the perspectives of multiple specialties can also be instrumental to epistemic success; see Solomon 1992.) In all such cases there is no conflict between the epistemic and the social dimensions of science.

The approaches discussed thus far regard the basic subjects of epistemic activity as individuals. Even the notion of a consensus practice is built up from individual practices; all cognitive states such as beliefs and acceptances (of hypotheses) seem to be attributed to individuals. However, don't we sometimes ascribe beliefs and/or knowledge to groups, that is, collective entities like companies, governments, and juries? So perhaps social epistemology should include—and even emphasize—collective entities as knowers. Several feminist epistemologists have gone even farther, proposing that the *only* knowers are communities. Lynn Hankinson Nelson writes:

> In suggesting that it is communities that construct and acquire knowledge, I do not mean (or "merely" mean) that what comes to be recognized or "certified" as knowledge is the result of collaboration between, consensus achieved by, political struggles engaged in, negotiations undertaken among, or other activities engaged in by individuals who, *as individuals*, know in some logically or empirically "prior" sense. . . . My arguments suggest that the collaborators, the consensus achievers, and, in more general terms, the agents who generate knowledge are communities and subcommunities, not individuals. (1993, 124)

Independent of feminist epistemology, an interest in collective subjects of "mental" states, including intention and belief, has grown in recent years, as reflected in book-length treatments by Margaret Gilbert (1989), Raimo Tuomela (1995), and John Searle (1995). They all share the idea that collective states of mind are philosophically legitimate, and if this is right, it should find a place within social epistemology. Is it necessary for this position to endorse ontological collectivism, that is, the view that there are collective minds above and beyond individual minds? Kay Mathiesen (2000) argues to the contrary. She claims that individuals can have "we intentions" by having appropriate mental contents, and that when a number of individuals share such an intention (and some further conditions are satisfied), it is appropriate to speak of a collective intention. The same idea might apply to collective beliefs.

It is presumably not sufficient for social epistemology that some notion of collective belief be legitimized. What must also be legitimized is the thesis that collective beliefs have epistemic properties. Only then could one speak of communities as knowers, as Nelson suggests. But perhaps this thesis is also defensible. Frederick Schmitt (1994) has argued that sense can be made of justification for group beliefs. So the door seems open to an enlarged conception of the "social" for social epistemological purposes.

Not everyone, however, is eager to embrace the notion of collective belief, or to make it pivotal in the development of social epistemology. More traditional approaches retain individuals as the agents or subjects of belief and knowledge, while emphasizing the massive effect of an individual's *relations to other agents* in the acquisition of knowledge. As we have seen, this is the core of Kitcher's approach in *The Advancement of Science,* and also of my approach in *Knowledge in a Social World.* Social epistemology can be built on social *relations* among individuals without committing itself to collective or socialized *agents* that bear epistemic properties.

Social Constructivism: A Metaphysics for Social Epistemology?

Earlier we examined some challenges to conceptions of social epistemology that are rooted in traditional epistemology. These were challenges to "realist" or objectivist conceptions of truth and justification. Another such challenge comes from the idea of social constructivism, an idea that serves as an underpinning for many radical social epistemologies. In its most interesting and relevant forms, social constructivism is ostensibly a kind of metaphysics. Its exact metaphysical position is difficult to pinpoint, however, and the metaphysical interpretations that make it significant are extremely difficult to sustain.

Though metaphysical in substance, the chief motivation behind social constructivism may well be political or reformist (Hacking 1999, chap. 1). A social constructivist typically begins by arguing that some X (gender, for example) is merely socially constructed rather than found "in nature." He proceeds to argue that X (or perhaps our conception of X) is merely contingent, not at all inevitable. Finally, he argues that X (or our current conception of X) is a bad thing and ought to be done away with or radically transformed. Our concern is not with the political or actional conclusions to be drawn, but rather with the metaphysical premises on which they are based. If social constructivists are right in saying, for example, that there are no objective facts or truths, or no facts independent of social construction, that might indeed pose difficulties for objectivist social epistemologies and tilt toward radical, nonobjectivist social epistemologies. This type of claim about facts is found in classic treatments of social constructivism, such as Bruno Latour and Steve Woolgar's *Laboratory Life: The Social Construction of Scientific Facts* (1979/1986) and Andrew Pickering's *Constructing Quarks* (1984).

It is essential to distinguish between weak and strong versions of social constructivism. The distinction hinges on what, exactly, is said to be constructed. Weak social constructivism is the view that *representations*—either linguistic representations or mental representations—are social constructs. When it is said that "gender" is constructed, a weak interpretation of this is merely that people's *representations* or *conceptions* of gender are socially constructed. Similarly, when it is said that scientific facts or entities are socially constructed, a weak interpretation of this is merely that scientists' *beliefs* or *theories* are socially constructed. This weak form of social constructivism is a rather innocuous doctrine, which would probably be agreed to by almost everybody (at least when applied to the sorts of cases just illustrated). But weak social constructivism poses no challenge to objectivism about facts or truth that classical epistemologists commonly endorse. That *representations* are socially constructed is compatible with there being mind-independent and community-independent *facts* that render such representations true or false, veridical or nonveridical. Strong social constructivism claims not only that scientists' *representations* of quarks or thyrotropin releasing hormone are socially constructed, but that *quarks themselves* and *thyrotropin releasing hormone itself* are socially constructed. This is a much more dramatic thesis, but also much more dubious.

What does strong social constructivism mean in saying that scientific facts or entities are socially constructed? What exactly is the metaphysical thesis? Andre Kukla (2000) distinguishes between *causal constructivism* and *constitutive constructivism*. Causal constructivism is the view that human activity causes and sustains the facts about the world (including scientific facts), whereas constitutive constructivism is the view that what we call "facts about the world" are really just facts about human activity (2000, 21). Causal constructivism would seem to be an empirical thesis, a thesis about causal relations. While it seems clear that human activity produces certain entities and facts, such as cabinets and computers, social constructivists about science (such as Latour and Woolgar or Pickering) seem to make the surprising claim that even (unsynthesized) biological chemicals and fundamental particles are so produced and sustained in existence. At least this would be the claim if they are interpreted as causal constructivists. But what could be the evidence that supports this? Could social scientists or "anthropologists" who study the laboratory have observed that these entities did not exist at one point in time and then started to exist after the scientists began their investigations? Could they have observed that these entities ceased to exist once humans stopped studying and talking about them? Surely not!

Perhaps scientific social constructivists mean to endorse constitutive constructivism. This position does not claim that human activity is causally responsible for (though ontologically distinct from) the entities in question; rather, it claims that human activity makes up, or constitutes, these entities. Kukla examines the possible details of such a metaphysical position and finds problems in every direction. One possible position is that the ultimate constituents of reality are social episodes such as negotiations and agreements, and that the rest of the world is made up of this primordial social material (Kukla 2000, 28). He calls this "metaphysical socialism." As Kukla indicates, however, this kind of reductionist metaphysics is very problematic. He also proceeds to amass a series of extremely serious problems for any attempt to develop strong social constructivism in any detail. The proper conclusion, I submit, is that strong social constructivism is a highly unpalatable metaphysical theory and that nobody should abandon objectivist or veritistic social epistemology because of it.

It should be emphasized, however, that there are important strands of social constructivism that survive the demise of *strong* social constructivism. Many social sciences are concerned with specific historical and/or cultural development of core social ideas: how people view gender or how they conceive of it. These inquiries fit comfortably under the heading of *weak* social constructivism, and nothing said here raises any quarrels with weak social constructivism.

Issues of Scope, Partition, and Methodology

There are many choices to make in developing a project of social epistemology. Among these are (A) choices of scope, (B) choices of partition, and (C) choices of methodology. Under the "scope" heading there is the question of whether social epistemology should subsume all types of social-intellectual endeavors or only selected endeavors. Let us call this a choice between a *universal* and a *special* conception of social epistemology.

The field of social studies of science, or science and technology studies, comprises the largest body of researchers in the general area of social epistemology (though they do not characteristically use this label). When they talk about issues of social epistemology, they focus exclusively on science; so this is one example of a "special" conception of the field. The science emphasis is hardly surprising, since science is generally regarded as the prototype of a knowledge-producing enterprise. Whatever knowledge is thought to be, science is "where it's at." So why shouldn't social epistemology train its microscope on the domain of science? This leaves open the question of how, exactly, social epistemology should study science. It might be studied in a purely descriptive-explanatory fashion, on the model of case studies illustrated earlier. Alternatively, it might be studied in a normative spirit, seeking to assess better and worse forms of science "policy," as Steve Fuller (1988, 1993, 2000) advocates under his conception of social epistemology.

A universal conception of social epistemology would study all forms of social interaction that have significant knowledge-producing or knowledge-disseminating properties. This is the sort of conception developed in my

Knowledge in a Social World. Under this conception everyday knowledge as well as scientific knowledge is of concern to social epistemology. Science as an institution is not the only institution of interest, but also such institutions and technologies as education, libraries, and the Internet. Legal policies that affect the flow of communication (and hence information) also fall within social epistemology's domain.

Suppose one accepts a universal conception of social epistemology. One then confronts the question of how to partition the field. Nobody can study everything at once, and some kinds of specialization seem imperative. So how should social epistemology be structured or organized? In *Knowledge in a Social World* I tackled this problem by distinguishing between "generic" and "domain-specific" social practices, what one might call "global" versus "local" practices. Global practices cut across all subject matters or fields of inquiry. Local practices are specific to a particular topic or field of endeavor. The global practices I selected were (i) testimony (communications intended to be understood as factual reports) (ii) interpersonal argumentation, (iii) the use of communication technologies, and (iv) general policies of supervising the flow of communication, including governmental policies on freedom of speech. The domain-specific practices I chose were (i) science, (ii) law, (iii) politics, and (iv) education. In the arena of law, for example, systems of legal adjudication were the target. Which trial methods constitute the best devices for courts to arrive at accurate judgments of guilt or innocence, liability or nonliability? How does the Anglo-American adversarial system compare with the so-called inquisitorial system of Continental Europe? Which specific rules of evidence would best promote accurate verdicts? Other special topics that might have received more attention are journalism and library science. One of the first calls for a social epistemology was made by a library scientist, Jesse Shera (1961, 1970); and many issues in contemporary library and information science fit into the perspective of a truth-based social epistemology (Fallis 2000).

Once a scope and domain are chosen, the social epistemologist must decide which methodologies or research paradigms to employ. Choices will partly depend, of course, on whether a descriptive or a normative approach is taken. In either case, however, a plethora of methodologies are available. In the history and sociology of science, case studies and "field" studies (of laboratories) are most typical. Another methodology is the application of rhetoric to scientific discourse (McCloskey 1985; Fuller 1993; Latour 1987). Philosophers who study argumentation and debate are more likely to turn to the tools of logic and probability theory. Indeed, probability theory, including Bayesian techniques, can be used for many segments and styles of social epistemology (Goldman 1999, chap. 4; Lehrer and Wagner 1981; Fallis 1999). A significant part of economics—namely, the economics of information—can be viewed as part of social epistemology, so the various techniques of information economics are part of the potential research tool kit. I have collaborated with an economist, James Cox, in applying economic analysis to two topics in social epistemology: journalism and the marketplace rationale for free speech (Cox and Goldman 1994; Goldman and Cox 1996). The main tool of information economics is game theory, and a game-theoretic approach has been used by William Talbott and me to analyze the adversarial process in civil litigation (Talbott and Goldman 1998). Deploying a more neoclassical style of economic analysis, the economists William Brock and Steven Durlauf (1999) have created a formal model of theory choice in science.

Normative Approaches

Having examined descriptive approaches to social epistemology in some detail (at least the science studies approach), I shall look more closely at normative approaches, especially because classical epistemology is traditionally a normative enterprise. In this section I illustrate the diversity of normative approaches by identifying four conceptions of epistemic normativity. In the following section I turn to yet a fifth specimen of normativity for social epistemology. The four conceptions presented in this section would each invite social epistemology to evaluate some designated social-epistemic practices in terms of their tendencies to promote or inhibit a distinctive goal or value. In other words, each would adopt some consequentialist foundation for normativity. The four goals or values are (A) true belief, (B) consensus, (C) rationality, and (D) cognitive democracy.

True belief (knowledge in the strict but weak sense) was discussed earlier, though not much in the context of normative approaches. The normative assessment of social practices in terms of true-belief conduciveness is the "veritistic" approach that characterizes *Knowledge in a Social World*. The idea is to assess a wide range of social practices in terms of their positive or negative contributions toward true belief. In contrast to the descriptive approach, normative veritism would not confine itself to social practices *actually* used by this or that community, but would equally concern itself with practices that *could* be adopted.

The truth-oriented approach fits comfortably with classical epistemology, but is also found in writers whose general orientation is frequently at odds with classical epistemology, for example, feminist epistemology. Here are some passages by a feminist epistemologist, Elizabeth Anderson:

> Social epistemology is the branch of naturalized epistemology that investigates the influence of specifically social factors on knowledge production: who gets to participate in theoretical inquiry, who listens to whom, the relative prestige of different styles and fields of research . . . and so forth. Feminist epistemology can be regarded as the branch of social epistemology that investigates the influ-

ence of *socially constructed conceptions and norms of gender and gender-specific interests and experiences* on the production of knowledge. (1995b, 54)

Some of [our belief-forming] processes are such that, once we reflect on how they work or what they do, we lose confidence in the beliefs to which they give rise, since they do not reliably lead to true beliefs. . . . Other processes satisfy the reflective endorsement test: reflecting on how they work or what they do leads us to endorse them and the beliefs to which they give rise. . . . A knowledge practice is rational to the extent that it promotes such critical self-reflections and responds to them by checking or canceling out the unreliable belief-formation mechanisms and enabling the reliable ones. (1995b, 55)

As the second passage makes particularly clear, Anderson is interested in practices that facilitate "reliable"—that is, truth-promoting—processes and that disable "unreliable"—falsehood-promoting—processes. Thus, the ultimate aim is one of promoting true belief and avoiding false belief. Under Anderson's picture of social epistemology, including the feminist branch of social epistemology, the aim is to contribute to the truth-promoting enterprise by examining specifically social factors that bear on knowledge production. Thus, Anderson's conception of social epistemology is fundamentally veritistic (though she adds explanation as a further desideratum beyond truth).

I turn next to the second type of goal: consensus, or agreement. Here I choose an example from the theory of argumentation, construed as a social, that is, interpersonal, practice. Although this is just one practice in the domain of social epistemology, it is an important one. A number of argumentation theorists, including Frans van Eemeren and Rob Grootendorst, conceive of argumentation as a practice aimed at settling disputes, or resolving disagreements. Under this conception it is natural to evaluate the goodness of arguments in terms of their ability to resolve disagreement, that is, to achieve agreement. Van Eemeren and Grootendorst (1984) advance a code of argumentative conduct for rational discussants, which features the following norm of rationality:

A language user taking part in an argumentative discussion is a rational language user if in the course of the discussion he performs only speech acts which accord with a system of rules acceptable to all discussants which furthers the creation of a dialectic which can lead to a resolution of the dispute at the center of the discussion. (18)

To illustrate the third goal, the goal of rationality, I turn to a specimen of social epistemology by Keith Lehrer and Carl Wagner (1981). Lehrer and Wagner are concerned with the question of how a subject should adjust his initial degree of belief in a proposition as a function of the beliefs by other people whom the subject "respects." There is no attempt to explain exactly how to assign respect or trust to others. But assuming that a subject does assign some levels of trust to various other individuals (as well as to himself),

Lehrer and Wagner pose the question of how such a subject should proceed from there, if he is to be rational. Taking a community of subjects who assign trust to one another, how should the profile of opinions in the community change over time if all the subjects in the community are rational? Lehrer and Wagner argue that it is rational for subjects to make *iterated* revisions of belief over indefinitely many stages. When a subject changes his degree of belief by taking account of others' opinions, that should not end the matter. He and the others (if they do the same) now have new degrees of belief, and these may still diverge. If so, the same operation should repeated. Rational agents will repeat the operation until there is consensus, and Lehrer and Wagner identify some fairly weak conditions under which such consensus will be reached. So the Lehrer-Wagner approach highlights rationality as the basis for social-epistemic conduct, though it also stresses consensus as a by-product of rationality.

Three democracy-based normative theorists of social epistemology are Jurgen Habermas, Steve Fuller, and Philip Kitcher. Habermas (1984) does not explicitly talk of social epistemology, but his ideal speech situation is clearly a sort of social-epistemic tool, and it is designed with a democratic goal or constraint in mind, namely, equal participation in the cognitive-epistemic sphere. Steve Fuller talks explicitly of social epistemology, and explicitly links it to democratic aims. "Social epistemology is devoted to recovering that lost space in the academic sphere [where the general ends and means of science can be debated] and contributing to a democratization of science in the public sphere" (2000, 7–8). In his most recent book, Kitcher (2001) treats the epistemic goal of science as subservient to the aims of democracy.

Justification-Based Normativity: The Epistemology of Testimony

I have reserved this final section for the most popular angle on social epistemology in current analytic epistemology, namely, the justification of testimony-based belief. The standard question in the epistemology of testimony is normative because it is usually formulated in terms of the normative terms "justified" or "warranted." This standard question concerns the conditions or circumstances in which a hearer is justified or warranted in accepting a speaker's testimony that p. What (if anything) must the hearer be justified in believing about the speaker to merit justification in believing p? Must he be justified in believing that the speaker is reliable and sincere? If so, can such supporting justification be based on other testimony, or must it ultimately be based on nontestimonial sources, for example, perception and inductive inference? In other words, is testimony a "basic" source of justification, or is it a "derivative" source that must inferentially rest on other kinds of sources? (See chapter 7 for a brief excursus into this question and for the citation of selected literature.)

It might be argued that a resolution of this issue is central to the status of social epistemology, because if testimony is a basic source of justification, this imports an irreducibly social element into the very core of epistemic justification. If testimonial justifiedness is merely derivative from other sources of justification, however, the social factor in justification reduces to nonsocial factors.

Whether testimony is a basic or a nonbasic source of justification, the problem of justification might be viewed as a problem for individual epistemology, because it concerns the question of how an individual doxastic agent should fix his beliefs. Whether the belief in question is about rocks, trees, or the credibility of a speaker, it is still a question for the doxastic agent, who must use his own cognitive resources—for example, his perceptual experiences, prior beliefs, and so forth—as evidence. Even if the question of trusting other people introduces a distinctively social dimension, the present position might claim that this social dimension is embedded in an individualist, or egocentric, perspective. From this vantage point, social epistemology is encased within individual epistemology.

In contrast with this vantage point, a few theorists of testimony (e.g., Burge 1993; Schmitt 1994b) propose a *transpersonal, transmissional,* or *preservationist* conception of justification. Under this conception a hearer is testimonially justified in believing p only if the *testifier* justifiably believes p. To confer justification on a hearer, the testifier must exist and must actually *be* justified in believing p. It is not sufficient that the hearer believe, or even justifiably believe, that the testifier is justified. This conception is analogous to a conception of memorial justification according to which S's later belief in p is justified only if that belief has a memory link with an earlier belief of S in p that was itself justified. Memory does not "create" justification out of nothing, but only preserves it from one temporal stage to another of the same person. Since transmissional justification depends on the (justificational) properties of both speaker and hearer, it is arguably more "social" than the purely personal conception of testimonial justification.

Under the transmissional conception of testimonial justification, testimonial justification would share certain generally recognized features of knowledge (in sense [4]). Since Gettier (1963), it is recognized that in order for someone's justified belief in p to qualify as knowledge, the belief in p must be true and other closely related beliefs must also be true. A justified true belief can fail to be knowledge because other things believed by the subject (for example, premises on which his belief in p is based) are false. Similarly, if we accept the transmissional conception of testimonial justification, then in order for a hearer to be justified in believing p it will not be sufficient that he is *justified* in believing that the testifier justifiably believes that p. In addition, this latter proposition must be *true:* the testifier must in fact justifiably believe that p. This feature of transmissional justification will obviously be unacceptable to a pure internalist about justification (see chapter 1), because the truth or falsity of a testifier's justifiedness is "external" to the hearer under any standard construal of "external" and "internal". Externalists about justification, however, would not have the same reason for qualms about the notion of transmissional justification. Still, the fact that it passes externalist muster, so to speak, doesn't mean that the transmissional notion is acceptable.

In fact, there are other reasons to question the acceptability of the transmissional notion, or theory, of testimonial justification. Consider this example. Ten people are witnesses to a given event, but the event occurs at dusk and no witness sees the relevant details with full clarity. Each believes proposition p concerning this event, but none of them is fully justified in believing p. All ten witnesses independently tell hearer H that p is the case, based on their personal observation. Suppose H infers that p is the case. Is H's belief in p fully justified? According to the transmissional conception, H cannot have full testimonial justification vis-à-vis p. No testifier could have transmitted such justification to H, because by hypothesis no testifier *had* such justification to transmit. However, it does seem as if H can have full justification in believing p, because H might be justified in believing that the ten observations were mutually independent and the witnesses were highly unlikely to arrive at the same judgment unless it were true. (On the importance and interpretation of independence, see chapter 7.)

The defender of transmissional justification might reply to this example as follows. Granting that H has full justification in this case, it is not clear that this full justification is (pure) *testimonial* justification. After all, part of what makes H fully justified in believing p is his ancillary information about the independence of the several witnesses. The defender of transmissional justification might advance his theory only as a theory of *pure* testimonial justification, which would not include the present example. However, I reply, if any ancillary information used by a hearer disqualifies a case from being pure testimonial justification, there may be very few cases, if any, of pure testimonial justification. The transmissional theory would then become quite uninteresting. An interesting theory would cover the full gamut of testimonial justification, but the proposed fix to avert the counterexample rules out that broad coverage.

Dropping the transmissional conception of testimonial justification would not, of course, eliminate the social dimension from testimonial justification. It just requires that the social dimension be examined from the perspective of the hearer. In other words, the social dimension enters as part of the propositional contents of the hearer's beliefs ("this person asserted p, that person denied it, etc."). In effect, this was my view in chapter 7, and the view that most epistemological treatments of testimony presuppose. This perspective does not conflict with treatments of social epistemology that address other epistemic concepts and proceed quite differently. For example, in a social-historical account of mathematical knowledge of the sort that Kitcher (1983) presents, the intellectual activities of generations of thinkers are critical. Whether "knowledge" is here used in sense (1), sense (3), or even sense (4), the account hinges on actual cognitive events and relationships among successions of cognitive agents. We can acknowledge the appropriateness and significance of this kind of social epistemological project applied to *knowledge* while still leaving room for a more "egocentric" or individualist perspective in the theory of testimonial *justification*, which retains its own distinctive manner of incorporating the "social." As the title of this chapter indicates, there is a smorgasbord of legitimate projects for social epistemology; we need not insist on a unique conception of the field.

Note

I am grateful to Steve Fuller, Joseph Shieber, and Holly Smith for helpful comments on this chapter.

References

Alston, William. 1973. Can Psychology Do Without Private Data? *Behaviorism* 1:71–102.

———. 1989. *Epistemic Justification*. Ithaca, NY: Cornell University Press.

———. 1993a. Epistemic Desiderata. *Philosophy and Phenomenological Research* 53: 527–51.

———. 1993b. *The Reliability of Sense Perception*. Ithaca, NY: Cornell University Press.

———. 1996. *A Realist Theory of Truth*. Ithaca, NY: Cornell University Press.

Anderson, Elizabeth. 1995a. Knowledge, Human Interests, and Objectivity in Feminist Epistemology. *Philosophical Topics* 23: 27–58.

———. 1995b. Feminist Epistemology: An Interpretation and a Defense. *Hypatia* 10 (3): 50–84.

Anton, G. 1899. Ueber die Selbstwahrnemung der Herderkrankungen des Gehirns durch den Kranken bei Rindenblindheit und Rindentaubheit. *Archiv fur Psychiatrie und Nervenkrankheiten* 32: 86–127.

Armstrong, D. M. 1973. *Belief, Truth, and Knowledge*. New York: Cambridge University Press.

———. 1980. What Is Consciousness? In *The Nature of Mind and Other Essays*. Ithaca, NY: Cornell University Press.

———. 1989. *Universals*. Boulder, Colo.: Westview.

Audi, Robert. 1989. Causalist Internalism. *American Philosophical Quarterly* 26:309–20.

———. 1993. *The Structure of Justification*. New York: Cambridge University Press.

———. 1995. Memorial Justification. *Philosophical Topics* 23: 31–45.

Bales, R. Eugene. 1971. Act-Utilitarianism: Account of Right-Making Characteristics or Decision-Making Procedure. *American Philosophical Quarterly* 8: 257–65.

Baars, Bernard. 1988. *A Cognitive Theory of Consciousness*. Cambridge: Cambridge University Press.

———. 1997. *In the Theater of Consciousness*. New York: Oxford University Press.

Barnes, Barry, and David Bloor. 1982. Relativism, Rationalism, and the Sociology of Knowledge. In M. Hollis and S. Lukes, eds., *Rationality and Relativism*. Cambridge, Mass.: MIT Press.

Baron-Cohen, Simon. 1995. *Mindblindness*. Cambridge, Mass.: MIT Press.

Basalla, G. 1988. *The Evolution of Technology*. Cambridge: Cambridge University Press.

Bauer, R. 1984. Autonomic Recognition of Names and Faces in Prosopagnosia: A Neuropsychological Application of the Guilty Knowledge Test. *Neuropsychologia* 22: 457–69.

Bealer, George. 1987. The Philosophical Limits of Scientific Essentialism. In J. Tomberlin, ed., *Philosophical Perspectives*, vol. 1. Atascadero, Calif.: Ridgeview.

———. 1996a. A Priori Knowledge and the Scope of Philosophy. *Philosophical Studies* 81: 121–42.

———. 1996b. On the Possibility of Philosophical Knowledge. In J. Tomberlin, ed., *Philosophical Perspectives*, vol. 10. Cambridge, Mass.: Blackwell.

———. 1998. Intuition and the Autonomy of Philosophy. In M. DePaul and W. Ramsey, eds., *Rethinking Intuition: The Psychology of Intuition and Its Role in Philosophical Inquiry*. Lanham, Md.: Rowman and Littlefield.

Benacerraf, Paul. 1973. Mathematical Truth. *Journal of Philosophy* 70: 661–79.

Bezuidenhout, Anne. 1998. Is Verbal Communication a Purely Preservative Process? *Philosophical Review* 107: 261–88.

Bigelow, John. 1992. The Doubtful A Priori. In P. Hanson and B. Hunter, eds., *Return of the A Priori*. Calgary: University of Calgary Press.

Blackmore, Susan. 1999. *The Meme Machine*. Oxford: Oxford University Press.

Block, Ned. 1995. On a Confusion about a Function of Consciousness. *Behavioral and Brain Sciences* 18: 227–47. Reprinted in N. Block, O. Flanagan, and G. Guzeldere, eds., *The Nature of Consciousness*. Cambridge, Mass.: MIT Press, 1997.

Bloor, David. 1976/1991. *Knowledge and Social Imagery*. Chicago: University of Chicago Press.

BonJour, Laurence. 1985. *The Structure of Empirical Knowledge*. Cambridge, MA: Harvard University Press.

———. 1992. A Rationalist Manifesto. In P. Hanson and B. Hunter, eds., *Return of the A Priori*. Calgary: University of Calgary Press.

———. 1994. Against Naturalized Epistemology. In P. French, T. Uehling, Jr., and Howard Wettstein, eds., *Midwest Studies in Philosophy* 19. Notre Dame: University of Notre Dame Press.

———. 1998. *In Defense of Pure Reason*. Cambridge: Cambridge University Press.

Boyd, Richard. 1985. Observations, Explanatory Power, and Simplicity: Toward a Non-Humean Account. In P. Achinstein and O. Hannaway, eds., *Observation, Experiment, and Hypothesis in Modern Physical Science*. Cambridge, Mass.: MIT Press.

Boyd, Robert, and Peter Richerson. 1985. *Culture and the Evolutionary Process*. Chicago: University of Chicago Press.

Braine, M., B. Reiser, and B. Rumain. 1984. Some Empirical Justification for a Theory of Natural Propositional Reasoning. In G. H. Bower, ed., vol. 18, *Psychology of Learning and Motivation*. New York: Academic Press.

Brewer, Scott. 1998. Scientific Expert Testimony and Intellectual Due Process. *Yale Law Journal* 107: 1535–1681.

Brock, William, and Steven Durlauf. 1999. A Formal Model of Theory Choice in Science. *Economic Theory* 14: 113–30.

Brodie, R. 1996. *Virus of the Mind: The New Science of the Meme.* Seattle: Integral Press.

Brown, James Robert. 1989. *The Rational and the Social.* London: Routledge.

Burge, Tyler. 1993. Content Preservation. *Philosophical Review* 102: 457–88.

———. 1998. Computer Proof, Apriori Knowledge, and Other Minds. In J. Tomberlin, ed., *Philosophical Perspectives* 12. Malden, Mass.: Blackwell.

Butchvarov, Panayot. 1970. *The Concept of Knowledge.* Evanston, Ill.: Northwestern University Press.

Byrne, R. 1993. Hierarchical Levels of Imitation. *Behavioral and Brain Sciences* 16: 516–17.

Byrne, R., and A. Russon. 1998. Learning by Imitation: A Hierarchical Approach. *Behavioral and Brain Sciences* 21: 667–84.

Campbell, Angus. 1981. *The Sense of Well-Being in America.* New York: McGraw-Hill.

Campbell, Donald. 1960. Blind Variation and Selective Retention in Creative Thought as in Other Knowledge Processes. *Psychological Review* 67:380–400.

———. 1974. Evolutionary Epistemology. In P. A. Schilpp, ed., *The Philosophy of Karl Popper,* vol. 1. La Salle, Ill.: Open Court.

Cantor, G. N. 1975. A Critique of Shapin's Interpretation of the Edinburgh Phrenology Debate. *Annals of Science* 33: 245–56.

Carroll, Lewis. 1995. What the Tortoise Said to Achilles. *Mind* 4: 278–80.

Cartwright, Nancy. 1983. *How the Laws of Physics Lie.* Oxford: Oxford University Press.

Casullo, Albert. 1988. Revisability, Reliabilism, and A Priori Knowledge. *Philosophy and Phenomenological Research* 49: 187–213.

Cavalli-Sforza, L. L., and M. W. Feldman. 1981. *Cultural Transmission and Evolution: A Quantitative Approach.* Princeton: Princeton University Press.

Chalmers, David. 1996. *The Conscious Mind.* New York: Oxford University Press.

Cheesman, J., and P. Merikle. 1986. Distinguishing Conscious from Unconscious Perceptual Processes. *Canadian Journal of Psychology* 40:343–67.

Cheng, Patricia, and Keith Holyoak. 1985. Pragmatic Reasoning Schemas. *Cognitive Psychology* 17:391–416.

Cherniak, Christopher. 1984. Computational Complexity and the Universal Acceptance of Logic. *Journal of Philosophy* 81:739–58.

Chisholm, Roderick. 1966. *Theory of Knowledge.* Englewood Cliffs, N.J.: Prentice-Hall.

———. 1977. *Theory of Knowledge.* 2nd ed. Englewood Cliffs, N.J.: Prentice-Hall.

———. 1989. *Theory of Knowledge.* 3rd ed. Englewood Cliffs, N.J.: Prentice-Hall.

———. 1990. The Status of Epistemic Principles. *Nous* 24: 209–15.

Church, R. M., and W. H. Meck. 1984. The Numerical Attribute of Stimuli. In H. Roitblatt, T. Bever, and H. Terrance, eds., *Animal Cognition.* Hillsdale, N.J.: Lawrence Erlbaum.

Clark, E., and K. Carpenter. 1989. The Notion of Source in Language Acquisition. *Language* 65:1–30.

Coady, C. A. J. 1992. *Testimony.* Oxford: Oxford University Press.

Cohen, Stewart. 1988. How to Be a Fallibilist. In J. Tomberlin, ed., *Philosophical Perspectives,* vol. 2. Atascadero, Calif.: Ridgeview.

Cosmides, Leda. 1989. The Logic of Social Exchange: Has Natural Selection Shaped How Humans Reason: Studies with the Wason Selection Task. *Cognition* 31: 187–276.

Cosmides, Leda, and John Tooby. 1992. Cognitive Adaptations for Social Exchange. In J. Barkow, L. Cosmides, and J. Tooby, eds., *The Adapted Mind.* New York: Oxford University Press.

———. 1994. Origins of Domain Specificity: The Evolution of Functional Organization. In L. Hirschfeld and S. Gelman, eds., *Mapping the Mind: Domain Specificity in Cognition and Culture.* Cambridge: Cambridge University Press.

Cox, James, and Alvin Goldman. 1994. Accuracy in Journalism: An Economic Approach. In F. Schmitt, ed., *Socializing Epistemology.* Lanham, Md.: Rowman and Littlefield.

Craig, Edward 1990. *Knowledge and the State of Nature—An Essay in Conceptual Synthesis.* Oxford: Oxford University Press.

Darwin, Charles. 1859. *On the Origin of Species by Means of Natural Selection.* London: Murray.

David, Marian. 1994. *Correspondence and Disquotation.* New York: Oxford University Press.

Dawes, Robyn. 1994. *House of Cards: Psychology and Psychotherapy Built on Myth.* New York: Free Press.

Dawkins, Richard. 1976. *The Selfish Gene.* Oxford: Oxford University Press.

———. 1993. Viruses of the Mind. In B. Dahlbohm, ed., *Dennett and His Critics.* Oxford: Blackwell.

Debner, J., and L. Jacoby. 1994. Unconscious Perception: Attention, Awareness, and Control. *Journal of Experimental Psychology: Learning, Memory, and Cognition* 20:304–17.

Dennett, Daniel. 1969. *Content and Consciousness.* New York: Humanities Press.

———. 1991. *Consciousness Explained.* Boston: Little, Brown and Co.

———. 1995. *Darwin's Dangerous Idea.* New York: Simon and Schuster.

DeRose, Keith. 1992. Contextualism and Knowledge Attributions. *Philosophy and Phenomenological Research* 52:913–29.

———. 1995. Solving the Skeptical Problem. *Philosophical Review* 104:1–52.

Descartes, René. 1955. *Philosophical Works of Descartes*, vol. 1, E. Haldane and G. R. T. Ross, eds. New York: Dover.

Devitt, Michael 1994. The Methodology of Naturalistic Semantics. *Journal of Philosophy* 91:545–72.

———. 1996. *Coming to Our Senses.* Cambridge: Cambridge University Press.

Diamond, Jared. 1997. *Guns, Germs, and Steel.* London: Cape.

Dimberg, U., M. Thunberg, and K. Elmehed. 2000. Unconscious Facial Reactions to Emotional Facial Expressions. *Psychological Science* 11:86–89.

Dretske, Fred. 1981. *Knowledge and the Flow of Information.* Cambridge, Mass.: MIT Press.

Dunbar, Robin. 1996. *Grooming, Gossip and the Evolution of Language.* London: Faber and Faber.

Ericsson, K. A., and H. A. Simon. 1980. Verbal Reports as Data. *Psychological Review* 87: 215–51.

———. 1984/1993. *Protocol Analysis: Verbal Reports as Data.* Cambridge, Mass.: MIT Press.

Eriksen, C. W. 1960. Discrimination and Learning Without Awareness: A Methodological Survey and Evaluation. *Psychological Review* 67:279–99.

Estes, William. 1975. The State of the Field: General Problems and Issues of Theory and Metatheory. In W. Estes, ed., *Handbook of Learning and Cognitive Processes*, vol. 1. Hillsdale, N.J.: Lawrence Erlbaum.

———. 1994. *Classification and Cognition*. Oxford: Oxford University Press.

Fallis, Don. 1999. Erring on the Side of Credulity. School of Information Resources, University of Arizona. Unpublished.

———. 2000. Veritistic Social Epistemology and Information Science. *Social Epistemology* 14 (4): 305–16.

Feigl, Herbert. 1953. The Scientific Outlook: Naturalism and Humanism. In H. Feigl and M. Brodbeck, eds., *Readings in the Philosophy of Science*. New York: Appleton-Century-Croft.

Field, Hartry. 1989. *Realism, Mathematics, and Modality*. Oxford: Blackwell.

Fine, Kit. 1985. Plantinga on the Reduction of Possibilist Discourse. In J. Tomberlin and P. van Inwagen, eds., *Alvin Plantinga*. Dordrecht: Reidel.

Feldman, Richard. 1988a. Epistemic Obligations. In J. Tomberlin, ed., *Philosophical Perspectives*, vol. 2. Atascadero, Calif: Ridgeview.

———. 1988b. Having Evidence. In D. Austin, ed., *Philosophical Analysis*. Dordrecht: Kluwer.

Feldman, Richard, and Earl Conee. 1985. Evidentialism. *Philosophical Studies* 48: 15–34.

Foley, Richard. 1987. *The Theory of Epistemic Rationality*. Cambridge, Mass.: Harvard University Press.

———. 1993. *Working Without a Net*. New York: Oxford University Press.

———. 1994. Egoism in Epistemology. In F. Schmitt, ed., *Socializing Epistemology*. Lanham, Md.: Rowman and Littlefield.

Forman, Paul. 1971. Weimar Culture, Causality, and Quantum Theory, 1918–1927: Adaptation by German Physicists and Mathematicians to a Hostile Intellectual Environment. In R. McCormmach, ed., *Historical Studies in the Physical Sciences*, vol. 3. Philadelphia: University of Pennsylvania Press.

Friedberg, M., B. Saffran, T. J. Stinson, W. Nelson, and C. L. Bennett. 1999. Evaluation of Conflict of Interest in Economic Analyses of New Drugs Used in Oncology. *Journal of the American Medical Association* 282:1453–57.

Gelman, R., and C. R. Gallistel. 1978. *The Child's Understanding of Number*. Cambridge, Mass.: Harvard University Press.

Frith, C. D. 1992. *The Cognitive Neuropsychology of Schizophrenia*. Hillsdale, N.J.: Lawrence Erlbahum.

Fuller, Steve. 1988. *Social Epistemology*. Bloomington, Ind.: Indiana University Press.

———. 1993. *Philosophy, Rhetoric, and the End of Knowledge*. Madison, Wis.: University of Wisconsin Press.

———. 2000. *Thomas Kuhn: A Philosophical History for Our Times*. Chicago: University of Chicago Press.

Gelman, R., and J. G. Greeno. 1989. On the Nature of Competence: Principles for Understanding in a Domain. In L. Resnick, ed., *Knowing and Learning: Issues for a Cognitive Science of Instruction*. Hillsdale, N.J.: Lawrence Erlbaum.

Gentzler, J. 1995. How to Discriminate Between Experts and Frauds: Some Problems for Socratic Peirastic. *History of Philosophy Quarterly* 3:227–46.

Gettier, Edmund. 1963. Is Justified True Belief Knowledge? *Analysis* 23:121–23.

Gibbon, J. 1981. On the Form and Location of the Psychometric Bisection Function for Time. *Journal of Mathematical Psychology* 24:58–87.

Gigerenzer, Gerd. 1991. How to Make Cognitive Illusions Disappear: Beyond "Heuristics and Biases." *European Review of Social Psychology* 2:83–115.

Gilbert, Margaret. 1989. *On Social Facts*. London: Routledge.

Ginet, Carl. 1975. *Knowledge, Perception, and Memory*. Dordrecht: Reidel.

Goldman, Alvin 1967. A Causal Theory of Knowing. *Journal of Philosophy* 64:357–72.

———. 1976. Discrimination and Perceptual Knowledge. *Journal of Philosophy* 73:771–91.

———. 1977. Perceptual Objects. *Synthese* 35:257–84.

———. 1979. What Is Justified Belief? In G. Pappas, ed., *Justification and Knowledge*. Dordrecht: Reidel.

———. 1985. The Relation Between Epistemology and Psychology. *Synthese* 64:29–68.

———. 1986. *Epistemology and Cognition*. Cambridge, Mass.: Harvard University Press.

———. 1987. Foundations of Social Epistemics. *Synthese* 73:109–44.

———. 1988. Strong and Weak Justification. In J. Tomberlin, ed., *Philosophical Perspectives*, vol. 2. Atascadero, Calif.: Ridgeview.

———. 1989a. Metaphysics, Mind, and Mental Science. *Philosophical Topics*: 131–45.

———. 1989b. Psychology and Philosophical Analysis. *Proceedings of the Aristotelian Society* 89:195–209.

———. 1989c. Interpretation Psychologized. *Mind and Language* 4:161–85.

———. 1991. Epistemic Paternalism: Communication Control in Law and Society. *Journal of Philosophy* 88:113–31.

———. 1992. *Liaisons: Philosophy Meets the Cognitive and Social Sciences*. Cambridge, Mass.: MIT Press.

———. 1994. Argumentation and Social Epistemology. *Journal of Philosophy* 91:27–49.

———. 1999. *Knowledge in a Social World*. Oxford: Oxford University Press.

Goldman, Alvin, and James Cox. 1996. Speech, Truth, and the Free Market for Ideas. *Legal Theory* 2:1–32.

Goldman, Alvin, and Moshe Shaked. 1991. An Economic Model of Scientific Activity and Truth Acquisition. *Philosophical Studies* 63:31–55.

Greco, John. 1992. Virtue Epistemology. In J. Dancy and E. Sosa, eds., *A Companion to Epistemology*. Oxford: Basil Blackwell.

Grice, H. P. 1989. *Studies in the Way of Words*. Cambridge, Mass.: Harvard University Press.

Grofman, Bernard, and Guillermo Owen. 1986. Condorcet Models, Avenues for Future Research. In B. Grofman and G. Owen, eds., *Information Pooling and Group Decision Making*. Greenwich, Conn.: JAI Press.

Haack, Susan. 1993. *Evidence and Inquiry*. Oxford: Basil Blackwell.

Habermas, Jurgen. 1984. *The Theory of Communicative Action*, vol. 1. Boston: Beacon Press.

Hacking, Ian. 1999. *The Social Construction of What?* Cambridge, Mass.: Harvard University Press.

Hanson, N. R. 1961. Is There a Logic of Discovery? In H. Feigl and G. Maxwell, eds., *Current Issues in the Philosophy of Science.* New York: Holt, Rinehart and Winston.

Hardwig, John. 1985. Epistemic Dependence. *Journal of Philosophy* 82:335–49.

———. 1991. The Role of Trust in Knowledge. *Journal of Philosophy* 88:693–708.

Harman, Gilbert. 1973. *Thought.* Princeton: Princeton University Press.

———. 1986. *Change in View.* Cambridge, Mass.: MIT Press.

Harsanyi, J. C. 1982. Morality and the Theory of Rational Behavior. In A. Sen and B. Williams, eds., *Utilitarianism and Beyond.* Cambridge: Cambridge University Press.

Hawthorne, John. 2000. Deeply Contingent A Priori Knowledge. Paper delivered at the Rutgers Epistemology Conference, New Brunswick, N.J.

Heil, John. 1983. Doxastic Agency. *Philosophical Studies* 40:355–64.

Hempel, Carl. 1952. *Fundamentals of Concept Formation in Empirical Science.* Chicago, Ill.: University of Chicago Press.

Hintzman, D. 1986. "Schema Abstraction" in a Multiple Trace Memory Model. *Psychological Review* 93:411–28.

Holender, D. 1986. Semantic Activation Without Conscious Identification in Dichotic Listening, Parafoveal Vision, and Visual Masking. *Behavioral and Brain Sciences* 9:1–23.

Holland, J., K. Holyoak, R. Nisbett, and P. Thagard. 1986. *Induction: Processes of Inference, Learning, and Discovery.* Cambridge, Mass.: MIT Press.

Hull, David. 1982. The Naked Meme. In H. C. Plotkin, ed., *Learning, Development, and Culture.* London: Wiley.

Hume, David. 1972. *Enquiries Concerning Human Understanding and Concerning the Principles of Morals.* L. A. Selby-Bigge, 2nd ed. Oxford: Oxford University Press.

Hursthouse, Rosalind. 1996. Normative Virtue Ethics. In R. Crisp, ed., *How Should One Live? Essays on the Virtues.* Oxford: Oxford University Press.

Irwin, T. H. 1992. Plato. In L. Becker and C. Becker, eds., *Encyclopedia of Ethics,* vol. 2. New York: Garland.

Jackendoff, Ray. 1983. *Semantics and Cognition.* Cambridge, Mass.: MIT Press.

Jeffrey, Richard. 1992. *Probability and the Art of Judgment.* Cambridge: Cambridge University Press.

Johnson, Marcia, and Carol Raye. 1981. Reality Monitoring. *Psychological Review* 88:67–85.

Johnson, Marcia, Mary Foley, Aurora Suengas, and Carol Raye. 1988. Phenomenal Characteristics of Memories for Perceived and Imagined Autobiographical Events. *Journal of Experimental Psychology: General* 117:371–76.

Johnson-Laird, Philip, and Ruth Byrne. 1991. *Deduction.* Hillsdale, N.J.: Lawrence Erlbaum.

Kant, Immanuel. 1965. *Critique of Pure Reason.* Trans. N. Kemp Smith. New York: St. Martin's.

Katz, Jerrold. 1981. *Language and Other Abstract Objects.* Totowa, N.J.: Rowman and Littlefield.

———. 1998. *Realistic Rationalism.* Cambridge, Mass.: MIT Press.

Kim, Jaegwon. 1988. What Is "Naturalized Epistemology"? In J. Tomberlin, ed., *Philosophical Perspectives,* vol. 2. Atascadero, Calif.: Ridgeview.

Kitcher, Philip. 1981. How Kant Almost Wrote "Two Dogmas of Empiricism" and Why He Didn't. *Philosophical Topics* 12:217–50.

———. 1983. *The Nature of Mathematical Knowledge.* New York: Oxford University Press.

———. 1992. The Naturalists Return. *Philosophical Review* 101:53–114.

———. 1993. *The Advancement of Science.* New York: Oxford University Press.

———. 1994. Contrasting Conceptions of Social Epistemology. In F. Schmitt, ed., *Socializing Epistemology.* Lanham, Md.: Rowman and Littlefield.

———. 1997. An Argument about Free Inquiry. *Nous* 31:279–306.

———. 2001. *Science, Truth, and Democracy.* New York: Oxford University Press.

Kripke, Saul. 1980. *Naming and Necessity.* Cambridge, Mass.: Harvard University Press.

Kornblith, Hilary. 1983. Justified Belief and Epistemically Responsible Action. *Philosophical Review* 92:33–48.

———. 1989. The Unattainability of Coherence. In J. Bender, ed., *The Current State of the Coherence Theory.* Dordrecht: Kluwer.

———. 1994. A Conservative Approach to Social Epistemology. In F. Schmitt, ed., *Socializing Epistemology.* Lanham, Md.: Rowman and Littlefield.

———. 1995. Naturalistic Epistemology and Its Critics. *Philosophical Topics* 23: 237–55.

———. 1998. The Role of Intuition in Philosophical Inquiry: An Account with No Unnatural Ingredients. In M. DePaul and W. Ramsey, eds., *Rethinking Intuition: The Psychology of Intuition and Its Role in Philosophical Inquiry.* Totowa, N.J.: Rowman and Littlefield.

Kuhl, P. K., and A. N. Meltzoff. 1996. Infant Vocalizations in Response to Speech: Vocal Imitation and Developmental Change. *Journal of the Acoustical Society of America* 100:2425–38.

Kuhn, Thomas. 1962/1970. *The Structure of Scientific Revolutions.* 2nd ed. Chicago: University of Chicago Press.

Kukla, Andre. 2000. *Social Construction and the Philosophy of Science.* London: Routledge.

LaBarge, Scott. 1997. Socrates and the Recognition of Experts. In M. McPherran, ed., *Wisdom, Ignorance and Virtue: New Essays in Socratic Studies.* Edmonton: Academic Printing and Publishing.

Latour, Bruno. 1987. *Science in Action.* Cambridge, Mass.: Harvard University Press.

Latour, Bruno, and Steve Woolgar, 1979/1986. *Laboratory Life: The [Social] Construction of Scientific Facts.* Princeton: Princeton University Press.

Laudan, Larry. 1977. *Progress and Its Problems.* Berkeley: University of California Press.

Lehrer, Keith. 1974. *Knowledge.* Oxford: Oxford University Press.

———. 1981. A Self-Profile. In R. Bogdan, ed., *Keith Lehrer.* Dordrecht: Reidel.

———. 1989. Knowledge Reconsidered. In M. Clay and K. Lehrer, eds., *Knowledge and Skepticism.* Boulder, Colo.: Westview Press.

———. 1990. *Theory of Knowledge.* Boulder, Colo.: Westview Press.

Lehrer, Keith, and Carl Wagner 1981. *Rational Consensus in Science and Society.* Dordrecht: Reidel.

Levi, Isaac. 1980. *The Enterprise of Knowledge.* Cambridge, Mass.: MIT Press.

Lewis, David. 1979. Scorekeeping in a Language Game. *Journal of Philosophical Logic* 8:339–59.

———. 1980. Psychophysical and Theoretical Identifications. In N. Block, ed., *Readings in Philosophy of Psychology,* vol. 1. Cambridge, Mass.: Harvard University Press.

———. 1986a. *On the Plurality of Worlds.* Oxford: Blackwell.

———. 1986b. Causation. In *Philosophical Papers,* vol. 2. Oxford: Oxford University Press.

Locke, John. 1959. *An Essay Concerning Human Understanding,* vols. 1–2, A. C. Fraser, ed. New York: Dover.

Longino, Helen. 1990. *Science as Social Knowledge.* Princeton: Princeton University Press.

———. 1993. Essential Tensions—Phase Two: Feminist, Philosophical, and Social Studies of Science. In L. Antony and C. Witt, eds. *A Mind of One's Own.* Boulder, Colo.: Westview Press.

Lycan, William. 1988. Moral Facts and Moral Knowledge. In *Judgment and Justification.* New York: Cambridge University Press.

———. 1996. *Consciousness and Experience.* Cambridge, Mass.: MIT Press.

Lynch, Aaron. 1996. *Thought Contagion: How Belief Spreads Through Society.* New York: Basic Books.

Lyons, William. 1986. *The Disappearance of Introspection.* Cambridge, Mass.: MIT Press.

Macnamara, J. 1986. *A Border Dispute: The Place of Logic in Psychology.* Cambridge, Mass.: MIT Press.

Maffie, James. 1990. Recent Work on Naturalized Epistemology. *American Philosophical Quarterly* 27:281–93.

Manktelow, K. I., and J. St. B. T. Evans. 1979. Facilitation of Reasoning by Realism: Effect or Non-effect? *British Journal of Psychology* 70:477–88.

Mannheim, Karl. 1936. *Ideology and Utopia.* New York: Harvest Books.

Marcel, Anthony. 1988. Phenomenal Experience and Functionalism. In A. Marcel and E. Bisiach, eds., *Consciousness in Contemporary Science.* Oxford: Oxford University Press.

———. 1993. Slippage in the Unity of Consciousness. In Ciba Symposium 174, *Experimental and Theoretical Studies of Consciousness.*

Markie, Peter. 1996. Goldman's New Reliabilism. *Philosophy and Phenomenological Research* 56: 799–817.

———. 1997. In Defense of One Form of Traditional Epistemology. *Philosophical Studies* 85: 37–55.

Mathiesen, Kay. 2000. What Do We Mean by "We"? A Philosophical Analysis of Collectives. Massachusetts College of Liberal Arts. Unpublished.

McCloskey, Donald. 1985. *The Rhetoric of Economics.* Madison: University of Wisconsin Press.

McGlynn, S., and D. Schacter. 1989. Unawareness of Deficits in Neuropsychological Syndromes. *Journal of Clinical and Experimental Neuropsychology* 11:143–205.

Meck, W. H., and R. M. Church. 1983. A Mode Control Model of Counting and Timing Processes. *Journal of Experimental Psychology: Animal Behavior Processes* 9:320–34.

Medin, D., and D. Schaffer. 1978. A Context Theory of Classification Learning. *Psychological Review* 85:207–38.

Meltzoff, A. N. 1995a. Understanding the Intentions of Others: Re-enactment of Intended Acts by Eighteen-month-old Children. *Developmental Psychology* 31: 838–50.

———. 1995b. What Infant Memory Tells Us About Infantile Amnesia: Long-term Recall and Deferred Imitation. *Journal of Experimental Child Psychology* 59: 49–515.

———. 1999. Imitation. In R. Wilson and F. Keil, eds., *MIT Encyclopedia of the Cognitive Sciences*.

Meltzoff, A. N., and M. K. Moore. 1983. Newborn Infants Imitate Adult Facial Gestures. *Child Development* 54:702–09.

———. 1998. Object Representation, Identity, and the Paradox of Early Permanence: Steps Toward a New Framework. *Infant Behavior and Development* 21:201–35.

Merikle, P., and S. Joordens. 1997a. Parallels Between Perception Without Attention and Perception Without Awareness. *Consciousness and Cognition* 6:219–36.

———. 1997b. Measuring Unconscious Influences. In J. Cohen and J. Schooler, eds., *Scientific Approaches to Consciousness*. Mahwah, N.J.: Lawrence Erlbaum.

Merton, Robert. 1973. *The Sociology of Science*. Chicago: University of Chicago Press.

Metcalfe, J., and A. Shimamura, eds. 1994. *Metacognition*. Cambridge, Mass.: MIT Press.

Miller, G., and G. Buckhout. 1973. *Psychology: The Science of Mental Life,* 2nd ed. New York: Harper and Row.

Milner, A. D., and M. A. Goodale. 1995. *The Visual Brain in Action*. Oxford: Oxford University Press.

Milner, B., S. Corkin, and H. Teuber. 1968. Further Analysis of the Hippocampal Amnesic Syndrome: Fourteen-Year Follow-Up Study of H.M. *Neuropsychologia* 6:215–34.

Moscovitch, M. 1982. Multiple Dissociations of Function in Amnesia. In L. Cermak, ed., *Human Memory and Amnesia*. Hillsdale, N.J.: Lawrence Erlbaum.

Moser, Paul. 1985. *Empirical Justification*. Dordrecht: Reidel.

Nelson, Lynn Hankinson. 1993. Epistemological Communities. In L. Alcoff and E. Potter, eds., *Feminist Epistemologies*. New York: Routledge.

Nelson, Thomas, ed. 1991. *Metacognition*. Boston: Allyn and Bacon.

Newell, Allen, and Herbert Simon. 1972. *Human Problem Solving*. Englewood Cliffs, N.J.: Prentice-Hall.

Nisbett, Richard, and Timothy Wilson. 1977. Telling More Than We Can Know: Verbal Reports on Mental Processes. *Psychological Review* 84:231–59.

Nozick, Robert. 1981. *Philosophical Explanations*. Cambridge, Mass.: Harvard University Press.

Pastore, N. 1961. Number Sense and "Counting" Ability in the Canary. *Zeitschrift für Tierpsychologie* 18:561–73.

Peacocke, Christopher. 1992. *A Study of Concepts*. Cambridge, Mass.: MIT Press.

———. 1998. Implicit Conceptions, Understanding, and Rationality. In E. Villanueva, ed., *Philosophical Issues. Vol 8: Concepts*. Atascadero, Calif.: Ridgeview.

Pickering, Andrew. 1984. *Constructing Quarks: A Sociological History of Particle Physics*. Chicago: University of Chicago Press.

Pinker, Steven. 1994. *The Language Instinct*. New York: Morrow.

Plantinga, Alvin. 1993a. *Warrant: The Current Debate*. New York: Oxford University Press.

———. 1993b. *Warrant and Proper Function*. New York: Oxford University Press.

Pollock, John. 1986. *Contemporary Theories of Knowledge*. Totowa, N.J.: Rowman and Littlefield.

———. 1989. *How to Build a Person*. Cambridge, Mass.: MIT Press.

———. 1990. *Nomic Probability and the Foundations of Induction*. New York: Oxford University Press.

———. 2000. A Theory of Rational Action. Unpublished manuscript. University of Arizona.

Popper, Karl 1959. *The Logic of Scientific Discovery*. London: Hutchinson.

———. 1962. *Conjectures and Refutations*. New York: Basic Books.

———. 1972. *Objective Knowledge: An Evolutionary Approach*. Oxford: Oxford University Press.

Pust, Joel. 2000. *Intuitions as Evidence*. New York: Garland.

Putnam, Hilary. 1960. Minds and Machines. In S. Hook, ed., *Dimensions of Mind*. New York: New York University Press.

———. 1979. Analyticity and Apriority: Beyond Wittgenstein and Quine. In P. French, T. Uehling, Jr., and H. Wettstein, eds., *Midwest Studies in Philosophy*, vol. 4. Minneapolis: University of Minnesota Press.

Quine, Willard van Orman. 1961. *From a Logical Point of View*, 2nd ed. Cambridge, Mass.: Harvard University Press.

———. 1969. Epistemology Naturalized. In *Ontological Relativity and Other Essays*. New York: Columbia University Press.

Quine, W. V., and Joseph Ullian. 1970. *The Web of Belief*. New York: Random House.

Railton, Peter. 1985. Marx and the Objectivity of Science. In P. Asquith and P. Kitcher, eds., *PSA 1984*, vol. 2. East Lansing, Mich.: Philosophy of Science Association.

Reichenbach, Hans. 1938. *Experience and Prediction*. Chicago, Ill.: University of Chicago Press.

Reid, Thomas. 1970. *An Inquiry into the Human Mind*. T. Duggan, ed. Chicago, Ill.: University of Chicago Press.

Rey, Georges. 1983. Concepts and Stereotypes. *Cognition* 15:237–62.

———. 1985. Concepts and Conceptions: A Reply to Smith, Medin, and Rips. *Cognition* 19:297–303.

———. 1998. A Naturalistic A Priori. *Philosophical Studies* 92:25–43.

Rips, Lance. 1994. *The Psychology of Proof*. Cambridge, Mass.: MIT Press.

———. 1995. Deduction and Cognition. In E. Smith and D. Osherson, eds., *Thinking: An Invitation to Cognitive Science*, 2nd ed. Cambridge, Mass.: MIT Press.

Rogers, James. 1983. *The Diffusion of Innovation*, 3rd ed. New York: Free Press.

Rorty, Richard. 1979. *Philosophy and the Mirror of Nature*. Princeton: Princeton University Press.

Rosen, Gideon. 1990. Modal Fictionalism. *Mind* 99:327–54.

Rosenthal, David. 1991. Two Concepts of Consciousness. In D. Rosenthal, ed., *The Nature of Mind*. New York: Oxford University Press.

———. 1997. A Theory of Consciousness. In N. Block, O. Flanagan, and G. Guzeldere, eds., *The Nature of Consciousness*. Cambridge, Mass.: MIT Press.

————. 2000. Consciousness and Metacognition. In D. Sperber, ed., *Metarepresentations*. New York: Oxford University Press.

Russell, Bertrand. 1912. *The Problems of Philosophy*. New York: Oxford University Press.

Schacter, Daniel. 1989. On the Relation Between Memory and Consciousness: Dissociable Interactions and Conscious Experience. In H. Roediger and F. Craik, eds., *Essays in Honor of Endel Tulving*. Hillsdale, N.J.: Lawrence Erlbaum.

Schmitt, Frederick. 1994a. The Justification of Group Beliefs. In F. Schmitt, ed., *Socializing Epistemology*. Lanham, Md.: Rowman and Littlefield.

————. 1994b. Socializing Epistemology: An Introduction Through Two Sample Issues. In F. Schmitt, ed., *Socializing Epistemology*. Lanham, Md.: Rowman and Littlefield.

————. 1995. *Truth*. Boulder, Colo.: Westview Press.

Schwarz, N. 1995. Social Cognition: Information Accessibility and Use in Social Judgment. In E. Smith and D. Osherson, eds., *Thinking: An Invitation to Cognitive Science*, vol. 3, 2nd ed. Cambridge, Mass.: MIT Press.

Schwarz, N., and F. Strack. 1991. Evaluating One's Life: A Judgment Model of Subjective Well-Being. In F. Strack, M. Argyle, and N. Schwarz, eds., *Subjective Well-Being: An Interdisciplinary Perspective*. Oxford: Pergamon.

Searle, John. 1995. *The Construction of Social Reality*. New York: Free Press.

Senor, Thomas. 1993. Internalist Foundationalism and the Justification of Memory Belief. *Synthese* 94: 453–76.

Shafir, Eldar, and Amos Tversky. 1995. Decision Making. In E. Smith and D. Osherson, eds., *Thinking: An Invitation to Cognitive Science*, vol. 3, 2nd ed. Cambridge, Mass.: MIT Press.

Shapin, Steven. 1975. Phrenological Knowledge and the Social Structure of Early Nineteenth-Century Edinburgh. *Annals of Science* 32: 219–43.

————. 1994. *A Social History of Truth*. Chicago: University of Chicago Press.

Shapin, Steven, and Simon Schaffer. 1985. *Leviathan and the Air-Pump*. Princeton: Princeton University Press.

Shera, Jesse. 1961. Social Epistemology, General Semantics and Librarianship. *Wilson Library Bulletin* 35: 767–70.

————. 1970. *Sociological Foundations of Librarianship*. New York: Asia Publishing House.

Shoemaker, Sydney. 1988. On Knowing One's Own Mind. In J. Tomberlin, ed., *Philosophical Perspectives*, vol. 2. Atascadero, Calif.: Ridgeview.

————. 1994. Self Knowledge and "Inner Sense." *Phenomenological Research* 54: 249–314.

————. 1996. *The First-Person Perspective and Other Essays*. New York: Cambridge University Press.

Skagestad, P. 1978. Taking Evolution Seriously: Critical Comments on D. T. Campbell's Evolutionary Epistemology. *Monist* 61: 611–21.

Smith, Edward. 1989. Three Distinctions About Concepts and Categorization. *Mind and Language* 4:57–61.

Smith, Edward, and Douglas Medin. 1981. *Categories and Concepts*. Cambridge, Mass.: Harvard University Press.

Solomon, Miriam. 1992. Scientific Rationality and Human Reasoning. *Philosophy of Science* 59: 462–503.

Sosa, Ernest. 1988. Knowledge in Context, Scepticism in Doubt: The Virtue of Our Faculties. In J. Tomberlin, ed., *Philosophical Perspectives*, vol. 2. Atascadero, Calif.: Ridgeview.

———. 1991. *Knowledge in Perspective*. New York: Cambridge University Press.

———. 1993. Proper Functionalism and Virtue Epistemology. *Nous* 27: 51–65.

Sperber, Dan. 1990. The Epidemiology of Beliefs. In C. Fraser and G. Gaskell, eds., *The Social Psychological Study of Widespread Beliefs*. Oxford: Oxford University Press.

———. 1996. *Explaining Culture: A Naturalistic Approach*. Oxford: Blackwell.

Steup, Matthias. 1988. The Deontic Conception of Epistemic Justification. *Philosophical Studies* 53: 65–84.

———. 1996. *An Introduction to Contemporary Epistemology*. Upper Saddle River, N.J.: Prentice-Hall.

Stich, Stephen. 1990. *The Fragmentation of Reason*. Cambridge, Mass.: MIT Press.

Strack, F., L. Martin, and N. Schwarz. 1988. Priming and Communication: The Social Determinants of Information Use in Judgments of Life-Satisfaction. *European Journal of Social Psychology* 18: 429–42.

Strack, F., N. Schwarz, and E. Gschneidinger. 1985. Happiness and Reminiscing: The Role of Time Perspective, Mood, and Mode of Thinking. *Journal of Personality and Social Psychology* 49: 1460–69.

Stroud, Barry. 1996. The Charm of Naturalism. *Proceedings and Addresses of the American Philosophical Association*, vol. 70, no. 2. Newark, Del.: American Philosophical Association.

Talbott, William, and Alvin Goldman. 1998. Games Lawyers Play: Legal Discovery and Social Epistemology. *Legal Theory* 4: 93–163.

Talmy, Leonard. 1983. How Language Structures Space. In H. Pick and L. Acredolo, eds., *Spatial Orientation: Theory, Research, and Application*. New York: Plenum.

Thagard, Paul. 1980. Against Evolutionary Epistemology. In P. Asquith and R. Giere, eds., *PSA 1980*, vol. 1. East Lansing, Mich.: Philosophy of Science Association, pp. 187–96.

Tomasello, M., A. Kruger, and H. Ratner. 1993. Cultural Learning. *Behavioral and Brain Sciences* 16: 495–511.

Tranel, D., and A. Damasio. 1985. Knowledge Without Awareness: An Autonomic Index of Facial Recognition by Prosopagnosics. *Science* 228: 1453–54.

———. 1988. Non-conscious Face Recognition in Patients with Face Agnosia. *Behavioral Brain Research* 30: 235–49.

Trianosky, Gregory. 1990. What Is Virtue Ethics All About? *American Philosophical Quarterly* 27: 335–44.

Tudge, C. 1995. *The Day Before Yesterday: Five Million Years of Human History*. London: Cape.

Tuomela, Raimo. 1995. *The Importance of Us: A Philosophical Study of Basic Social Notions*. Stanford: Stanford University Press.

Tversky, Amos, and Daniel Kahneman. 1982. Judgment under Uncertainty: Heuristics and Biases. In D. Kahneman, P. Slovic, and A. Tversky, eds., *Judgment Under Uncertainty*. New York: Cambridge University Press.

———. 1983. Extensional Versus Intuitive Reasoning: The Conjunction Fallacy in Probability Judgment. *Psychological Review* 91: 293–315.

Unger, Peter. 1984. *Philosophical Relativity*. Minneapolis: University of Minnesota Press.

van Eemeren, Frans, and Rob Grootendorst. 1984. *Speech Acts in Argumentative Discussions*. Dordrecht: Foris.

van Fraassen, Bas. 1989. *Laws and Symmetry*. Oxford: Oxford University Press.

Velmans, Max. 1991. Is Human Information Processing Conscious? *Behavioral and Brain Sciences* 14: 651–69.

Watson, John. 1913. Psychology as the Behaviorist Views It. *Psychological Review* 20: 158–77.

Weiskrantz, Lawrence. 1986. *Blindsight: A Case Study and Implications*. Oxford: Oxford University Press.

———. 1988. Some Contributions of Neuropsychology of Vision and Memory to the Problem of Consciousness. In A. Marcel and E. Bisiach, eds., *Consciousness in Contemporary Science*. New York: Oxford University Press.

Wilson, T. D. 1985. Strangers to Ourselves: The Origins and Accuracy of Beliefs About One's Own Mental States. In J. Harvey and G. Weary, eds., *Attribution: Basic Issues and Applications*. New York: Academic Press.

Wood, D. 1989. Social Interaction as Tutoring. In M. Bornstein and J. Bruner, eds., *Interaction in Human Development*. Hillsdale, N.J.: Lawrence Erlbaum.

Wynn, Karen. 1992a. Evidence Against Empiricist Accounts of the Origins of Numerical Knowledge. *Mind and Language* 7: 315–32.

———. 1992b. Addition and Subtraction in Human Infants. *Nature* 358: 749–50.

Young, A., and E. de Haan. 1993. Impairments of Visual Awareness. In M. Davies and G. Humphreys, eds., *Consciousness*. Oxford: Blackwell.

Zagzebski, Linda 1996. *Virtues of the Mind*. Cambridge: Cambridge University Press.

Index